Introduction To Music Education

Of related interest . . .

Charles R. Hoffer
Teaching Music in the Secondary Schools, Third Edition

Charles and Marjorie Hoffer
Basic Musicianship for Classroom Teachers: A Creative Musical Approach

William O. Hughes
A Concise Introduction to School Music Instruction, K–8, Second Edition

Robert and Vernice Nye, Neva Aubin, and George Kyme
Singing with Children, Second Edition

Bessie Swanson
Music in the Education of Children, Fourth Edition

Michael Combs
Percussion Manual

Vincent Oddo
Playing and Teaching the Strings

Jay Zorn
Brass Ensemble Methods for Music Educators

Introduction To Music Education

Charles R. Hoffer

INDIANA UNIVERSITY

Wadsworth Publishing Company

Belmont, California

A Division of Wadsworth, Inc.

Music Editor: Sheryl Fullerton

Production Editor: Toni Haskell

Interior and Cover Designer: Patricia Girvin Dunbar

Copy Editor: Jonas Weisel

MT I
H 723
1983

Printed in the United States of America

3 4 5 6 7 8 9 10—87

ISBN 0-534-01375-9

Library of Congress Cataloging in Publication Data

Hoffer, Charles R.
    Introduction to music education.

    1. School music—Instruction and study. I. Title.
MT1.H723 1983   780'.7'   82-21891
ISBN 0-534-01375-9

To Andrew Allan Hoffer

Contents

Section 3 The Music Curriculum 57

Section 4 The Process of Teaching 153

Section 5 Evaluating Results 195

Section 6 The Music Education Profession 223

Preface

IN THE PAST few years a number of colleges have instituted an introductory course in music education for prospective music teachers. The purposes of the introductory course are to provide students with an overview of the field, to acquaint them with the process of teaching, and to encourage them to consider themselves in terms of becoming a teacher. Usually this course precedes the methods courses in which the students learn techniques for teaching various aspects of music.

For the most part, instructors in the introductory course have relied on lectures and assigned readings from journals and textbooks to provide the subject matter. Lectures and assigned readings are only partially successful in this course, as I learned when I taught it. The students can read the materials (if they have not been misplaced) only in the library, and they have to resort to taking notes on the lectures. My experience with this arrangement convinced me that a book would be a much more efficient and effective means of providing information to the students. And so the idea for *Introduction to Music Education* was born.

In considering the topics to be included in an introductory book, I realized that certain chapters not dealing with methods in *Teaching Music in the Secondary Schools* would be useful. Therefore, these chapters have been adapted slightly and included in this book. In addition, three new chapters have been written.

Introduction to Music Education is divided into six sections. The first deals with the process of teaching music and music teachers. The next four sections introduce students to the four aspects of the teaching process: why music is a part of the school curriculum, what is (or should be) taught in music classes, how generally music should be taught, and with what results. The book closes with a chapter on the music education profession.

Theoretical and practical considerations are combined whenever possible in this book, because each aspect is vital and each influences the teaching of music. The writing has been made practical, clear, and alive, and it speaks directly to the reader at some points.

I would like to thank the many persons who encouraged and enlightened me in my efforts to be a teacher and writer. Citing a few names here would not be fair to the greater number who would not be mentioned. I can only thank them as a group, therefore, and hope that this is adequate. Specific recognition is due Linda Crowe of Southeast Missouri State University for her review of the material on Jaques-Dalcroze and Eugenia Sinor of Indiana University for her review of the material on the Kodály approach. I also wish to acknowledge the following persons for their reviews of the manuscript: Barbara Bennett, Baylor University; Russell A. Hammar, Kalamazoo College; William D. Hughes, Florida State University; Gary M. Martin, University of Oregon; Samuel D. Miller, University of Houston; James Scholten, Ohio University.

Charles R. Hoffer

Introduction To Music Education

1 | *Music Teaching and You*

AN INTRODUCTORY BOOK or course in music education logically begins with a look at music teaching and music teachers. The quality of teaching has an enormous effect on the results, which is part of the reason for starting with teachers and teaching. The teacher bears much of the responsibility for guiding the teaching process so that learning can take place.

Teachers who truly understand that process have a much better chance of guiding it successfully, which is another reason for beginning with teaching and teachers. An understanding of this process is a solid foundation on which the other aspects of being a teacher can be developed. Chapter One briefly describes this process.

Chapter Two examines the characteristics of the people who guide learning in music, the teachers. Should they have a particular type of personality? What competencies should they possess? Are good music teachers the result of special inborn qualities, or are they developed through knowledge and hard work? These and other questions should be of interest to anyone considering music teaching as a career. With a better understanding of what is needed to be a successful music teacher, the prospective music educator will have a basis on which to look at himself or herself in terms of being a music teacher.

C H A P T E R   O N E

IF YOU ARE PREPARING to teach music in the schools, you have chosen a profession that is interesting, challenging, and important. To begin with, it involves working with music in all its infinite variety of types and styles—and its beauty and enjoyment. There aren't many jobs in which a person can work with one of the arts; people who operate computers or sell auto parts or thousands of other jobs don't enjoy this privilege.

Then there are the students in the schools. Whatever else may be said about them, no one has accused them of failing to make things interesting and lively in classrooms. Students come in all shapes and sizes, and they have widely differing interests and abilities. A set or "cookbook" approach to teaching them music will often not be successful because of the great differences among them as individuals and the wide variations among the thousands of teaching situations across the United States. Imagination and intelligence need to be applied in coming up with ways to meet the challenges and opportunities these differences offer to every music teacher. For these reasons, among others, music teaching is not for the lazy or fainthearted.

In addition to being interesting and challenging, teaching music is an important field of work. For reasons that are described more fully in Chapter Three, music and the other fine arts should be included in the education of every student. They are too much a part of life in contemporary society for the schools to ignore, and they are too vital in people's lives for anyone not to be informed about them.

Where do you start in learning how to teach this interesting, challenging, and important subject? A good way to begin is by making sure you have a clear idea of what the words *music* and *teach* really mean. Although their meaning may appear to be obvious, they both have implications that are basic to what music teachers do or should do. First, the word *music*.

What Is Music? | *T*he nature of music seems like a simple matter, but is it? Is a crash of a cymbal or an eerie sound from a synthesizer music? Why is a boom from a bass drum considered musical and booms from other sources thought of as noise? The difference is not so much in the sounds themselves as in the context in which they are heard. If they appear in a planned sequence of sounds, then they become music; if not, they are just random noises. The key to the matter is organization. In fact, music has often been defined as "organized sound."

The organizing of sounds in a span of time is something that human beings do. Music was not preordained by the cosmic laws of the universe and therefore something that people find. Music is created by humans for humans. It is a human activity, and it varies in the forms it takes as much as other human creations like language, clothing, and food.

The world of music is vast and complex. Not only does it include all the music that people have created—folk, symphonic, instrumental, vocal, electronic, rock—it also encompasses musical activities such as singing, listening, analyzing, and creating. In fact, music is both an *object* in terms of being composed or improvised works and a *process* in terms of the actions involved in producing or reproducing music.

The vastness of the world of music forces teachers to make choices about what to teach and how to teach it. Fortunately, the definition of music as organized sounds does offer a clue to the most important responsibility of music teachers: guiding students to understand and appreciate organized sounds. The processes of performing and creating music often help in achieving this goal. For example, creating melodies helps students to understand better the organizing of sounds, and so does singing or playing melodies on a clarinet.

Sometimes teachers emphasize one aspect of music so much that other aspects are largely ignored. Some teachers, for example, concentrate so much on the techniques of singing, playing, or creating music that the students never get around to understanding where the activity fits into the world of music. In other cases teachers devote so much attention to factual information that the students fail to think of music as an art form consisting of organized sounds.

Successful music teaching requires a balanced view of the world of music. Both musical objects and processes are needed, as is a variety in the type of music the students study. And both information and activities should be related to organized sound.

What Is Teaching? | *T*eaching is the organizing and guiding of the process in which students learn. Simply put, a teacher's role is to bring about the acquisition of information, understanding, and skills by the students. The way in which this role is accomplished can take a number of different forms. Sometimes it consists of providing the students with information, while at other times it involves setting up a learning situation and then stepping aside as the students work on their own. In some instances it means deciding on tasks for students to do individually, while in other cases it consists of leading a group in a unified effort such as singing a song. Whatever form the teaching takes, the essential characteristic is that the students learn. Results are what the process of teaching is all about, not the particular actions teachers take when working with students. It is important not to confuse the essential goal of teaching with its different styles.

The definition of teaching as a process in which students learn also has implications for the attributes of teachers. Although a teacher may exhibit charm and good looks, lecture brilliantly, manage a classroom well, and use this or that method, if no learning takes place, he or she has not been successful as a teacher. In fact, occasionally (but not typically) a person who appears to violate the usual assumptions about what is needed to be a teacher turns out to be highly effective in getting students to learn. Teaching is so subtle and complex an endeavor that such a situation can happen every so often.

Teachers' jobs usually include duties in addition to leading the learning-teaching process—checking out instruments, taking attendance, keeping order in the classroom. Most of these duties are important and necessary, but they are not really part of the process. A person can be a good manager of classrooms and still not be a good teacher.

The Components of Music Teaching

*W*hat is included in this process called teaching? When all is said and done, it comes down to five simple but basic components that can be stated as questions: (1) *Why* have music in the schools? (2) *What* should be taught in the music class? (3) *How* will it be taught? (4) *To whom* will it be taught? (5)*What are the results*? Because these questions are the essential elements of teaching, they form the basic outline of this book. Each component is discussed in subsequent chapters, but first a brief introduction to each.

Why Have Music in the Schools?

The most basic question concerns why there are music classes in the schools and teachers to teach them. The answer to that question should provide teachers with a sense of direction, and to some degree it affects the answers to the other four questions of "What?," "How?," "To whom?," and "With what results?" Teachers who lack a clear understanding of what they are about are like rudderless ships floundering in the seas of education.

Different answers to the question of "Why?" lead to quite different practical actions. For example, a teacher who sees school music primarily in terms of entertainment for the public teaches quite differently from a teacher who tries to give students a better understanding of music as organized sounds. These two teachers will choose different types of music, teach different skills and information, often use different methods, and evaluate their teaching and students differently.

Fortunately, it is not necessary to return to the question of "Why?" when thinking about every class or rehearsal. If you can express your reasons for teaching music with a reasonable degree of confidence, your answer can give direction and consistency to your teaching. However, it is a good idea to rethink from time to time the fundamental reasons for teaching music. Maturity, experience, and changed circumstances call for a periodic review of a person's views. The topic is too important to be decided once and for all at the age of twenty. Develop some solid answers now to the question of why music should be taught in schools, but don't "chisel your beliefs in stone" this early in your career.

What Should Be Taught in Music?

The question of the content of music classes deals with the "stuff" of music—musical works, facts, fingerings, patterns of sound, understanding of the process of creating music, interpretation, and similar things. It includes all types of information, skills, and attitudes, and it should light the spark of creativity and individual expression within the students.

Deciding what to teach is an enormously complex matter. As pointed out earlier, the world of music is huge, which makes choices about what to teach difficult. Other factors also contribute to the complexity of making these decisions, including practical considerations such as the musical background of the students, the amount of time available, the traditions of the community, the size of the class, and the amount and type of materials available.

It must also be remembered that students learn not only in music classes or under the guidance of teachers. After all, students spend only about 1000 of their 8736 hours each year in school, so it is not reasonable to credit or blame the school for everything students learn or know. The fact remains, however, that not much learning or understanding of music will usually take place without organized, competent instruction in school.

Unlike the question of "Why?" the matter of what to teach needs to be spelled out specifically for each lesson or class. It isn't enough merely to "put in time" in music. There should always be clearly stated objectives in terms of what the students are to learn.

How Should Music Be Taught?

This question of how music is taught focuses on the ways of organizing and structuring instruction, as well as selecting the manner of presentation. Some people who have never taught falsely assume that teaching is a job in which you merely stand up in front of the students and talk. If that were the case, teaching would indeed be easy! However, that is not the way it is, even if some experienced teachers make it look easy, just as a fine violinist makes the difficult passages of a concerto sound effortless.

The suggestions in methods textbooks are geared to what might be called the "typical" school situation. Readers should realize, however, that there are almost no typical schools, and certainly each student is unique. The ideas presented apply to perhaps a solid majority of all teaching situations. As much as an author would like to, it is impossible to offer specific ideas on how to teach music in each of the thousands of schools in the United States.

The difficulty in specifying procedures for all situations is not characteristic of several other professions. For example, since nearly everyone's appendix is in approximately the same part of the body, surgeons can be taught a specific surgical procedure for its removal. Unfortunately, human behavior is much less consistent than human anatomy. Not all students have the same interests, musical background, and mental ability. For this reason identical teaching procedures sometimes produce exactly opposite results in different classrooms, especially when different teachers are involved. Part of the challenge of teaching is being adaptable enough to meet a variety of situations.

Deciding on which methods are most appropriate for teaching specific material to a particular group of students is one of the challenges of teaching. Suppose a teacher wishes to teach a second grade class to sing a song with pleasing tone and accurate pitch. Because the song is simple, it presents the teacher with no technical obstacles. The children are enjoyable to work with and tractable, offering the teacher few problems in guiding the class. The challenge comes in presenting the art of music so that it becomes meaningful to the seven-year-old youngsters. How can the contour of the melodic line be impressed on children who don't know what the word *contour* means? How does a teacher make second graders conscious of the pitches and accurate when they sing them? Certainly not by merely telling them, "Watch your intonation!" How can the phrases of the song be presented so that the students will understand better the function of phrases in the song? Does a gentle sweep of the arm really aid children in perceiving phrases, or are there other means that would be more effective? These questions have just scratched the surface of the pedagogical matters that are involved in teaching a song.

A sizable amount of information exists about learning and the conditions under which it takes place, but much remains unknown. This available information should be the "stuff" of music methods courses. Ideas on teaching change as new evidence becomes available from research and practical experience. For example, it was once believed that language reading should be introduced by teaching letters of the alphabet first, since words are made up of letters. When the alphabet had been learned, they were put into words and finally into sentences.[1] This method (known as the ABC method) seems logical, but what is logical is not always the way people function. Today teachers know that words are comprehended as a whole, not letter by letter. Without this knowledge and without training in how to use it, teachers would waste much time and introduce habits that would have to be broken later. A fluent reading ability and a gracious way with children are not sufficient qualifications for teaching reading. The same is true of teaching music.

To Whom Is Music Being Taught?

Music is taught to someone, and the capabilities and motivation of the students are essential components in the teaching process. Not only must teachers consider such obvious matters as the range of voices and previous musical knowledge, but they should also be aware of the probable use the students will make of what they learn. A seventh grade general music class and a high school orchestra may both study a Bach fugue, but each will approach the work in a different way and with a different degree of technical information.

The "To whom?" question requires that teachers put themselves in the place of the students in order to recognize better their varied interests, needs, and backgrounds. Teachers must try to see the subject through the eyes of the pupils. This ability is needed not only to know how to adapt methods and materials but also to establish a teacher-class relationship that will encourage a positive attitude in the students. Students are often slow to distinguish between their feelings toward the teacher and their feelings toward the subject. And in a subject such as music, in which so much depends on feeling and perception, the students' attitudes are especially important. When the students realize that the teacher is sensitive to their interests, the relationship between pupils and teacher is greatly improved, and more learning takes place.

What Are the Results?

The fifth component in the teaching process is finding out the results of a class or lesson. What do the students know or what are they able to do after the class that they did not know or do before? Exactly and precisely, what was accomplished?

Teachers cannot determine the amount of learning by trusting to luck or by watching the students' facial expressions. Instead what is needed is evidence in terms of what students can do as a result of the learning experience. The term *observable behavior* does not refer to classroom deportment, although there is some relationship between the quality of teaching and classroom conduct. Rather it refers to specific learning revealed through the students' abilities to answer questions, to signal when a theme returns, to sing or play the third of a triad when asked, or to add an improvised phrase to a line of music.

Why? What? How? To whom? With what results? The answers to these questions are the essential parts of the process called teaching. If teachers fail to think through each one of these questions, they run the risk of producing educational failures marked by wasted time and lost opportunities for the students. Teaching is similar in this respect to getting an airplane off the ground. If any important part is missing or not working, the plane will not take off. Because educational failures are less dramatic and less immediately visible than airplanes failing to become airborne, some teachers are able to hold their jobs without thinking carefully about what they are doing. Only their students are the losers. Sometimes the material is too difficult, too easy, or meaningless; sometimes the hours spent in music classes add up to little additional knowledge or skills for the students; sometimes teachers and classes wander, not knowing what they are trying to accomplish or if they have learned anything. When any of these situations occurs, the lack of learning can correctly be called an "educational failure."

The five questions discussed in this chapter provide an approach for thinking and learning about teaching. They also give focus to thoughts that would otherwise be a formless blob in one's mind. Analyzing and understanding the teaching process are the first steps in becoming a good teacher.

Reference
[1]James B. Stroud, *Psychology in Education* (New York: Longmans, Green, 1946), pp. 164–169.

C H A P T E R   T W O

ARE PEOPLE BORN with the ability to teach music well, or do they become good teachers by hard work and self-improvement? What characteristics do most good music teachers possess? Where do preprofessional experiences and student teaching fit into the training of teachers? These and other questions are concerned with the type of persons music teachers should be, the skills and knowledge they need to have, and the ways they can continue to improve their ability to teach after they get a job. Because music programs can be no stronger than the people who teach them, the quality of music teachers is vitally important.

Personality and Ego

The research and writings on the topic of the personality of good teachers have tended to reaffirm what nearly everyone already knows: warm, friendly, understanding teachers are more effective than those who aren't; businesslike and organized teachers are more effective than teachers who are careless and disorganized; and imaginative and enthusiastic teachers surpass in effectiveness those who are routine and dull.[1] One writer concludes that a good teacher is "held to embody most human virtues along with a great many qualities more frequently attributed to divinity."[2]

A few points can be stated with confidence, however, about the personality of successful music teachers. They should be adults in the fullest sense of the word, and they should be conscious of the needs and feelings of others. The whims and idiosyncrasies of an "artistic" temperament have no place in the schools.

It does seem that music teachers are susceptible to greater ego involvement in their work than are most other teachers. It may be that the "leader" role that many music teachers have as part of their jobs attracts people with greater ego needs. It could be that the circumstances of the job tend to encourage a heightened sense of personal involvement; as someone has pointed out, the applause of an au-

FUNKY WINKERBEAN   **Tom Batiuk**

dience is "heady wine." It may be that some music teachers would really rather be performers. Whatever the reasons, many music teachers tend to view their work as an extension of themselves. For example, a number of times the author has heard music teachers almost boastfully relate how the choir or band "fell apart" after they left a particular teaching position. Some teachers work hard with students who have ability because they help bring recognition to the teacher but have little time for the less talented students. The situation pictured in the comic strip on this page in which the teacher draws attention to himself or herself has actually happened in football programs and yearbooks; only the size of the director's face was less prominent.

Music teachers need to face the fact that the pressures of ego involvement will be present throughout their teaching career. What they need to do—and do often—is remind themselves that the role of teacher is one in which you gain satisfaction through observing the learning of your pupils. Music exists in the schools for the benefit of the students, not for the aggrandizement of teachers. The *Final Report* of the Teacher Education Commission of the Music Educators National Conference (MENC) makes the point clearly: "The ego-satisfaction of the music student in college is often gained through personal performance whereas that of the music educator is gained largely from creating opportunities for students' music expression."[3]

The preceding paragraph about where the satisfactions in teaching are found may sound like a teacher's role is one of self-sacrifice. That would not be the correct conclusion. It is not so much a sacrifice of ego and self as it is a different way of achieving satisfaction. When you teach so that the students learn something they would not have learned without your efforts, that is truly gratifying. There is something deeply satisfying about knowing that you make a difference in the lives of people, especially young people. Such satisfactions can hardly be thought of as making a sacrifice; far from it. They are much more rewarding than a career devoted to beating out someone for better chairs in an orchestra or solo parts in oratorios. When all is said and done, there is a lot more enjoyment in doing something for others than in worrying so much about oneself, and such activity carries with it its own type of ego satisfaction.

The grooming and appearance of teachers is a subject that has occasionally produced heated discussions, but it probably has little effect on the students' learning *as long as it does not distract from or interfere with the respect and confidence the students have in the teacher.* It is everyone's right as a citizen to wear any hairdo or clothing style they wish. But if a person's appearance causes the students to look upon the teacher as a freak or egoist, then it is simply not worth the loss of learning that results. Each college and each school has its own standards, both written and unwritten, on this matter. New teachers and student teachers should find out what those expectations are and abide by them. In most cases common sense is a reliable guide for personal appearance.

The speaking voice of teachers should be pleasing, and, more important, it should carry a quality of decisiveness. During student teaching the complaint is sometimes leveled at a novice teacher that his or her voice cannot be heard in the back of the room. This problem usually disappears as the young teacher gains confidence and experience and makes an effort to improve in this area.

In the final analysis, there is something beyond personality, grooming, and voice: a sense of commitment to being a good teacher. David Ausubel, the noted educational psychologist, has written: "Perhaps the most important personality characteristic of a teacher . . . [is] . . . the extent of the teacher's personal commitment to the intellectual development of students. . . . It determines in large measure whether he will expend the necessary effort to teach for real gains in the intellectual growth of pupils or will merely go through the formal motions of teaching."[4] Myron Brenton is more blunt about it: "The best teachers wear a large invisible button that reads, 'I give a damn.'"[5]

The Importance of Being Yourself

When authors or groups such as the Teacher Education Commission write about what teachers should be like, they are presenting an ideal or model, not a set of minimum competencies that must be met. They realize that teachers are human beings and that no one can fulfill every suggested quality. The reason that all the qualities are mentioned is to make readers aware of what is desirable in a music teacher.

Every one of us has strong and weak points in terms of being a teacher. It is obvious that we should utilize our strengths to the fullest in order to compensate for our weaker points. With some teachers their strength is their ability to play piano, with others it is an ability to inspire students, and with others it is their knowledge of music and their intelligence. Each person develops somewhat different ways to fulfill the role of teacher.

Many young teachers who have studied under a dynamic, extroverted individual or observed such a person in full swing at a workshop may have wondered, "Is it necessary for me to have that kind of personality to be successful?" Beginning teachers may find that when they stand before a performing group, it is all they can do to give the necessary directions and go through the conventional conducting gestures. No matter how hard they try, they cannot seem to break out of their shell. This timidity happens to some degree to beginning teachers in general music classes, too. When this situation happens, does it mean that the person has chosen the wrong line of work? Probably not.

Extroversion does not guarantee a teacher's ability to convey ideas and teach effectively. Suppose a teacher puts on a red shirt and conducts groups something like a cheerleader. At first that would probably grab the attention of the students, but what about the fiftieth or hundredth class? What was once attention grabbing could become pretty annoying. And what does the red-shirted teacher do *then* to get attention?

Many good music teachers are not extroverts and would only look silly if they tried to be. Instead of extroversion what is needed is a quality of decisiveness, of knowing what is needed, and letting the students know that you are competent and in charge. Good teachers cannot be weak and "mousy." The way in which each individual achieves this quality of competence depends on his or her unique personality, but it must be achieved, especially when teaching in the secondary schools. Two conditions can help achieve the impression of competence: (1) A firm belief that what you are teaching is worth the students' knowing, and (2) the confidence that arises from understanding what you are about as a teacher. Beyond these basic understandings the quality of decisiveness (not aggressiveness—there is a difference) is something that many future teachers must work on and develop through experience and training.

Human Qualities and Professional Competence

It is easy to point out that teachers should be sensible, fair, decisive, and interested in the students' learning. But how do these attributes relate to the ability of teachers to work with people, something that is central to teaching? The Teacher Education Commission presents the following thoughts on the subject in its *Teacher Education in Music: Final Report:*

Like all teachers, music educators need to be first and foremost live and growing human beings. The fact that they have elected music as their particular discipline places certain special requirements on them but in no way relieves them of their need to be outstanding persons.

Music educators must:

Inspire others. They must demonstrate qualities of leadership that will enable them to excite the imagination of students. They must be able to communicate their enthusiasm for music.

Continue to learn in their own and in other fields. They must develop an attitude of intellectual curiosity that will assist them to find answers not provided in their preservice education.

Relate to individuals and society. They must develop empathy with students and colleagues of varying backgrounds, and restore positive attitudes and commitments toward children of all cultural backgrounds to effect the common goals of mankind. The strengths and qualities valued by cultural minorities must be incorporated to alter, temper, or strengthen traditional goals for the ultimate benefit of a humane and effective society.

Relate to other disciplines and arts. They must be familiar with the scientific method and its application to the physical and social sciences, and know the similarities and differences between their own and other arts. They must seek relationships between music and other disciplines.

Identify and evaluate new ideas. They must develop an attitude that enables them to seek and evaluate new ideas. They need to welcome and utilize technological, experimental, and exploratory developments in musical composition, teaching procedures and aids, and sound-generating devices.

Use their imaginations. They must learn to be creative not only with musical materials but also in the way they approach learning problems and their dealings with colleagues.

Understand the role of a teacher. They must understand that many attitudes and values that are common and appropriate among college music students need to mature substantially for effective music teaching. The desired maturity in attitude must be initiated during prospective teacher training. For example, the ego-satisfaction of the music student in college is often gained through personal performance whereas that of the music educator is gained largely from creating opportunities for students' musical expression.

Most importantly, music educators must demonstrate their understanding that the level of performance and the literature performed must be appropriate to the needs of a specific group of learners. They must also understand that the nature of performance reinforces the teacher-dominant classroom and that the music educator needs to give special attention to overcoming this tendency.[6]

Personal Efficiency.　　Proper planning requires personal efficiency and organization. Unless teachers have these qualities, both they and their students are apt to find themselves in a state of confusion. Music teachers have been known to forget to order chairs or risers for a performance, to lose their own music, to fail to keep track of uniform and instrument numbers (or worse yet money from ticket sales!), and to wait to the last moment to prepare a program for a concert. What excitement these fumblings create! But when confusion reigns, the educational results are reduced. Musicians, along with almost everyone else, may dislike "administrivia"; but trivial or not, details must not be neglected.

Relations with Professional Colleagues. In some instances a music program is hampered because of poor relationships between music teachers and the people with whom they work. For example, if a teacher is personally disagreeable, the school guidance counselors may be hesitant about encouraging students to enroll in music courses. Some instrumental music teachers consider themselves to be in competition with choral music teachers, and vice versa. Not only do the two factions fail to work together, but occasionally the teacher of one group belittles the other in an attempt to build up his or her group. Such friction undermines the total music program and is a waste of emotional energy for the teachers.

Music teachers sometimes overlook the school clerical and custodial staff, or they feel superior to them and let those feelings show. A successful music program depends on the assistance of the nonteaching staff, but thoughtless music teachers occasionally take this help for granted and fail to acknowledge it in any way.

Music teachers need to take an active interest in school activities. They cannot say on the one hand that music is an integral part of the curriculum and then shy away from serving on schoolwide curriculum committees because they feel that music is a "special" area. Nor should they display little interest in the fate of the football team or the winter play, especially if they want the support of the physical education and drama departments for the music program.

Professional Preparation

*V*irtually every state has developed a set of minimum requirements for the certification of music teachers. In most cases these are only minimums and are far below the amount of training that is actually desirable for preparing competent music teachers. Usually these requirements are stated in terms of credit hours for various courses or areas of study.

The Teacher Education Commission and the National Association of Schools of Music (NASM) have emphasized competencies rather than course requirements. They are more interested in saying what teacher education graduates should be able to do than in stating the hour requirements those graduates must fulfill. Competencies can be stated somewhat generally or quite specifically. In Part I of the *Final Report* the Teacher Education Commission is rather general in its statements, with the specific competencies regarding teacher education programs in music presented in Part V. The general competency statements are as follows:

Skills in Producing Sounds (Performance)

All music educators must be able to:

Perform with musical understanding and technical proficiency. Their performance ability on an instrument or with their voice must be sufficient to enable them to interpret representative works of past and present. They must be able to improvise rather than be limited only to performance through reading music. Their performance opportunities during their education should have included solo, small ensemble, and large ensemble experience.

Play accompaniments. They must be able to perform single accompaniments on the piano and on instruments such as the guitar or accordion, and be able to employ these instruments as teaching tools.

Sing. Music educators must have a basic understanding of the human voice as a musical instrument and be able to use their own voices effectively. Not everyone possesses a solo voice, but all music teachers must be able to sing passages for illustrative purposes and lead singing.

Conduct. They must demonstrate conducting techniques that will enable them to elicit from ensembles musical performances appropriate to the compositions being performed.

Supervise and evaluate the performance of others. Music educators must be able to instruct others in developing performance skills. They must have a broad knowledge of repertoire in many areas of music performance, and must develop a knowledge of ethnic instruments and materials suitable for instructional activities in musics of other cultures. Those who plan to teach instrumental music must develop sufficient technique to demonstrate and supervise beginning students on all kinds of instruments, including electronically amplified equipment. They should be familiar with current devices for sound modification and be equipped to explore new developments as they appear.

Organizing Sounds (Composition)

All music teachers must be able to:

Organize sounds for personal expression. Through handling sounds creatively, the musician develops a greater understanding of musical expression as well as enthusiasm for his art.

Demonstrate an understanding of the elements of music through original composition and improvisation in a variety of styles....

Demonstrate the ability to identify and explain compositional choices of satisfactory and less satisfactory nature. Aural discrimination encompasses the ability to identify the most effective devices to realize expressive requirements.

Notate and arrange sounds for performance in school situations. The ability to create and adapt music to fit the achievement level of performers permits a wider variety of repertoire and enables the teacher to sustain the musical challenge without overwhelming the learners.

Skills in Describing Sounds (Analysis)

All music educators must be able to:

Identify and explicate compositional devices as they are employed in all musics. They must be able to apply their knowledge of music to diatonic and non-diatonic Western and non-Western art, dance, and folk music, to such popular idioms as rock, soul, jazz, and country-and-western music, and to traditionally nonmusical sounds.

Discuss the affective results of compositional devices. They must know the ways in which composers in various cultures combine the elements of music to elicit particular responses in the listener.

Describe the means by which the sounds used in music are created. Music educators should be familiar with the tone-production capabilities of conventional instruments, instruments of other cultures, and electronically amplified instruments, electronically controlled tone-altering devices, and electronic sound synthesizers. They must be equipped to explore new developments as those appear.

Professional Qualities

The ability to communicate with students is essential for teachers. Therefore music educators must be able to:

Express their philosophy of music and education. They must establish a commitment to music as an art and component of education. They should be able to communicate this commitment not only verbally and in written form, but also through their professional attitudes and activities.

Demonstrate a familiarity with contemporary educational thought. They must know how people learn and be able to apply this knowledge in teaching music. They must be familiar with the latest media of instruction and various schemes of educational organization.

Apply a broad knowledge of musical repertory to the learning problems of music students. Familiarity with comprehensive musical resources permits the teacher to respond imaginatively and significantly to the diverse situations and demands that arise in the classroom.

Demonstrate, by example, the concept of a comprehensive musician dedicated to teaching. Musical expertise and inspiration are essential leadership qualities that can command of students their most dedicated efforts.[7]

Each future music educator and each music teacher education program should examine these competencies and decide how well they are being met. Although the *Final Report* is certainly not infallible or the ultimate word on the subject, its recommendations merit careful consideration.

Some preparation in both vocal and instrumental music is valuable in music teacher education programs. Not only is this requirement musically and philosophically desirable, it is a practical necessity for many teachers. Although the figures vary from state to state and college to college, several surveys indicate that between a tenth and a fifth of all first-year music teachers have responsibilities in music areas other than their main teaching area.[8] Beginning teachers most often have dual responsibilities because they are likely to work in school systems too small to warrant hiring specialists for each of the various areas of music and because the new person sometimes gets the odds and ends that the teachers already in the system have left behind.

There is another reason for a broad undergraduate preparation. Suppose that it could be determined just what you needed to know to be a music teacher, and you were given only those courses. That situation would be like buying only the amount of blanket needed to cover you at night. You would lie on your back with your hands at your side as your tailored blanket pattern was traced and then cut. Yes, this procedure would save blanket material, but a problem would come up if you wanted to change positions as you slept, because you would have no cover for any other position. A narrow teacher education program provides little "cover" for different positions in music education and may inhibit advancement in the profession. As an undergraduate it is impossible to be able to predict exactly what will be useful to you in the future.

The concept of preparing music teachers for all grades, kindergarten through grade 12, is certainly justified. The vast majority of jobs available to music teachers involve teaching on more than one level.[9]

Knowledge of Teaching Techniques

Good teachers know how to teach what their students are to learn. For example, if a band plays a passage in a staccato style, how does the teacher get the idea of staccato over to the players so that they can execute it correctly? Without knowing how to do this, the teacher must resort to pleading, "Now, make those notes *short!*" This procedure is all right as a beginning, but experienced teachers know that telling the students to play short notes is not enough to teach staccato, except for a few short notes that might happen by trial and error.

Teachers should have in mind numerous examples, analogies, and explanations for use in teaching. They cannot stop a class, run to their desks, and thumb through a book to find this technique or that bit of information. Whenever possible, music teachers should anticipate the problems that might be encountered in a certain piece. If a work requires staccato playing, they can review various ideas for playing staccato (it's not the same on every instrument) prior to presenting the piece to the group.

In teaching a performing group, teachers should teach their students to do more than execute the printed music symbols and follow the conductor's gestures. Singing and playing can easily become mechanical, so that the students make music in a parrotlike fashion without any understanding of what they are doing. Playing and singing are fine, but they are only a part of music education. Students should also be taught something about the style, harmony, form, rhythmic structure, and composers of the more substantial works the group performs. Specific techniques for doing so are presented in *Teaching Music in the Secondary Schools*, third edition.

Preprofessional Experiences

Observations. Many states and colleges require that future teachers have contacts with schools and students prior to the student-teaching experience. These contacts are called by a variety of names, with "field experiences" perhaps being the one most commonly used. The purpose of field experiences is to encourage future teachers to think about and be aware of school situations well before the last semester of the undergraduate preparation, when student teaching is usually taken. In fact, some colleges and states specify contacts with schools beginning in the freshman year, and sometimes the observation of handicapped or ethnic minority children is also stipulated. The Teacher Education Commission also encourages such experiences as early and as often as possible.[10]

Usually field experiences take place in a variety of school situations so that future teachers gain a perspective of the total music curriculum. Many of them are for one time only in any one school or with any one teacher. Occasionally a small-project type of teaching is done in conjunction with a music methods class, such as when a committee of three students develops and teaches a lesson on playing the autoharp to a third grade classroom.

The usefulness of these pre-student-teaching experiences depends to a great extent on the attitude of the future teachers. If they look upon them as just putting in time to fulfill a requirement, then they probably will receive the minimum benefit from them. On the other hand, if they go into school situations and try to analyze the teaching process (*not* the teacher as a person) and learn from what they see, they can benefit a great deal from them.

And what should future teachers attempt to analyze as they observe school music classes? The teaching process as described in Chapter One. (Surprised?) Since these experiences present only a limited time to observe a teacher, and since there is an ethical question about future teachers attempting in an hour or two to guess the motivation of a teacher, the five questions presented in Chapter One should probably be reduced to four for purposes of the observation experiences. For each class, then, the observing students should answer these questions:

1. What was the teacher trying to have the students learn?

2. What methods did the teacher employ to help the students learn?

3. What appeared to be the musical background and interests of the students?

4. What were the observable results of the instruction?

In addition, student observers will find it useful to notice how the teacher managed some of the routine matters of teaching. Such matters include the setup of the room, the distribution of music, the promptness and orderliness with which the class is started and conducted, the assignment of seats for the students, and the manner in which attendance is taken. In no sense are such actions equal in importance to the amount of learning that takes place, but they can affect the educational results, and are therefore worth observing.

Student Teaching.   Student teaching has three purposes. First, it provides the student with the opportunity to observe and work with an established, successful teacher. A student teacher in a real sense is an apprentice to an experienced teacher. This apprenticeship permits an intensive observation and testing experience that is considered essential in all teacher education programs. Supervising critic teachers (the term often assigned to such teachers) are selected because they are considered to be better than average. The critic teacher accepts student teachers largely out of a sense of professional commitment, not to make his or her job easier or to gain extra income.*

The second purpose of student teaching is to provide a guided in-

---

*The stipend for supervising a student teacher is only a token payment, if there is any at all.

duction into teaching. Student teachers can move step by step into situations structured by critic teachers; consequently, student teachers are not just pushed into jobs in which they must either sink or swim.

The third purpose of student teaching is to establish the fact that the student teacher can in fact teach. A prospective employer wants to know, "How did this candidate do when actually in front of a classroom?" A good college record and good character recommendations are fine, but there is no better test of teaching ability than actually teaching in a "real life" situation.

It helps if you are clear on what everyone's role is in the student-teaching situation. Your role as student teacher has already been pointed out: an apprentice or intern. (There are slight differences between those two words, but the essential role is the same.) It is an in-between situation. You will be a teacher, but yet not quite. You will be closer in age to the students than their teacher, but you are expected to act like a teacher, not a student or an intermediary between the class and the teacher. The students know that you are a student teacher and that after awhile you won't be around anymore. They also suspect that you won't have a lot to say about their final grades or their seats in the clarinet section. In a real sense the position of student teacher is one of a "guest" or "temporary resident." You will be working with someone else's classes in a school in which you are not a permanent employee. You will not be in a position to make significant decisions without the approval of the critic teacher, to fill out requisitions unless the supervising teacher approves them, or to negotiate a different schedule for music classes.

Yet you will be a teacher. By that time you will have had much specialized training for what you are doing. Your role will be that of teacher, and you will be expected to show up promptly each day school is in session. You will be allowed some initiative in what is taught, but such undertakings should be cleared with the critic teacher ahead of time.

The role of a critic teacher is that of mentor to the student teacher. A mentor is one who guides, offers constructive help, and answers questions. Offering suggestions for improvement is part of that process, as are commendations for assignments that are done well. Student teachers need not agree with every suggestion they receive, but the critic teachers' thoughts should be given careful consideration and in most cases given a try. In addition, the critic teacher is responsible for a report to the college about your teaching and usually is asked to write a letter of recommendation. For all of these reasons the usefulness of the student-teaching experience depends very much on the critic teacher.

College supervisors usually do not have a major role in the student-teaching situation. This situation is so for one simple reason: the number of times they can visit a student teacher is usually quite limited.

Even if three or five visits are possible, these usually last for only a couple of classes. The college supervisor's role consists more of making the initial placement and then serving as a coordinator between the college and the critic teacher. If important problems arise in the student-teaching situation, then the college supervisor's role becomes very significant. Also, if a college supervisor has observed your teaching, he or she can write a letter of recommendation for you that is more credible than letters from other professors because it can report on your teaching.

The amount and type of teaching that a student teacher undertakes depends on the critic teacher's opinion of the particular needs of the program. Usually the first week or so is spent observing and learning about the situation. Gradually the student teacher is given more responsibility. Often this initial responsibility consists of working with individuals or small groups and doing menial chores such as passing out books, moving chairs, and typing tests. After awhile the student teacher is given entire classes and eventually most of the critic teacher's schedule.

For student teachers who demonstrate initiative, optimism, and a willingness to learn, the student teacher experience is most rewarding.

The Music Teacher and the Community

Professional Musicians

School music programs are affected by the other music activities and interests in the community. A city or town with an active musical life helps the school music program, and, in turn, effective school music programs contribute to the level of the arts in communities. For these reasons music educators should promote musical activities in the community. Also, music teachers should work to bring professional performers into the school through such programs as Young Audiences, Inc., and Artists in the Schools. These programs and others are designed for schools, and usually a portion or all of the costs are paid from nonschool sources. To the extent possible, in-school performances by professional performers and the educational concerts should be jointly planned ventures between the school music teachers and the performers. The benefits are greater when such cooperation takes place.

Attempts have been made to define the "turf" or domain of professional musicians and of school groups. In 1947 the MENC, the American Association of School Administrators, and the American Federation of Musicians drew up a comprehensive Code of Ethics that specifies which activities are the domain of school music groups and which should be left to professional musicians. The code has been reaffirmed every seven years since 1947. All music educators should be familiar with and abide by the provisions of the code.

Music Merchants

Contacts between music teachers and music merchants should also be conducted ethically. Because music teachers are employed by the public, and therefore should treat everyone equally, they should not accept personal favors or commissions from merchants. The acceptance of gratuities has a way of obligating the teacher and gives the appearance of favoritism. The choice of store and purchases made should be determined solely on the basis of the quality of goods and services in relation to the cost. When purchases amount to $50 or more, it is wise (and usually required by law or school regulation) that bids be secured. Competitive bidding encourages the best price from the merchants and provides proof that business transactions are handled fairly and openly.

An especially delicate situation exists when there are a small number of local music merchants whose prices and services are not as good as those of merchants from neighboring communities. In such cases music teachers should make all pertinent information available to the students and their parents but should make no recommendations about merchants. When this practice is followed, the responsibility for which merchant is selected becomes a matter for the individual family, not the music teacher. The same policy should be followed with regard to brands of instruments. Instrumental music teachers should make a list of acceptable brands and types available. Unacceptable brands need not be listed, a procedure that is preferable to denigrating them in written form for someone to challenge.

Private Music Teachers

The same practice should be followed with regard to music teachers' recommendations of private instructors. Never should the work of an incompetent private teacher be deprecated publicly; that person should simply not be recommended. Whenever possible, music teachers should provide interested parents with the names of more than one competent private teacher. The level of the school music program can be advanced considerably by the efforts of good private music teachers. This is especially important in the case of instrumental students who have progressed beyond intermediate levels. Because few instrumental teachers know the advanced techniques on more than one or two instruments, the progress of the school band or orchestra depends in part on the availability of private instruction.

Community Organizations

Community service clubs and organizations, and especially a local arts council, should not be ignored. Service clubs sometimes provide scholarship help to enable worthy music students to study, and they also contribute travel monies on occasion. These groups also are a good means of getting information about the music program to the public. The arts council represents a ready-made group that supports the arts, and such support can be valuable if the music program faces financial cutbacks.

Parents and Public

The most useful contacts music teachers have with the public are the parents of the students. Information should be supplied to the parents periodically about the activities and goals of the music program. Slide shows, videotapes, and brochures can be prepared explaining the program. In some instances parent support groups have been of great help in furthering high school performing groups, especially bands. It is hoped that over time music teachers will steer the interests of such organizations toward the entire music program, not just one segment of it.

For a number of years in March or April the MENC has led a nationwide effort to promote music in the schools; it is called Music in Our Schools Week. Not only does the MENC national office supply prepared materials and posters, it also secures some national publicity for school music. Teachers are encouraged to secure proclamations from mayors and state organizations from governors. Such proclamations provide favorable publicity for school music and let everyone know that music education is indeed alive and well. When music teachers have taken advantage of the Music in Our Schools Week through special performances and programs, they have reported quite positive results in terms of the public's response.

Parents look to music teachers for guidance when their child is contemplating a career in music. School guidance counselors may also be involved in such matters, but their knowledge about music is usually quite limited. To assist students who are considering music teaching and other music careers, both the MENC and the American Music Conference have prepared materials on careers in music. These materials may be secured for a small charge by contacting the appropriate organization.[11]

School Administrators

Clearly the matter of promoting the music curriculum with school boards and administrators is of great importance. A special section is devoted to this topic in Chapter Three.

Continued Growth and Self-Evaluation

*C*ontinued professional development of music teachers after graduation from college is necessary for several reasons. If you graduate from college at the age of twenty-two, you have forty-three years remaining before you reach the age of sixty-five, which is the most common mandatory retirement age for school teachers. Think of it, forty-three years! This is a very long time just to think about, but it is an even longer time to remain fresh, vital, and interesting. Without continued growth teachers run the risk of repeating one year's experience forty-three times rather than improving with each year of experience. No one should want to stay "in a rut" for their entire career.

What can teachers do to continue growing professionally? The most obvious means, and one required in most states before permanent certification can be attained, is to continue study at the graduate level during summers or evenings.

Another means of growth is membership in professional organizations such as the MENC and its state and local affiliated associations. These organizations keep teachers informed about current happenings in the field through their publications and meetings. Most colleges and universities have student MENC chapters in which prospective music teachers should take an active part.

Keeping informed about pertinent research in music education also improves teachers' professional capabilities. Teachers should be aware of the results of studies of music teaching and of practices in music education, many of which have never been subjected to rigorous and thorough intellectual examination. Research results are reported at MENC meetings and in its publications. Music teachers should not be satisfied with answering the question, "Does this teaching procedure work?" In addition, they should ask, "Would another procedure work better?" Being satisfied with something just because it happens to work is like being content to spend a lifetime hopping about on one leg. Undoubtedly hopping works, but there is a more efficient way to get around; it's called walking.

Even after taking advantage of every opportunity and graduating from a good music education program, beginning teachers should realize that they must still teach themselves to teach. No course or series of courses, no professor, no book, no college can impart enough information about the particular school, its students, and its unique nature to train teachers fully for the job they will undertake. Teachers finally must succeed or fail on their own. They must undergo the sometimes difficult process of looking objectively at themselves and improving on their own work.

Fortunately, there are some guidelines for going about the process of evaluating your own teaching. They are presented in Chapter Eleven on evaluation. That chapter is not nearly as concerned with grading pupils as it is with improving instruction. Basically the idea is to decide when planning the lesson or class what it is that the students should be able to do as a result of the instruction. They may be able to answer certain questions, or play certain notes, or tell when a modulation has taken place, or demonstrate similar actions related to what they were taught. Such observable actions aid teachers by letting them know which portions of a lesson seem to have been learned by most of the students and which were not learned so well. Then knowing that, a teacher can do a better job of planning for the next class.

Although self-evaluation has the obvious disadvantage of being somewhat subjective, it is the only practical means open to most music teachers. For one thing, self-evaluation is a continuous process. It is not something that occurs once or twice a semester; it should go on in one form or another during every class. For another thing, it is done with full knowledge of what one is trying to teach and of the total school situation.

Evaluations by outsiders are of limited usefulness. School administrators seldom know much about music. Visits by school principals to classrooms often bring forth comments about things other than the learning of music—"The students seemed to enjoy the class" and statements like that. Even adjudicators at contests, who are competent in music, are listening to the performance of a few prepared works with no knowledge of the school situation. School music supervisors can offer the best critiques for teachers. However, their time available for such work is limited, and many school districts do not have music supervisors.

Teacher Rating Forms

The use of forms for evaluating teachers is a standard at the college level for professors seeking promotion or tenure, but such forms are not found often in the schools. Even at the college level, rating forms are of limited value. The ratings given are only partly the result of the instructor's actions. For example, instructors of required classes for freshmen and sophomores seldom rate as high as instructors of junior and senior-level courses in the students' major area. Rating forms seem to work best with mature students; they are of little worth in elementary and middle schools. The other problem with teacher rating forms is that the responses must be only general reactions about the teacher. A general statement that one is or is not a good teacher is not very helpful in improving instruction. The use of specific objectives and the evaluation of teaching in terms of the students' learning of those objectives is a more valid and useful way of analyzing instruction than is a teacher rating form.

Playback of Classes

Another specific means of self-evaluation is the use of a videotape or tape recorder. Some teachers make a recording of their classes or rehearsals. Before the next class with the same group, they listen to the tape and evaluate what they hear. The recordings serve two purposes: they allow a more leisurely and thoughtful study of what the class has done, and they enable teachers to evaluate their own efforts in teaching the class or rehearsal. In analyzing a tape for self–evaluation purposes, teachers can ask themselves these questions:

1. Were there unnecessary delays and wasted time?

2. Were the points on which I corrected the group really those that needed attention?

3. Did my suggestions to the group actually result in improvements?

4. Were my statements clear and decisive?

5. Did I repeat certain words and phrases—such as "OK?" "You know," "Right"—so frequently that they became annoying?

6. Did I stay long enough or too long with one point of musical learning?

7. Were there relaxing breaks in the rehearsal or class routine—a little humor or something done just for the pleasure of it?

8. Specifically, what was accomplished in the class?

9. Did I encourage the students to discover and learn some points for themselves, or did I direct every action?

Supplementary Employment

Some teachers undermine their effectiveness by assuming work loads that would frighten Hercules. Many teachers are hard-pressed financially, especially those who are supporting a family, and outside work such as teaching private lessons or directing a church choir may be necessary. The problem is that teaching is already a full-time job, and beginning teachers find that the duties connected with it consume all of their time and energy. They must consider the ethical and practical considerations of how much outside work they can do.

One of the pioneers in music education used to schedule one night a week that he spent at home reading, practicing, or in other ways improving himself professionally. His example might well be copied by all music teachers.

No one has ever achieved the status of "perfect teacher." Teachers are human. However, each teacher's unique strengths and weaknesses give him or her a distinctive way of teaching. Such individuality is desirable and can be developed along with the requisites of sensitive musicianship and personal maturity. Music teachers need to relate their educational efforts to the efforts of other professionals in music and in education, and to inform the community about what happens in school music classes. Finally, teachers must look objectively at their work if they are to achieve their potential as teachers of music.

Questions

1. Think of two good school music teachers you have had and of two that you felt were not as good. What in their personality and work made them successful or unsuccessful?

2. Being as objective as you can be, do some self-examination of your own personality and how it relates to teaching music. What are your strong points? What needs improvement?

3. Think of a community that you know well. If there are professional musicians in it, what efforts are made to promote coordinated efforts between them and the school music teachers? What is the relationship between private music teachers and the school music teachers? Between music teachers and music merchants?

4. Suppose that you are responsible for planning a set of slides to explain the music program to parent groups. How many pictures would you use, and what would they depict? What would you say to accompany the pictures?

5. Suppose that you wish to study current research on an aspect of music teaching. Where would you find pertinent articles?

6. During your first year in a new job, you take your musical instrument to a local music store for repair. As you pick it up, the merchant says, "Forget the bill. It's on the house." Should you accept this favor? Why or why not?

Projects

1. Make a tape recording of yourself teaching a segment of a music methods class or a class in the schools. If this cannot be arranged, record yourself teaching a lesson to a fellow student on your major in-

strument or in singing. Evaluate the effectiveness of what you said, the amount of talking you did, the pertinence of your comments about the student's work, and the general pace of your teaching.

2. Visit two identical classes (high school bands, fifth grade general music, and so on) in two different schools. Make some evaluation of the comparative musical maturity of the students, their musical ability, equipment, schedule, and other factors. Make a list of the areas in which the two classes differ.

References

[1] D.G. Ryans, *Characteristics of Teachers* (Washington, DC: American Council on Education, 1960), pp. 360–361.

[2] J. M. Stephens, "Traits of Successful Teachers: Men or Angels?" *Theory into Practice*, II, no. 2 (April 1963), p. 59.

[3] *Teacher Education in Music: Final Report* (Reston, Va.: Music Educators National Conference, 1972), p. 5.

[4] David Ausubel, *Educational Psychology* (New York: Holt, Rinehart & Winston, 1968), p. 412.

[5] Myron Brenton, *What's Happened to Teacher?* (New York: Avon Books, 1970), p. 40.

[6] *Teacher Education in Music*, pp. 4–5. Used by permission.

[7] Ibid., pp. 5–7. Used by permission.

[8] David J. Ernest, "Ten Years of Placement in Music," *Gopher Music Notes*, February 1981, pp. 14–15.

[9] Ibid.

[10] *Teacher Education in Music*; p. 10.

[11] Music Educators National Conference, 1902 Association Drive, Reston, Va. 22091. American Music Conference, 100 Skokie Boulevard, Wilmette, Ill. 60091.

2 | *Why Teach Music?*

THE FIRST and foremost question to answer before beginning to teach is, "Why should students learn music?" The answer to it is the foundation on which so much else rests. It may determine whether or not it will be done, or if you will do it, because people generally do not undertake something unless they consider it worthwhile. The answer to the question of "why" very much influences the kinds of things that a teacher does in the class or rehearsal room. For those reasons, anyone considering teaching as a career should carefully and logically seek to answer this question. Chapter Three provides a beginning in doing this.

The Reasons for Music in the Schools

C H A P T E R   T H R E E

MANY MUSIC TEACHERS don't want to be bothered with fundamental questions about why music should be a part of the school curriculum. Why not just go ahead and do a good job of teaching and leave the philosophical questions to college professors? There are at least four reasons why every teacher needs to think through such matters for himself or herself.

Reasons for Considering Basic Goals

*F*irst of all, teachers cannot avoid taking positions on the question of "Why is music being taught in the schools?" through things they do and decisions they make when teaching.

John Marsh believes that the main purpose of music in the schools is to entertain audiences. He selects music for its audience appeal and then drills the performers on it. His students gain very little understanding of how the music is organized or of the meaning of the texts of the songs. Only the best students are selected for the performing groups; the average students are ignored.

By his actions John Marsh has provided a clear statement of his beliefs about music in the schools. The correctness of his opinions is not the issue here. The point is that through what he does he reveals a philosophy—a set of beliefs—about music education.

Second, there is a need to "sell" music in the schools. Most of the time the problem is not one of coping with obvious and deliberate doubts about the value of music instruction. Very few people are opposed to having music in the schools. Rather teachers have to do some convincing so that more staff can be added when needed, schedule conflicts can be worked out, and sufficient money can be budgeted for supplies and equipment.

Sandra Petrocelli, teacher of general music at South Middle School, has discovered that the number of sections of seventh grade general music will be reduced and each class will be 50 percent larger than it was last year. Sandra realizes that she needs to convince the school administration of the importance of realistic class sizes for general music classes, and that the employment of another teacher for a couple of periods each day is a good use of school funds.

If Sandra Petrocelli is to make a case for reasonable-sized classes, she must first know what should be accomplished in the classes, and then make clear the probable effect of class size on student learning. In most school situations, by the way, it must be the music teachers who need to educate the school administrators on the nature and needs of the music program. Many districts do not have music supervisors, which is unfortunate, so the responsibility cannot be left to someone else. Even in districts with supervisors, often the intraschool solutions to problems such as scheduling and room assignments are left up to the teachers who teach in the building. More is said about educating administrators and the public later in this chapter.

Third, for their own sake teachers need to be clear on what they are trying to accomplish.

Marian Knowles is tired. It's been a hard day; nothing has seemed to go right. The classes have been talkative, and their singing dull and often flat. As an added disappointment, she has just realized that she has used up most of the money in the budget for new music, with none of the music for the spring concert purchased yet.

As she drops into a chair in the teachers' lounge after school, a veteran teacher notices her dejected air and says, "Don't worry so much, Marian. Why work so hard? After all, who wants to be the best teacher in the graveyard?" Marian wonders, "Is it really worth all the work and worry?"

Marian Knowles had better be able to answer the question about why teaching music is worth it, if for no other reason than to keep her sense of perspective. If she can, she will be a happier and more effective teacher.

Fourth, teachers need to be clear about their goals in order to be consistent.

Last fall was Neil Gorton's first year as band director at St. Marks. He was anxious to have a prize-winning marching band, so he enrolled anyone who would carry an instrument or flag. He worked hard on the corps style of marching, with its careful attention to the one show to be used for many performances. The results were only mixed. Some of the better musicians became unhappy with the limited type of music and quit, but a few other students were motivated to join the band. Other, more experienced bands won the contests that St. Marks entered, but at least Neil could talk about winning "next year."

At the end of the marching season, he realized that he didn't need many of the students who were enrolled. In order to have a good concert band, he tried to convince the less able players to drop out for a semester (to return next fall, of course). Also, he made rigorous demands for extra rehearsals and caustic remarks in the hope that the less able students would quit. The band members became indifferent to the band and to Neil, and a couple of good players dropped out.

In March, prodded by his conscience and some talks with the principal, Neil changed to a more pleasant approach and showed more interest in his students as persons. But the time was late. The students did not quickly forget the way things had been over the past few months. His more relaxed attitude initially produced more talking and fooling around. After a month the behavior improved, and the band made an effort to prepare for the spring concert. As the year closes, Neil wonders what he will do next fall when he again wants to enter marching contests. He feels torn between a desire to create a public image as a "winner" and an interest in teaching music to his students.

Neil Gorton's vacillating sense of direction is making him miserable, and it is keeping him from doing anything well. He must make a choice of goals and then stick consistently to them, so that the actions he takes in October will not undo what he wants to accomplish in February.

At first glance, thinking about the basic goals of music in the schools may seem impractical, but in a real sense such efforts may be the most practical thing teachers can do. Wandering about with no sense of direction is wasteful and impractical.

The Value of Music and the Fine Arts

*Y*ou may have noticed that the heading for this section includes music and the fine arts. At the basic, general level the same points can be made for each of the fine arts. The differences among them lie in the medium of expression. Music is organized sound, painting is organized shapes and colors on a two-dimensional surface, and dance involves both form and movement in a span of time. While the arts are not identical, especially in terms of the technical factors present in each, they have the same basic reasons for existence and for being included in the school.

It is not difficult to establish the point that music and the other fine arts are important in human life. It can be done in several ways. One way is to assemble data on the amount of money people spend for instruments, recordings, and sound-reproducing equipment. Also, the number of people attending concerts in the United States each year is truly impressive; it is larger than the number who attend sports events such as major league baseball and college football.[1] Also, millions of Americans play musical instruments and sing in church choirs.

Another way is to point out the fact that music is present in every area of the world, even among the remote Aborigines in Australia. It has been present in every historical era since the dawn of civilization. The walls of Egyptian buildings picture people playing instruments and singing, and the Bible tells how David soothed King Saul with his music. Clearly, there must be something important about an activity when it is so pervasive today and in the past. Music is not just another pastime like roller skating or macrame.

More than logic and objective data are available to music educators in seeking support for music in the schools. Most people, when they hear a group of children sing or young people play their instruments, have a good feeling about it. Intuitively they sense—correctly—that making music is a constructive, worthwhile thing for children and teenagers to do. Usually they can't say just exactly why they feel this way, but that is not necessary. If this feeling that music is good for school students is true of most people, it is especially true of persons involved with education and, of course, parents. For years music educators have observed the enthusiasm of parents for the music events in which their children are involved, even if the music is not particularly well performed. The scene from the musical *The Music Man* in which the parents enthusiastically respond to awkward sounds of the children taught by Professor Harold Hill's phoney "think system" is not far from the way it really is.

The objective evidence about the important place of music in life can be combined with good feelings people have for music and school students in order to present a stronger case for music. This approach might be called, for lack of a better name, the "Let's not cheat the kids" approach. For many years the most successful fund raiser for the local arts fund in one community was a businessman who called on other businessmen and said something like this: "Look, you and I don't know much about the arts, but do you want the young people of this community to grow up as ignorant about art and music as we are?" His choice of words is clearly not recommended for music educators, but he was correct in his essential approach, and he was very effective.

It is on the demonstrable and intuited significance of music in people's lives that music educators should build their case when communicating with school administrators and the public about why music should be in the schools, a topic discussed more fully on page 49. Although objective, logical evidence does not (unfortunately) always carry the day in education and other areas of life, having the facts on your side is a much more useful and stronger position than not having them.

What About Music Is Valued?

The question of why music and the arts are important to people is usually not a particularly interesting one to nonmusicians. They are not won over by assertions like "Music is a tonal analogue of emotive life."[2] In fact, the matter is not of much interest to many music teachers, but it should be, because it has quite a bit to say about what music teachers should teach and how they should teach it.

There are a number of different theories about why the arts are valuable to people, but they are more nearly intellectual guesses than they are established facts. One view, perhaps best represented by the twentieth-century American writers on philosophy and aesthetics John Dewey and Susanne Langer, holds that in the arts humans reexperience in a roundabout way feelings associated with life, and through them they gain insight into subjective reality. Others, such as the nineteenth-century philosopher Arthur Schopenhauer, maintain that music is "transfigured Nature" transcending the world and revealing the realm of the ultimate Will (God).[3] And there are other views. As profound as these theories are, it seems probable that no single explanation can account for the workings of the human mind, especially when doing something as complex as listening to music. It is important to remember, however, that the lack of agreement among aestheticians and philosophers about why the arts are valuable does not alter the fact that they make a fundamental and important contribution to the quality of human life; on that point there is wide agreement.

Essentially the arts represent an important difference between existing and living. Animals exist in the sense that they manage to survive; that's their objective in existing. Humans live; they attempt to make life interesting, rewarding, and satisfying. Humans are not content merely to get by, to survive. Music, painting, and dance all enrich life and bring to it their special meanings and provide an avenue of expression. People admire the shifting surf, the color of a sky at sunset, and the beauty of a flower. They also create objects that they can contemplate and with which they can enrich their lives. For example, although a rather large cardboard box could serve as a nightstand by your bed and it would cost nothing, you really would rather have a wooden table or stand with a little bit of grace and beauty. This compulsion of humans to reach beyond their immediate, practical needs is not just a nice luxury; it is an essential quality of being human.

Aesthetic Experiences

The arts involve an aspect of human experience called *aesthetic*, a word that is often heard and seen in writings on music education. For about two decades now music educators have been exhorted to emphasize the aesthetic aspects of music, to make youngsters aesthetically sensitive, and to involve themselves in aesthetic education. Fine; but what does the word *aesthetic* mean? What makes an aesthetic experience different from ordinary experiences like eating a hamburger or going to class?

One basic difference between aesthetic and ordinary experiences is the nonpractical nature of aesthetic experiences. They are valued for the insight, satisfaction, and enjoyment they provide, not for any practical benefits. Looking at a bowl of fruit (a scene frequently painted by artists) is aesthetic when you contemplate the color and shape of the pieces of fruit; it is nonaesthetic when you are thinking about how the fruit reminds you that you are hungry. An aesthetic experience is an end in itself; it is done only for the value of doing it.

A second characteristic of an aesthetic experience is that both intellect and emotion are involved. When you look at a painting aesthetically, you are consciously aware of considering thoughtfully its shapes, lines, and colors. That is the intellectual part. At the same time you are reacting to what you see; you have feelings about the painting, even if it is abstract art. Seldom are these reactions so strong that you start laughing or crying, but you react to some degree; your feelings are involved.

Because intellectual contemplation is required, recreational activities like playing tennis and purely physical sensations such as standing under a cold shower are not considered aesthetic. Neither are purely intellectual efforts such as working multiplication problems, although even in that case a reaction is often involved, as when you see $3 \times 9 = 28$.

A third characteristic of aesthetic experiences is the fact that they are experiences. You cannot tell someone else about a painting or a musical work and expect that person to derive the same amount of enjoyment from the work as you did. In fact, telling about a piece of music or a drama seems to ruin it. For this reason aesthetic experiences have no answers, as do problems in a math class. Listening to the last minute of Beethoven's *Fifth Symphony* is not the "answer" to that symphony. Anyone who tries doing that will be cheating himself or herself out of the aesthetic enjoyment that the symphony provides.

A fourth characteristic of aesthetic experiences is a focusing of attention on the object being contemplated. This centering of attention is on the object as an object and not on a task to be accomplished, such as hitting the ball out of the infield in a baseball game. When you listen to a song aesthetically, you concentrate on its musical qualities and how they enhance the text, not just on the message of the words or the singer's appearance.

Where does the notion of beauty enter into the discussion of aesthetic experiences? In one sense it doesn't enter in very much. Not all aesthetic experiences need be beautiful in the usual sense of the word. Hundreds of works of art ranging from Stravinsky's *The Rite of Spring* to the Ashcan school of painting of Edward Hopper and George Bellows have demonstrated that the aesthetic and the beautiful are two different considerations.

Pointing out what an aesthetic experience is *not* may help to clarify further what it *is*. The opposite of *aesthetic* is not *ugly* or *unpleasant* but rather might be thought of as *anesthetic*—no feeling, no life, nothing. Perhaps the clearest example of "anesthetic" behavior that comes to mind happened one day while I was observing a rather bad junior high school band rehearsal. A sousaphone player was talking to one of the drummers when the band director started up the band without waiting for players who were not paying attention. After a few moments the young sousaphone player realized that he should be playing along with the others. Although he didn't know where or why, he pulled the mouthpiece to his mouth and started blatting away without any sense of what was happening musically.

Teaching for Aesthetic Awareness

The example of the boy playing the sousaphone without any idea of what he was doing points out an important obligation of all music teachers: teach for an awareness of the aesthetic properties in the music. Precisely what does that mean? Should the young player have known facts about the composer of the piece and its stylistic characteristics? That would have been nice, but such information is not aesthetic. Should he have been taught about the technical features of the music? Nothing wrong at all in learning analytical skills, but they are not aesthetic either. Should he have known how to play the correct notes at the right time? That would have been valuable, too, but it isn't aesthetic. Rather, the properties of the music that can cause aesthetic experiences include such aspects as the rise and fall of the melodic lines, the greater and lesser tensions in the chord progressions, the timbres caused by the various instrumental combinations, the repeating or developing of melodic and rhythmic ideas, and the changing dynamic levels. Those and similar points are the aesthetic features of music that students need to be taught to notice.

Perceiving music aesthetically is a complex human action that has two aspects. One aspect consists of cognitive processes like identifying, comparing, analyzing, and classifying. In general, these processes are objective, and they can be practiced, tested, and taught. The other aspect consists of feelings, which are, of course, subjective. Feelings and reactions can only be hinted at in words, and they cannot be analyzed, tested, or taught in any direct way. Therefore teachers must devote their efforts to what is teachable and encourage and hope for aesthetic reactions. Teachers can only set up situations in which reactions can happen, much as one might set up the pins in a bowling alley in the hope that the bowler will knock them down.

To teach the more objective aspects of aesthetic experience, teachers can draw the students' attention to the properties in the music either through asking questions or sometimes telling about them. The teacher of the band in which the sousaphone player was a member might have asked him such questions as these: "How should the smooth melodic line affect the way you play your accompanying bass part?" (The student would need to think about the relation between his part and the melody.) "When the piece changes from major to minor at letter G, how does that change seem to affect the quality of the music?" (The student would have to listen and think about the quality of the music.) "Do you have a fragment of the melodic line in your part a couple of measures after letter E?" (The student would need to compare his part with the melodic line.) "Where should you take a breath in the passage after letter C?" (The student would be encouraged to think about phrasing and its effect on the music.) "In the first four measures of the melody at letter D, which is the most important note?" (The student would need to consider the relationship among the notes of the melody and which one seems most significant to it.) There are literally hundreds of such questions that can be raised about the qualities of any work of music.

The teaching for an awareness of the aesthetic qualities in a piece of music can take place concurrently with learning to play or sing the music, as well as with the learning of some information about it. It is not necessary to neglect one aspect of music to learn another. Traditionally music teachers have taught performing skills and a little bit of information about the music, but not nearly often enough have they drawn attention to the qualities of the music. This is too bad, because aesthetic experiences are the "payoff" for being involved in the arts; they are what the arts are all about. Therefore music teachers should make the teaching for aesthetic awareness as important a goal as the learning of skills and information.

On the basis of educational priorities, John Marsh's main goal of entertaining audiences (p. 37) can be faulted. He is giving his students a limited education in music, one confined to performing a certain type of music in an attractive way. Any awareness that his students gain of the aesthetic qualities of the music they sing will be on their own initiative and ability. There are some additional weaknesses in John Marsh's goals that will be discussed in Chapter Four on the music curriculum.

From the points that have been presented in these pages, it is evident that the reason why music and the other fine arts are important does have something to say about what teachers should do when they stand in front of music classes. The reasons why music is valuable to human beings may not be fully appreciated by nonmusicians, but they are an important guide to music teachers.

*M*usic has a long tradition of being included in schools for reasons such as citizenship, character development, team spirit, and health benefits. Plato in his *Republic* cites the need for music in the education of every citizen. His reasons were based on the ancient Greek idea of *ethos*—the belief that each mode promoted certain qualities of character in a person. Music was also much more broadly conceived in his day and included aspects of poetry and physical education. Since music was closely allied with mathematics during the Middle Ages, music was taught in the medieval universities partly because scholars were fascinated with the acoustical ratios of musical sounds. They wondered if the ratios might reveal secrets about the universe. During other periods of history music was included in the curriculum primarily because a knowledge of music was a mark of an educated person. In 1837, when Lowell Mason was given permission to begin music in the Boston schools, the subject was justified because it contributed to reading and speech and provided "a recreation, yet not a dissipation of the mind—a respite, yet not a relaxation—its office would thus be to restore the jaded energies, and send back the scholars with invigorated powers to other more laborious duties."[4]

The practical benefits of music were still being stressed through the era of the Seven Cardinal Principles of Education and the progressive education movement during the first half of the twentieth century. As late as 1941 such eminent music educators as Peter Dykema and Karl Gehrkens were emphasizing nonmusical outcomes with their philosophy that "the teacher teaches children through the medium of music."[5] The clear implication was that music is included in the schools to achieve some goal greater than itself.

Not until the late 1950s did music educators begin publicly to question the validity of statements about music's usefulness in promoting nonmusical goals. There were three reasons for their doubts. One was the lack of research demonstrating that music classes influence students to become better citizens or healthier individuals. Granted, music does not encourage poor citizenship, loose morals, or failing health. However, claims that say "it doesn't hurt people" are not very convincing when it comes to getting music in the school curriculum.

A second factor that weakened the traditional utilitarian claims for music was the realization that other curricular and extracurricular activities can do the job better. Courses in history and government are more pertinent to citizenship than are music courses, and physical education is more beneficial than music for health and physical fitness. If school administrators wish to strengthen these areas, they are not likely to select the music program as the means of achieving such ends.

A third reason for the change was the awareness that music and the fine arts are significant and valuable in their own right. Just as biology and history teachers do not claim to teach something "through the medium of biology or history," music educators realize that their subject is valid too. Unsupported claims for nonmusical outcomes only make them appear weak, illogical, and uncertain about the value of their subject. Today most music educators agree that music is an area of study that is equal in worth to other subjects of the curriculum.

The interest in the nonmusical values of music has never completely been abandoned, however, and renewed interest in them has been seen in recent years as more music programs have faced the possibility of cutbacks. Happily, music can be two things at the same time. It can be an art filled with aesthetic qualities, and it can serve as a means of nonmusical ends such as leisure-time diversion, emotional release, and social activity. In any case these nonmusical values merit further discussion.

Transfer to Other Subjects

If you study one subject, and what you learn in that subject contributes to your understanding of a second subject, transfer of learning has taken place. Does instruction in music transfer to other areas of the curriculum? If so, which areas, and how much? Unfortunately, the research on the topic of transfer is limited, and some of what has been done is suspect in quality. Almost all the studies of transfer have been done in elementary schools; little can be said about transfer at the secondary school level. It appears that a program infused with study and activity in the arts contributes to a better attitude toward school. A better attitude, in turn, results in more learning and less absenteeism on the part of the students.[6] The area holding the greatest prospects for transfer from music appears to be language arts. Reading may be aided by music study.[7] Music also helps with certain types of speech problems, especially stuttering.[8]

After a thorough review of the available research on transfer, Karen I. Wolff concludes:

The weight of evidence gleaned from the research leads one to believe that there may be measurable effects of music education on the development of cognitive skills and understanding. This seems to be true for both general transfer, i.e., "learning how to learn," and specific transfer. Specific transfer is particularly apparent in its effect on performance in the language arts.[9]

Mental Health

The old belief was that music has the power to "soothe the savage breast." That may be an overstatement, but music therapy has demonstrated that music can affect human behavior and aid mental health. It may be that music allows for the venting of emotions in a socially acceptable way. Young people have for years said that music helps them when they are "feeling low" and contributes to a sense of well-being.

In many communities music has been promoted with slogans such as "A boy who blows a horn will never blow a safe." Although guiding adolescent behavior is far more complex than that statement indicates, it does suggest that there are some psychological benefits for students who study music.

Avocational Value

While the average life expectancy has been increasing, the average workweek has been decreasing. These facts mean that more time for leisure is available. Music is an important avocational activity in many countries, including America. One listing of community orchestras contains over 1400 entries, and there are thousands of church choirs and other amateur choral groups.[10] An even greater number of people listen to music. For these reasons the training for intelligent listening is an important challenge for music educators.

Two significant points should be kept in mind about the nonmusical outcomes of music instruction:

1. *There are valid and supportable reasons for including music in the elementary school curriculum, apart from any nonmusical benefits.* The nonmusical benefits can be thought of as "bonuses" for instruction that the schools should be offering anyway. The place of music in the schools does not depend on them, but its position may be stronger because of them.

2. *There is little a teacher can do directly to make these transfer, psychological, and avocational benefits happen.* The self-image of students, their social and psychological needs, and their choice of what to do with their leisure time are all influenced by circumstances over which teachers have little control. Teachers cannot use a teaching procedure that ensures any nonmusical benefits, although good teaching can help create a situation in which they are more likely to happen.

Students or the Subject?

The fact that students can learn the subject of music while gaining personal and social benefits should lay to rest a long-standing but false dilemma: Should teachers teach the subject or the students? They should teach both; it is not an either-or proposition. Students are not helped if they are left ignorant about what they are supposed to learn, no matter what their personal problems may be. On the other hand, teachers cannot ignore the fact that they teach human beings. They need to be flexible and sensitive to the students' needs so that they can do the best possible job of teaching.

Teachers and Educational Goals

Teachers have both opportunities and limitations in determining the goals in public education. They must accept the broad goals endorsed by the society and its educational system. Teachers who act contrary to these goals reduce the total effectiveness of the schools, to say nothing of possibly losing their jobs. For instance, teachers cannot ignore the many for the benefit of the few or teach the violent overthrow of the government without detracting from the results the schools seek to achieve. These broad mandates apply to music teachers just as much as they do to other teachers. Music is a specialized area of study, but so are other school subjects. Specialization is not a grounds for exemption in this matter.

The educational mandates guiding teachers are broad and general. They are something like the directions a passenger gives a taxi driver. The rider gives the destination, but decisions about the best way to get there are the driver's, because he or she is the "expert" in getting around that city. There are some general restrictions, such as not hitting other cars and not driving on the sidewalk, that the passenger doesn't need to state specifically. Taxi drivers, like teachers, make the detailed decisions about the process of reaching the destination and implement them as intelligently and efficiently as possible.

Who finally decides what the specific objectives are for music classes—administrators, boards of education, governmental agencies, or teachers? The forces that affect educational goals and objectives are diverse and often conflicting. States authorize local school boards to oversee education, and school boards then employ administrators to guide the daily efforts of education. But the matter does not stop there. Teachers can also influence decisions within school systems. Because administrators rarely know as much about each subject matter area as the teachers who are specialized in an area, they must depend on the music faculty members for guidance and leadership concerning the music program. Then after considering the other needs in the school system, they will try to render a fair and equitable decision about how fully the recommendations of the music teachers can be implemented. Unless administrators are informed by the music faculty members about what is needed, they will assume that the present situation is satisfactory and will tend to continue it.

The detailed, within-class decisions are the responsibility of each teacher. There is no way for administrators to oversee such matters. There simply isn't time for them to look over the shoulder of every teacher, and (except for music supervisors) they lack the knowledge of music to make specialized decisions. Very few school administrators know the correct embouchure for the French horn or what the Kodály-Curwen hand signs are!

Music Teachers and School Administrators

Music teachers tend to place much importance on the quality and amount of support provided music programs by school administrators. (Many school administrators feel that the powers attributed to them by teachers are exaggerated, however.) It is true that school administrators can have a significant effect on the success of a music program. Sometimes teachers have devoted much attention to their teaching but forgotten to work with the school administration so that conditions exist in which the teaching of music can take place.

If, as hoped, music teachers do communicate with school administrators about the music program, what do they say that is (1) understandable and meaningful to nonmusicians and (2) true? Part of the answer to the first question was given earlier in this chapter on pages 40–41. Music teachers must build a solid case for music on (1) its significant place in American society and (2) the administrators' positive intuitive feelings about music and children. Important as these points are, they are only the first step.

The second essential point to get across is that music needs to be taught in school in a systematic way by trained personnel. As in the case of mathematics and language skills, when music moves beyond the rudimentary level of singing a few simple songs, it exceeds the teaching capabilities of most families. There is too much to learn that is too complex for the family to teach. That is one reason virtually all societies have found it necessary to establish a system of schools. Although there would be some music in America without music instruction in the schools, the amount and type of music would be only a shadow of the subject as we know it. Young people would be truly limited in their knowledge and understanding of music, the point on which the successful fund raiser mentioned on page 40 built his appeal. In no way can radio disc jockeys and record players adequately replace music teachers.

People who know music only superficially usually regard it as a recreational activity. And it is true that music is often merely a pastime. However, there is a big difference between singing a song around a campfire for fun and singing a song to gain a greater understanding of its musical properties. One is recreation, while the other is education. For these reasons music teachers must make the point that music is a subject requiring consideration and esteem equal to what is given other school subjects. If this point is made, music teachers are of course obligated to teach children and young people music and not just consider music classes as an entertaining pastime.

Many times music has been sold to the public and school administrations for its public relations value. This is where the "true" criterion mentioned earlier for communicating with administrators comes in. Sometimes an administrator has been urged to buy a certain instrument because the band needs it to look good on the football field or to win a higher rating at contest time, and not because the instrument will help students learn more adequately how the music should sound. The "We don't want to be shown up" argument is not a valid one; administrators should not be urged to do the right thing for the wrong reasons.

Often school administrators have been given the nonmusical benefits of music as the reason for including music in the schools. As was mentioned earlier in this chapter, such reasons are shaky, and many school administrators know it. They know, for example, if improvement in reading is the goal, it is better to add more time or teachers for reading than to increase the amount of attention given music, even if music instruction does contribute to reading skill.

A brief example of how one teacher dealt with the school administration can serve as a successful example of communicating with administrators.

Margaret Coppock teaches strings in several Centerton schools. For a number of years it was clear that strings were not faring well when it came to enrolling beginning instrumental students for the classes in the sixth grade. The band teachers recruited intensively through the use of their jazz bands, and the attraction of the shiny instruments and vibrant music presented tough competition for the gentler sound of violins and cellos. She became convinced that Centerton should follow the practice of a number of other school districts of offering string instruction one year earlier than instruction was offered for the winds. The other full-time string teacher in the district was supportive but not interested in working on the idea, so she proceeded on her own.

Although the administration had not asked for ideas for improving the music program, Margaret prepared a proposal in writing for the administration in which she spelled out the requested change and the reasons why it was desirable and needed. The first pages of the proposal presented a brief statement of what the string program was trying to accomplish and why strings are a necessary part of the total music curriculum. Then the suggested improvements were described, including how instruments could be secured and the amount of additional instructional time that would be needed. The response to her proposal was a polite letter from the superintendent indicating interest in the idea but expressing regrets that funds did not permit instituting the change for the coming year.

The next year Margaret sent a slightly revised version of the proposal to the administration, with about the same results. The proposal was prepared and sent a third year, again with about the same response.

There was no music supervisor in the Centerton district, and so one year the administration asked that a committee of music teachers be formed to formulate suggestions for program improvement. The idea of starting strings a year ahead of the winds was proposed by Margaret to this committee. After about a year and a half of meeting sporadically, the committee developed a list of recommendations, of which the string proposal was one. Margaret's earlier proposal was touched up and served as documentation in the committee report. After several months the administration decided to move ahead with the idea, and the following fall string instruction was offered to fifth graders for the first time.

Her efforts did not end there. During the first year she and the new string teacher believed that a massed performance of all the fifth grade string players in the district was necessary to demonstrate the success of the program. A performance was scheduled (and starting time moved ahead thirty minutes to accommodate the superintendent) for early April. Preparing for the performance was quite a bit of work, and the musical results were modest, but the large group performing some simple music reasonably well established an image of success in the audience's mind. Figures on enrollment and attrition were also presented to the administration after the first year.

No two cases are the same, of course, but certain facts about this example merit attention. First, the teacher communicated with the administrators, even when such information was not specifically requested; she didn't wait for their invitation before presenting a needed improvement in the program. Second, the teacher persisted in seeking the improvement. It is not enough to make a point once and then forget about it. Sometimes it takes several years to convince the administration that a change is needed. Third, it helps a great deal if the music faculty can make its recommendations in a somewhat unified manner. A group statement has more impact than an individual's views, although an individual is better than no one speaking up at all. The idea became a reality after it achieved group endorsement. Fourth, it is not possible in this case to determine what influenced the administration to adopt the idea. In a sense it doesn't really matter, but such knowledge might have been useful to teachers in presenting proposals in the future. Probably there was not just one cause, because such matters are usually complex ones. Fifth, the requests, both by the teacher and the committee, were organized, well thought out, and put in writing. When these steps are followed, the proposal being made to the administration is presented in the best possible manner. Sixth, the efforts at informing the administration continued even after the new program had been instituted.

Public Relations

Music teachers should also attempt to generate more understanding of and support for the music program among members of the community. There are several means for doing so. One of the most effective is the students themselves. Their interest and favorable attitude toward their music experiences can do much to encourage support among parents and relatives. For this reason there is a relationship between effective music teaching and the support of the program among a portion of the public.

Another avenue of contact with the public is through newspaper stories, radio spots, and the like. The details of a press release will not catch the attention of every reader, but many people notice and remember that something appeared in the newspaper about the school music program. The use of photographs helps draw attention to the story. Not every item given newspapers is printed. Their space needs differ from day to day, and so one can never be sure how much of a story will be published. Newspapers like stories written from a newsy "angle," not just another concert announcement. The material should be written as a news story and provide the essential who-what-where-when information.

Some school districts prepare an attractive brochure about the music program. Such brochures should be economical in the amount of text they carry and liberal in the number of attractive photographs. Sometimes a question-and-answer format is effective in such publications. For example, a question such as "Does the school rent instruments to students who wish to begin taking lessons?" offers the chance to provide readers with information about the availability of instruments.

Speaking appearances by music teachers and performances by school groups before organizations such as the PTA and Rotary are other accesses to the public. The MENC has produced several audiovisual packages for use on such occasions.[11]

Strong, articulate teacher guidance is vital in establishing an effective music curriculum. To provide guidance teachers themselves must know why music should be included in the curriculum of the schools. Then they need to educate the school administration and the public in the merits of school music instruction.

Questions

1. Is John Marsh's devotion to entertainment (p. 37) as the main goal of his performing groups defensible in terms of music education? Why or why not?

2. Suppose that you are Sandra Petrocelli (p. 38). What points would you make to the school administration for reasonable class sizes?

3. This chapter stressed that the main reason for teaching music in the schools is to give students an understanding of its aesthetic qualities. Is this goal also the primary function in art education? English? History? Extracurricular activities such as scouts and interscholastic athletics? If the reasons are not the same, in what ways are they different?

4. Assume that you are asked to give a fifteen-minute talk to a local service club on the school music program. How would you explain in simple, practical terms the goals of aesthetic sensitivity? Or would you just ignore the subject and talk about the more obvious features of the program?

5. How consistent with the objectives of education in America are the following statements by music teachers?

(a) "You can't make a silk purse out of a sow's ear. No use straining yourself over a kid who just doesn't have talent."

(b) "I've got one of the best positions in the state. Three fine junior highs feeding me well-trained players, and I use the best of them."

(c) "I know that not many youngsters take choral music. But if the few I have get a good music education—not just the trash so many teachers dish out today—then it will have been worth it."

(d) "I don't care how poor or lacking in talent they are, I'm determined to teach them as much as possible about music and what makes it tick."

Suggested Readings

Meyer, Leonard B. *Emotion and Meaning in Music*. Chicago: University of Chicago Press, 1956.

―――. *Music, the Arts, and Ideas*. Chicago: University of Chicago Press, 1967.

Reimer, Bennett. *A Philosophy of Music Education*. Englewood Cliffs, N.J.: Prentice-Hall, 1970.

Toward an Aesthetic Education. Reston, Va.: Music Educators National Conference, 1971.

References

[1]*U.S. News and World Report*, 28, no. 20 (May 23, 1977), p. 63.

[2]Susanne K. Langer, *Feeling and Form* (New York: Charles Scribner's, 1953) p. 27.

[3]Arthur Schopenhauer, *The World as Will and Idea*, 4th ed., vol. 1, trans. R. B. Haldane and J. Kemp (London: Kegan, Paul, Trench, Trubner, 1896), p. 333.

[4]Edward Bailey Birge, *The History of Public School Music in the United States* (Reston, Va.: Music Educators National Conference, 1966), p. 43.

[5]Peter W. Dykema and Karl Gehrkens, *The Teaching and Administration of High School Music* (Evanston, Ill.: Summy-Birchard, 1941), pp. 380–381.

[6]J. David Boyle and Robert L. Lathrop, "The IMPACT Experience: An Evaluation," *Music Educators Journal*, 59, no. 5 (January 1973), p. 42.

[7]Edwin A. Movesesian, "The Influence of Teaching Music Reading Skills on the Development of Basic Reading Skills in the Primary Grades" (Ph.D. dissertation, University of Southern California, 1967).

[8]Richard M. Graham, comp., *Music for the Exceptional Child* (Reston, Va.: Music Educators National Conference, 1975), p. 35.

[9]Karen I. Wolff, "The Nonmusical Outcomes of Music Education: A Review of the Literature," Council for Research in Music Education Bulletin no. 55 (Summer 1978), p. 19.

[10]American Symphony Orchestra League, P.O. Box 669, Vienna, Va. 22180.

[11]Music Educators National Conference, 1902 Association Drive, Reston, Va. 22091.

3 | *The Music Curriculum*

WHAT SHOULD STUDENTS learn in music classes? Are some areas more important than others? On what basis are decisions about the subject matter content of music classes made? Should there be a common content for all students? These questions are part of the second major area in the teaching process: the content that teachers teach and students presumably learn. Chapter Four explores some of the topics and questions related to what students learn in music classes.

Chapter Five describes the form that music education has taken in the public schools of the United States. Such knowledge is useful to someone entering the field. Also useful is some information about recent developments in the field, which is the subject of Chapter Six. Chapter Seven provides an introduction to four significant approaches to teaching music that have come to America from other countries: the methods of Jaques-Dalcroze, the Orff *Schulwerk*, the Kodály approach, and the Suzuki Talent Education program.

Preparing for performances is a major part of many music teachers' jobs. The nature and type of performances are both a result of and an influence on what other learning takes place in the class or rehearsal. Because it is such a significant topic for music teachers, Chapter Eight is devoted to it.

The Subject Matter of Music

C H A P T E R

MUSIC TEACHERS are largely responsible for the the content of the music classes they teach. In many school situations there is no district-wide plan or course of study that teachers are expected to follow, and where such plans do exist, they are the products of committees made up mostly of teachers. Furthermore, many state and school district curriculum guides are not very specific, a fact that gives teachers quite a bit of latitude in and responsibility for what is taught.

Often, it seems, discussions of curriculum and course content make one feel a bit like the sorcerer's apprentice, who, desperately trying to stop the broom from carrying buckets of water, grabs an ax and chops the broom into pieces, only to see each new piece begin carrying water. When curricular topics are examined, each idea and its ramifications seem to multiply, and before long the topic is cluttered with questions about ends and means, goals, content, methods, skills, concepts, maturation, and countless other interrelated topics. So that this chapter is kept within manageable proportions, it is confined largely to subject matter content. What is being discussed is content—the "stuff" taught in music classes—not methods. A distinction between them needs to be kept in mind to avoid confusing *what* is taught with the *way* it is taught.

Learning in Music

The chorus at Middlebury High School is singing the black spiritual "There Is a Balm in Gilead." What should the students be learning from singing this beautiful song? At least five things:

1. patterns of musical sounds—the syntax of music
2. the song as a work of music
3. understandings about musical processes and organization
4. skills in performing and listening to music
5. attitudes about the particular piece and about music in general

Each of these five outcomes of learning merits further discussion.

Musical Syntax

If music is organized sound, as it was defined in Chapter One, then a sense of organization and patterns of sounds is absolutely required for a person to hear the sounds as music. Otherwise they are just a random jumble, as when a cat walks on the keys of a piano.

The analogy between language and music is not a perfect one, but in a number of ways they are much alike. When learning language, children find out that "runs big slowly dog black the" is not an understandable pattern. They need similar learning in music, except with musical sounds, of course. Apparently a sense of syntax in language, and probably in music as well, is developed through experience with speaking and listening. Children enter school with several years' experience in hearing and speaking words. Then only after they have had much practice and experience with spoken language are they given the visual symbols for the words they already know aurally.

There is another similarity between language and music. Research studies indicate that the learning of syntax and the pronunciation of words develop early in life.[1] By the age of ten, the ability for such learning begins to decrease. For this reason it is very important that children in the primary grades of elementary school be given many opportunities for gaining a sense of musical syntax and learning to be accurate in singing pitch.

It is easy to overlook the importance of learning the syntax of music. (Actually, throughout the world and history there have been many different syntaxes that were considered music by someone, but American children should learn first Western "common practice" syntax.) This is true because syntax is sensed and is not so easily testable. Also, its acquisition is quite gradual, at least by the age when children enter elementary school. In fact, all of us are still improving our sense of syntax for the types of music with which we are still involved. At our "mature" stage of experience in music, the increments of improvement in our syntactical sense are very small, but we are still improving.

The syntax of music is probably the first type of learning that students should acquire in music, because without it the other four areas of learning won't mean much. It alone can carry a person quite a distance in the world of music. For example, most of the early jazz musicians had little formal training and could not read music, yet their great intuitive sense for musical patterns more than compensated for these limitations. However, they were limited in what they knew about music, and music educators would not want their students today to be similarly restricted in what they know and can do in music.

Musical Works

The amount of music created throughout the world over the past couple of thousand years is massive beyond comprehension. Not only is there art music ranging from the 3800 works by Telemann to the 1600 trouvère and troubadour melodies to Haydn's 104 symphonies, but also thousands and thousands of works of folk music and popular songs. No one, even the most avid listener to music, could in an entire lifetime hear each work even once. And the amount of music increases each day.

One of the things students should learn in music classes is where a particular piece of music fits into the world of music. In the case of "There Is a Balm in Gilead" the singers should acquire some understanding of the text, melodic characteristics, social setting, and similar information about this work and other black spirituals, as well as other types of black music. It is not enough just to sing a song without knowing anything about it as a piece of music.

A difficult problem for teachers is the selection of music. With the time available for music instruction in schools so very limited, teachers can barely skim the surface of the deep waters of available music. Therefore some hard decisions must be made, and many fine works of music simply have to be left out. Some suggestions for making the necessary choices are presented later in this chapter.

Intellectual Understandings

The intellectual understandings of music involve the formation of concepts about music, the manner of thinking about music, and some knowledge of the process of creating music. Of the three, concept formation seems to be the most important.

Concepts. The dictionary definition of *concept* is quite useful in understanding what concepts are and how they are formed: "the resultant of a generalizing mental operation; a generic mental image abstracted from percepts."[2] Concepts, then, are generalizations about phenomena.

Some concepts such as music are quite broad in scope, while others such as phrase are more specific. The structuring of concepts of differing comprehensiveness is somewhat like the system of classification used in biology—phylum, genus, species, and so on. In music there are conceptual ideas about melody, harmony, form, rhythm, and so on. Subconcepts of melody include ideas about contour, motive, theme, expression, and so on. And each of these subconcepts can be divided further into more specific categories.

A concept is not the same as its verbal symbol or definition; in fact, a concept can exist without a verbal symbol. A definition is merely an attempt to assign a verbal "handle" to something already formed in the mind. It is more accurate, for example, to think of the generalized quality of "dogness" as the concept rather than the more specific word *dog*.

People form concepts as they notice similarities and differences among objects and in the process organize and classify them. For example, they form a concept of dogness as animals with four legs and one tail, with an ability to bark and an acute sense of smell, but unable to climb trees or see in the dark, and with all the other features that make up the quality of dogness. Without previous experience with animals, definitions ("A dog is . . .") and factual statements ("Dogs can bark . . .") are largely meaningless. A concept must first exist on which to affix the verbal symbol. What this means is that teachers are limited to establishing situations in which the students can form the desired concepts. The generalizing process essential for concept formation must happen within each student's mind; it cannot be accomplished by outside forces. Like the sense of musical syntax, concepts are refined somewhat with each experience. This fact is the main reason for the "spiral curriculum" of Jerome Bruner and others. Concepts are never learned once and for all. Instead, they need to be revisited and refined often.

The reason that teachers should be interested in concept formation is that concepts facilitate the ability to think. The fact that words are mental tools as well as a means of communication is well established.[3] Students who have no concept of melody are seriously impaired in their ability to think about, understand, and appreciate melodies. Furthermore, since concepts are generalized ideas, they are far more versatile and flexible than specific ideas. The concept of melody can be applied in all kinds of pieces of music, but the melody to "There Is a Balm in Gilead" is specific to only that one piece of music. A third virtue of conceptual learning is that basic, general ideas are remembered much better than specific facts, a point that is cited again in Chapter Nine.

Way of Thinking. Every field of study—science, history, music—has its mode of thinking, its way of looking at things. A physicist, for example, is interested in the physical properties of sounds; a social scientist is interested in the effect of sounds on human behavior; a musician is interested in how sounds are manipulated and the tonal effects and compositions that can be created with them. Part of what students should learn in school is to think as scientists in science class, as social scientists in a social science class, and as musicians in a music class. Appropriate thinking and mental approach is as much a part of the subject as the factual information associated with it.

And how does musicianlike thinking differ from other thinking? If you question the proverbial "man on the street" about his views on music, the chances are that you will find that he thinks of music as something for accompanying other activities—whistling songs while painting a fence and playing music on the car radio while driving to work. Almost never will he talk about music as an object for careful consideration by itself. On the other hand, musicians value organized sounds; they think that the way Mozart put sounds together in the last movement of his Symphony no. 41 is pretty impressive. In fact, they don't want distractions like painting a fence while listening to the *Jupiter* Symphony. Also, musicians analyze the sounds they listen to; they are interested in figuring out what Mozart did with the sounds. Because they value sounds and analyze them, musicians enjoy music more and know more about it than do most nonmusicians.

Creative Process.   Learning in music should not be confined to the re-creation of what others have done. At a level consistent with their musical development, students should engage in creating music through composition and/or improvisation. Creative activity is valuable because it requires students to think about how sounds are manipulated, which is a central feature of the way musicians think. It also educates students about the process of creating music, including its mental trial and error and just plain hard work. In addition, creative activities allow students to explore their own music potential and in that sense to know themselves better.

As valuable as creative activities are for students in learning music, they are only a part of the subject. Students should not be confined to only those works that they themselves create, anymore than they should be limited to works that someone else has created.

Skills and Activities

The words *skills* and *activities* are not synonymous. Skills refer to physical activities such as vibrato on the violin, tonguing the clarinet, and sight singing. Some music classes have the acquisition of skills as a major part of their content. This fact is true of the instrumental music classes and of private instruction in singing or on an instrument. Other music classes include some learning of skills.

Activities are actions that the students engage in as a means of learning. Other things being equal, students who sing a song are more likely to understand and appreciate the song than students who just listen to it, especially if the students have not had much musical experience. For example, when English teachers want their students to understand drama, they have them read a drama and discuss its purpose, literature, and technical production. To increase their understanding of certain points, English teachers may have the students act out a portion of a play in the classroom. The activity furthers learning about drama, just as activities in music can aid learning in music.

Activities, however, cannot substitute for subject matter content. Singing one song after another, class after class, does not contribute much to the students' understanding of music or their aesthetic sensitivity. At one time, music programs in the elementary schools were described entirely in terms of activities: singing, playing instruments, rhythmic movement, reading, creating, and listening. Although it may seem like hairsplitting, these were activities, not subject matter content. It would have been more accurate to say what students learned through the activity of singing or listening. The goal of music education is not just to do something in music. Rather it is to educate students in music, and it happens that this education is often furthered through the use of appropriate activities.

Attitudes

How a person feels about what he or she knows is important. This statement is probably truer for music than for the traditional academic subjects. All of us use the ability to read and write daily, regardless of whether or not we enjoyed reading and writing when we were taught them in school. Nearly everyone needs to balance checkbooks and compute income taxes regardless of how he or she felt about arithmetic in school. Not so with music. People who don't like music can refrain from buying recordings and attending concerts. If forced to listen to music in the supermarket, they can psychologically "tune it out." Much of the ultimate success of music instruction depends on how the students feel about the subject after the classes are over. And students do acquire attitudes about the subject whether or not teachers realize it. The question is not, "Will the students form feelings about music?" but rather, "What feelings will they develop?"

What influences the attitudes people adopt? Some generalizations can be offered in terms of tendencies, but no rules can be stated that people invariably follow. One generalization concerns familiarity. If there be truth in the statement "I know what I like," there is also truth in the words "I like what I know." Social scientists have discovered this fact in a variety of situations ranging from people to words to pictures.[4] Music teachers can support this finding also. Many teachers have found that a good musical work that was not liked when it was introduced to the students gradually became well liked.

People tend to like things that are similar to what they already know and like. A person who likes Broadway musicals can more easily acquire a favorable attitude toward art music than can a rock-ribbed lover of country music.

People are influenced by the person who is suggesting a change. A teacher who is liked is more effective in changing attitudes than one who isn't. Part of the reason for this tendency lies in the fact that the students have a pleasant association with the subject when they like the teacher. And the associations people make with music can influence their attitude toward it.

Attitudes are also influenced by what one's friends and peers think, and this is especially true of students in the secondary schools. If all your friends like a particular piece of music, the chances are greatly increased that you will like it, too. This is so partly because you respect and like your friends, partly because you don't want the friction involved in disagreeing with them, and partly because you tend to "go with the flow" of their feelings as you perceive them.

The family has a significant influence on children's attitudes. If the parents listen to symphonies on their record-playing equipment, the chances are much greater that the children will end up listening to that type of music when they are mature.

Attitudes and knowledge are complementary. People cannot have intelligent reactions to something they don't know. If asked, "Do you like aardvarks?" they will probably answer, "I don't know." So a teacher's first task is to remove ignorance so that at the least there can be intelligent preferences and at the best there can be what the educator-philosopher Harry Broudy refers to as "enlightened cherishing."[5] Few people, including music teachers, enjoy all types of music equally well. Being educated about something does not mean that you must like it. Rather education offers the opportunity to make intelligent choices.

Some practical actions that music teachers can take to encourage positive attitudes on the part of their students include the following:

1. Seize upon every opportunity to make students familiar with the music that it is hoped they will learn to like.

2. Avoid direct attempts to teach an attitude; for example, don't say, "This is a great piece of music that you ought to like." Attitudes are in a sense "caught" in a more indirect way, including observing how other people react.

3. Make the learning of music as pleasant and positive an experience as possible. True, a few students will tolerate very negative experiences and still like music. However, the great majority of students try to avoid such situations, and in doing so, they avoid music. If a classroom is a situation with constant pressure, carping by the teacher, and little feeling of success, few positive attitudes will be engendered.

4. Try to have the students enjoy a feeling of success in music. People like better the things they believe they do well. For example, if you throw many gutter balls when bowling, you will avoid bowling whenever possible; if your average is over 200, you will seek chances to demonstrate your bowling skills—and in the process become even better at bowling.

Nonmusical Outcomes

Nonmusical benefits also result from the study of music. For instance, a student may derive emotional release from singing a song. Whether or not such a release happens depends primarily on the inclinations of the particular individual and not on any direct action of the teacher, as was pointed out in the preceding chapter. As long as the classroom atmosphere is not repressive, emotional release and other nonmusical outcomes can happen as by-products of the class.

The outcomes of music teaching—syntax, knowing musical works, understandings, skills, and attitudes—are very much interrelated. For example, the syntax of a style is presented in every musical work, and intellectual understandings take on meaning when they are associated with a musical work. Skills aid in learning about a work of music and are largely worthless unless involved in bringing about a greater understanding of music. Understanding more about music usually contributes to liking it better, and, in turn, positive attitudes motivate students to learn a subject better.

Who Decides on Content?

*I*n recent years a number of writers on education have advocated changing the role of the teacher from one of a leader in the learning process to one of helper. The concept of the teacher as leader connotes making decisions about what is to be learned, while the view of the teacher as helper means, for some advocates at least, giving the students a great deal of choice about what they will learn and when they will learn it. The term used by some educational writers for teachers assuming the helper role is not teacher but rather facilitator, enabler, or similar words.

The theoretical case for the helper role is quite interesting and attractive. Students do learn better when left to pursue their own interests. However, in the area of music there are some practical problems with allowing the students the dominant voice in deciding what they will learn. If the music specialist can visit each elementary school classroom only twice a week for a total of fifty or sixty minutes (a typical schedule), then time is a very valuable commodity. It is nearly impossible to permit much time for exploring what the students may want to do or to devote much attention to the variety of topics they might select. Also, seldom does an entire class decide on the same thing to do, so large-group activities such as singing songs are greatly reduced, if not eliminated.

There is an even more serious problem with student-selected content. People can make intelligent choices only about things they know. Students rarely decide to study something about which they know little or nothing, and the result is a severe limitation in their education. Their music study becomes a perpetuation of what they already know, which is usually what they hear on the radio or the latest record hits. Such a situation violates an important guideline to be suggested shortly, one that says students should learn things in music classes that they do not know or would not learn without instruction.

It is not being "authoritarian" or "dominating" to realize that teachers who have a college degree in music know more about music than the average twelve-year-old. Furthermore, it does not seem unreasonable to use this much greater knowledge of the subject to render most of the decisions about the educational needs of the students in music. These decisions will, of course, be more effective if they take into consideration the interests and backgrounds of the students. Considering the interests of the students is important in achieving the best teaching. That is not the same, however, as turning over most of the curricular decisions to them.

Guidelines for Selecting

Because time is limited for music instruction, teachers must make some difficult decisions about what to teach. In doing so, they may consult students and parents and consider their wishes. Even when this is done, however, the teacher has to make choices. The following guidelines may help in doing this.

Educational.   The first guideline sounds like a simple one: the students should gain information, skills, or attitudes that they did not have prior to the class or course and probably would not acquire without instruction in school. This idea seems basic to any educational undertaking. Without it, education becomes merely baby-sitting or a recreation program.

While the guideline is a simple but important one, it has sometimes not been followed, for a number of reasons. Some teachers have felt that the effort to teach something would not be worth it, or that it would not make any difference to the students, or that there is not really anything to learn in music. Whatever the reason, the students were the losers. Here is how Raymond Lopez, a consultant in the Los Angeles Public Schools, puts the matter:

> As soon as you can establish rapport, then you can introduce Brahms and Wagner. You don't have to stoop to "all they can sing is pop." In one school, all they were doing was drivel, in any old way. There was no attempt to organize it. The kids could just as well have been walking down the street—and maybe that's what we're preparing them for. We say that we are preparing the student for the world of reality. But shouldn't we always be struggling for enrichment? Why not acquaint the kids with those in the stream of time who have created outstanding music? I have heard a teacher say, "Why give them that stuff (a great composer's music)? They've never heard it. They'll never know it, and it won't make any difference to them." If I had had teachers like that maybe today I wouldn't know the difference. My teachers exposed me to the greats in music and that enriched my life. I'm better off for those teachers.[6]

One practical question for the criterion of being educational is, "What would the students learn about music if they had no instruction in school?" Is there some music and information about music that, like riding a bicycle, would probably be learned without a music teacher? The music that can be learned outside of school can be left to others, and other subject matter content can be taught in the schools.

Valid.   Music is an established academic discipline, a recognized field of knowledge and study. Teachers should ask themselves, "Is what is being taught a legitimate portion of the field of music? Would most trained musicians (performers, musicologists, teachers) recognize and accept this content as a part of the field?" For example, a few teachers of violin with elementary school children use a kind of notation in which notes are identified not by pitch but by the name of the string and fingering: A1, D3, and so on. The system cannot indicate relative pitch, note values, or sharps and flats. It must be unlearned as the students progress. No music theorist, symphony musician, or musicologist uses this system in studying or playing music. Therefore it is not valid in the field of music.

The call for validity is a logical one. Why teach something under the name of music that is not really part of the field of music? It is neither logical nor honest to transform a subject, even in the hope of aiding learning.

Fundamental.   Closely related to validity of content is the belief that students should learn the basic ideas of the subject, not just factual minutiae. Knowing the keys of the thirty-two Beethoven piano sonatas is not as useful as understanding his development of themes and motives. When information is associated with a concept, it is useful, but memorizing insignificant facts is not effective learning. Fundamental ideas—tonality, development of themes, the 2:1 ratio in rhythmic notation, and the unity of words and music in art songs, to cite a few examples—are valuable because they are comprehensive and have wide application in music.

Representative.   If the music curriculum is limited to only a few types or aspects of music, then the students are not being given a well-balanced education in music. The band director who has the band play one march after another and the general music teacher who spends all the class time working with the synthesizer are both guilty of shortchanging their students, because both are omitting many other important areas of music. Sometimes teachers give the students very little art music—music that contains a sophisticated handling of sounds. Their students continue to think of music only as a pastime or entertainment and are never introduced to the idea that music is an aesthetic, expressive human creation.

One way of checking out the representativeness of music selected is to take a piece of paper or a chalkboard and divide it into boxes according to categories. On the horizontal plane one might put style periods: pre-Renaissance, Renaissance, Baroque, Classical, Romantic, and Twentieth-Century. On the vertical plane could be put types of music appropriate for the class, such as folk songs, show tunes, art songs, oratorio-opera, and religious works for a choral group. Making a mark in the appropriate category for each piece of music provides a good picture of the distribution of the music used.

Contemporary.   The music and information taught in music classes should be up to date. This criterion refers not only to the date when composed but also to the style. Some works composed in the 1960s and 1970s are still in a style that is a century old. The main problem for teachers in this matter is the technical difficulty of many twentieth-century works. They would like to have the students sing or play them, but many times the music is too hard. It requires some searching, but contemporary works that are not technically so demanding can be found.

Relevant. The word *relevant* has been used in several ways in recent years. To some people it means those things vital for survival and living; to others it means topics that one happens to like or be interested in; and to others it means the relationship between a person and a given subject. It is in the third sense that the word is used here.

As mentioned in Chapter Three, sometimes the interests of the students and the requirements of valid subject matter have appeared to be in conflict. The pendulum has swung back and forth between these extremes several times in the rather short history of music education in America. Proponents of subject matter validity ask, "What good is a subject that has lost its integrity and character?" The advocates of relevance answer, "What good is a subject that seems meaningless and worthless to the students?" Both views have a fair claim for the attention of teachers, and the two positions need not be mutually exclusive.

Relevance is probably affected more by the method of teaching than by the content. Topics and subjects have little inherent relevance; people make things relevant. A topic that is important and interesting to one person couldn't matter less to another. Relevance results when a topic is given meaning through a teacher's attitude and skill in organizing the subject. Teachers need to teach so that the real content of music becomes relevant to the students. For example, figuring out minor scale patterns is not relevant to most students because it is not particularly helpful to them in understanding music. Achieving relevance is quite an assignment, but as the opening sentence of this book says, the job of teaching music is not an easy one.

Learnable. The music curriculum must be learnable by most of the students. It is useless to teach something for which they are not prepared. While the students' backgrounds and interests should be considered, these are not the only things that teachers should think about. Teaching something that is of a suitable level of difficulty for the students should be determined in relation to the other guidelines, as well as to a host of practical matters such as amount of class time, books and materials, and performance obligations. A good teacher can build on the interests the students already have without abandoning the subject. If students seem uninterested in a topic, perhaps another approach to it is called for instead of giving up on it entirely.

Some of the guidelines presented here may appear to be contradictory, and to a degree this is so. The need to offer substantive instruction seems to work against the idea of relevancy, and contemporary content appears to contradict the idea of representative samples of the subject. In the case of education versus relevancy the solution lies in the proper methods of teaching. However, some of the time teachers need to strike a balance in making curricular decisions between conflicting needs. None of the guidelines are absolute and overriding, which means that teachers have to account for a number of divergent factors in their teaching.

Evaluating Musical Works

It is nearly impossible to discuss the content of music classes without touching on the sometimes emotional and foggy question of the quality of musical works. Is there a difference, or is it simply a matter of what a person happens to like? The answer is that there are differences, but they are difficult to state in words. A few points can be stated, however.

1. Because music is a human creation done in a particular cultural setting, there are no universal criteria for evaluating musical works. For example, it is impossible to claim that a Japanese piece of music is superior or inferior to a Mozart piano sonata. Each should be considered within its own cultural context.

2. The purpose or type of music should be considered in evaluating works. Some music is not intended to be listened to intently (film music, hymns, most popular songs, and so on) and should not be evaluated in terms of concert music. And the opposite is true; music written for careful listening should not be evaluated in terms of its usefulness around a campfire or for social dancing.

3. Works of music do not fall into neat categories: great, incompetent, OK. Instead they seem to exist on a continuum ranging from very simple to very complex.

4. Judgments can seldom be made on the basis of the technical features of the music—the amount of syncopation, range and contour of the melody, percentage of tonic chords, and so on. Most attempts at identifying technical characteristics of "good" music ended up excluding some works generally considered to be of good quality.

5. It appears likely that some judgments can be made in comparing the quality of similar works. Briefly, the music considered to be of better quality provides listeners with a greater challenge and variety as it progresses in ways generally expected of music; less significant music is less challenging and more obvious. This theory of music quality is developed fully in the writings of Leonard B. Meyer and others.[7]

In addition to considering the greater complexity of music that Meyer and others cite, what practical actions can teachers take to gain a clearer idea of the quality of works they are considering using? Here are some practical, intuitive criteria that may be applied. They certainly will not provide conclusive or final answers to the quality of a musical work, but at least they can serve as a starting point.

1. Does the work seem to stick with you after you are away from it for a few minutes, or is it quite forgettable?

2. Does the work seem to "wear well" over the days of rehearsal, or do you become tired of it rather easily? Quality works have something about them that can stand—indeed almost seem to require—working with them time and again. Each time you find something in the music that you had not noticed before.

3. In the case of a work that has been around for a generation or so, has it "stood the test" of time? For example, there is a quality in the marches of John Philip Sousa that people find interesting nearly a century after many of them were composed, and that quality has not been found in many other marches. Time has a way of sorting out what is of better quality.

4. The content of the music series books has been subjected to careful evaluation by the books' authors. The fact that a song is included in these books means that it has passed a screening process. An attempt is made in these books to offer a wide variety of good music. The contest lists for high school bands, orchestras, and choral groups often contain selections of high quality. The quality of these lists is not consistent, however.

5. If you have a choice between a work by a recognized composer and one you have never heard of, it is wiser to stay with the known composer. Bach, Brahms, and Bartok are not esteemed names in the world of music because they had clever managers or because someone proclaimed their music to be good. Rather musicians over the years have found that their music possesses qualities that makes it stand out in the world of music. Such recognition should influence teachers in deciding which pieces of music to study in their music classes.

A quality music curriculum results not only from drawing up a list of courses but also from providing a varied and quality program of music education. Deciding what to teach requires thoughtful attention to subject matter validity, relevance, and the selection of music.

Most important, music teachers should realize that they are teaching a subject and that in their classes students should learn music, both as an academic area and as an art.

Questions

1. Should a performing group hear and study musical works that it does not perform for the public? Why or why not?

2. What are some characteristics of musicianlike thinking?

3. What are the values of music activities in music classes?

4. What does the term *subject matter validity* mean? What does the term *relevance* mean?

5. On what basis do Meyer and some other scholars make value judgments about musical works?

6. What does the word *syntax* refer to? Why is it important that students recognize it?

7. Why is creative activity important in music education?

Projects

1. Select a book designed for use in a general music class and evaluate its content according to the guidelines suggested on pages 67–71.

2. Select three songs or other musical works and evaluate them for their music quality.

3. Secure a curriculum guide or course of study for a music course. Evaluate it in terms of the suggested guidelines of pages 67–71.

Suggested Readings

Ernst, Karl D., and Charles L. Gary, eds. *Music in General Education*. Reston, Va.: Music Educators National Conference, 1965.

Klotman, Robert H. *The School Music Administrator and Supervisor: Catalysts for Change in Music Education*. Englewood Cliffs, N.J.: Prentice-Hall, 1973. Chapter 4.

Madeja, Stanley S., and Harry T. Kelly. "The Process of Curriculum Development for Aesthetic Education." In *Toward an Aesthetic Education*. Reston, Va.: Music Educators National Conference, 1971.

Reimer, Bennett. *A Philosophy of Music Education*. Englewood Cliffs, N.J.: Prentice-Hall, 1970. Chapters 8 and 9.

References

[1]Wilder Penfield and Tamar Roberts, *Speech and Brain—Mechanisms* (Princeton, N.J.: Princeton University Press, 1959), pp. 240–255.

[2]*Webster's Third New International Dictionary* (Springfield, Mass.: G. & C. Merriam, 1965), p. 469.

[3]Tamotsu Shibutani, *Society and Personality* (Englewood Cliffs, N.J.: Prentice-Hall, 1961), pp. 187–191.

[4]Jonathan L. Freedman, J. Merrill Carlsmith, and David O. Sears, *Social Psychology* (Englewood Cliffs, N.J.: Prentice-Hall, 1970), pp. 71–72.

[5]Harry S. Broudy, "The Case for Aesthetic Education," in *Documentary Report of the Tanglewood Symposium*, ed. Robert A. Choate (Reston, Va.: Music Educators National Conference, 1968), p. 13.

[6]*Music Educators Journal*, 56, no. 5 (January 1970), p. 96. Used by permission.

[7]Leonard B. Meyer, *Music, the Arts, and Ideas* (Chicago: University of Chicago Press, 1967), Chapter 2.

The Music Program in the Public Schools

C H A P T E R   F I V E

IT IS IMPORTANT for prospective teachers to be informed about and interested in the entire music program—kindergarten through high school, general, choral, and instrumental. The reason for an interest in the total program is the fact that it is a single entity. At each level or in each type of class students are learning music, and in the long run each portion of the music program affects to some degree the other parts.

Goals of the Music Program

*A*ll parts of the music program also operate under the same broad goals. Although the amount of attention given to certain goals differs according to the type of class, all music classes should be attempting to educate students in music. Various writers and groups in music education have formulated lists of goals for the music program. Probably the most significant of these efforts are two publications of the MENC: *Music in General Education* (1965)[1] and *The School Music Program: Description & Standards* (1974).[2] *Music in General Education* states its goals in terms of what all students should be able to do in music by the time they finish high school. The goals and statements describing them are presented here in full.

Skills

I. He will have skill in listening to music.

The generally educated person listens with a purpose. He recognizes the broad melodic and rhythmic contours of musical compositions. He is familiar with the sounds of the instruments of the orchestra and the types of human voices. He can hear and identify more than one melody at a time. He can recognize patterns of melody and rhythm when repeated in identical or in altered form. He can concentrate on sounds and the relationships between sounds.

II. He will be able to sing.

The generally educated person is articulate. He uses his voice confidently in speech and song. He sings in a way that is satisfying to himself. He can carry a part in group singing. His singing is expressive.

III. He will be able to express himself on a musical instrument.

A generally educated person is curious. He is interested in how instrumental music is produced and willing to try his hand at making music, if only at an elementary level with a percussion instrument, a recorder, or a "social-type" instrument. He experiments with providing accompaniments for singing and rhythmic activities. He is familiar with the piano keyboard.

IV. He will be able to interpret musical notation.

The generally educated person is literate. He understands arithmetical and musical symbols. He is able to respond to the musical notation of unison and simple part songs. He can follow the scores of instrumental compositions.

Understandings

V. He will understand the importance of design in music.

The generally educated person understands the structure of the various disciplines. He knows the component parts of music and the interrelationships that exist between melody, rhythm, harmony, and form. He is able to recognize design elements aurally, and he uses musical notation to confirm and reinforce this recognition. He realizes that the active listener can, in a sense, share in the composer's act of creation. By understanding how music communicates he has come to gain insight into what it communicates.

VI. He will relate music to man's historical development.

The generally educated person has historical perspective. He recognizes that music has long been an important part of man's life. He understands that its development in Western civilization is one of the unique elements of his own heritage. He is familiar with the major historical periods in that development and the styles of music which they produced. He has acquaintance with some of the musical masterpieces of the past and with the men who composed them. He relates this knowledge to his understanding of man's social and political development.

VII. He will understand the relationships existing between music and other areas of human endeavor.

The generally educated person integrates his knowledge. He has been helped to see that the arts have in common such concepts as design resulting from repetition and variation. Sociology and politics are recognized as pertinent to the development of art as well as to economics. He understands how literature and music enhance one another and together illuminate history. The mathematical and physical aspects of music are known to him through aural experiences as well as through intellectual inquiry.

VIII. He will understand the place of music in contemporary society.

The generally educated person is aware of his environment. He understands the function of music in the life of his community and he accepts some responsibility for exercising his critical judgment to improve the quality of music heard in church and on radio and television. He is aware of the position of the musician in today's social structure and understands the opportunities open to him to engage in musical endeavor both as a vocation and as an avocation.

Attitudes

IX. He will value music as a means of self-expression.

A generally educated person has developed outlets for his emotions. He recognizes music not only as a source of satisfaction because of its filling his desire for beauty, but also because of the unique way in which it expresses man's feelings. If he is not prepared to gain release by actually performing music, he has learned to experience this vicariously. He looks to music as a source of renewal of mind and body, as an evidence of beneficence in his life. He recognizes the importance of performers and composers and is grateful for the pleasure and inspiration which they give him.

X. He will desire to continue his musical experiences.

The generally educated person continues to grow. He seeks additional experiences in areas in which he has found satisfaction. He looks for community musical activities in which he can participate. He attends concerts and listens to music on radio, television, and recordings. He keeps informed concerning happenings in the world of music by reading newspapers and magazines.

XI. He will discriminate with respect to music.

The generally educated person has good taste. He has learned to make sensitive choices based on musical knowledge and skill in listening. He evaluates performances and exercises mature judgments in this area. He is not naive about the functional use of music for commercial purposes, nor to the commercial pressures which will be exerted to obtain what money he can spend for music.[3]

The *Description & Standards* book was developed by the National Commission on Instruction of the MENC in conjunction with the National Council of State Supervisors of Music. It adheres to the three main processes advocated by the Comprehensive Music Project (CMP, see Chapter Six). It advocates experiences in performing, organizing, and describing for each level and each instructional setting, and it states that the categories should be interpreted broadly.

Performing

Those skills related to the production of musical sound:
1. The use of the body as an instrument
2. The use of the voice
3. The manipulation of environmental sound sources
4. The playing of instruments

Organizing

Those skills related to the creation of music through the determination of the sequence of musical sounds:
1. The spontaneous development of musical ideas through improvisation
2. The communication of one's musical intent through composition or arrangement

Describing

The skills of:
1. Listening to music and demonstrating understanding through
   a. Fundamental movement or expressive dance
   b. Visual representation, including diagrams and abstract drawings
   c. Verbal description, including both image terms and technical terminology
   d. The use of traditional notation and contemporary notational schemes
2. Reading music:
   a. Translating the score into sound
   b. Verbal description, including both image terms and technical terminology[4]

The book goes on to list activities under the headings of the three activities for five different age-level groupings.

Each of these sets of goals is useful for music educators and merits consideration. The establishment of broad goals is only part of the building of a music program, however. Such goals need to be implemented in class and rehearsal rooms. The form of this implementation in the schools is described and discussed in the remainder of this chapter. The presentation is divided into two parts: elementary schools (kindergarten through grades 5 or 6) and secondary schools (grades 6 or 7 through 12).

Elementary School Music Program

*M*ost college students have only vague memories of their instruction in music back when they were eight or ten years old. In many cases they didn't receive much music instruction in school, so there isn't much to remember. In other cases the passage of ten or more years has dimmed their impression of what took place in those classes. What memories they have may consist mostly of singing songs. The experiences of the musicals and contests in high school are fresher and usually seem much more exciting. Many prospective music teachers (as well as many teachers and administrators and much of the public) associate music education largely with the high school performing groups.

This limited association and attention is indeed unfortunate. Music classes in elementary or junior high-middle schools are not only as important in terms of education as the performing groups, but also they can be a musically rewarding experience for everyone. The author once heard a musicologist ridicule music in the elementary schools as just the singing of songs like "The Little Red Caboose." His inaccurate perception is probably shared by quite a few people. If this view of elementary school music was ever accurate—and it may have been at one time in some places—it is certainly not the correct one today. To begin with, the content of the classes consists of much more than the singing of songs. Stepping into an elementary classroom during music, you may see students creating pieces out of sounds they find around the room; you may observe them listening to and then analyzing a short work by Mozart or Villa-Lobos or an African percussion piece; you may see the students working with classroom instruments to gain a better feeling for rhythmic or pitch patterns; and, yes, you may listen to them sing some songs, including songs in the popular idiom, folk songs, and a few art songs.

If an elementary school music class is dull, the blame falls on the teacher, who is not using the myriad of musical possibilities available to him or her.

The claim here is not that music in the elementary or junior high-middle schools operates at the same technical level as the high school performing groups. The technical level of the music is only one aspect of music, however. A well-shaped phrase and expressive performance can happen just as easily in simpler music as it can in complex works (maybe more easily). When performed expressively, William Billions's "Chester" is a stirring work, whether it is sung by a classroom of sixth graders or played by a high school band. Musical satisfaction should come from the expressive qualities of the music, not from its technical difficulty. Because music is music regardless of its difficulty, teaching music in the elementary schools can be musically satisfying.

The reasons for the importance of the general or classroom music program in the elementary or junior high-middle schools are very compelling. First, it is the portion of the music curriculum that involves every student. For many of them it is the *only* formal instruction they receive in music. Second, it represents the foundation on which subsequent efforts in music must be built. A child who had a hard time "carrying a tune" in the primary grades and developed doubts and fears about his or her musical ability is not a good candidate for the high school choir or band and in later years is unlikely to be supportive of music in the schools as a voter or school board member. All music educators should work for a strong and successful program of music in the elementary schools. Furthermore, teaching such classes can be as rewarding in terms of musical and educational satisfactions as teaching at other levels.

Types of Classes

Most of the music program in the elementary schools consists of classroom music; that is, music is taught to all of the children in a particular classroom at the same time for the purpose of educating them in music, not to prepare for a performance. It is required of all students and is general in nature, which implies a wide variety of activities and content. The subject matter for these classes is discussed more fully later in this chapter.

Many elementary schools offer a few music activities on an extra-curricular basis. Probably the most frequent offering of this type is the glee club for students in the upper grades. Sometimes it meets during school time, but more often it utilizes a time such as noon hour or recess. Some schools offer recorder classes on this basis. Usually the method of allowing students to join such groups is by the student's expression of interest, a "selection-by-election" approach. Students are not usually auditioned for places in elementary school music groups.

Instrumental music is offered in many districts at about the fifth grade level, and in some schools a grade or two earlier or later. Many schools allow any interested student to begin instrumental study, but in some schools the size of the beginning classes is limited. In such cases, a means is found by the teachers to select the students who will be allowed to begin instrumental study. Sometimes aptitude tests are used for screening purposes, and other times reports and recommendations of the students' school music teachers are used; in some school districts students are allowed to start in a summer program, and only those students who show sufficient interest and ability are allowed to continue in the fall.

Traditionally, most of the classes consist of all wind or string instruments, but rather often families of instruments are taught together. Instrumental instruction is done by an instrumental music specialist who travels among several schools. Usually the classes meet twice a week for thirty or forty minutes. The students are excused from classroom activities according to the instrumental music teacher's schedule, since he or she usually has little flexibility in setting up the times for classes and schools. The classes tend to be small (five to fifteen students), although great size variations are found.

Amount of Time

The typical schedule for music instruction in elementary schools is two times a week for thirty minutes each time. A few schools have a little more time for music, but a great many have less. A recent survey by Barbara Amen of classroom teachers in Virginia, for example, indicated that 39.4 percent of them taught no music at all, and another 39.1 percent taught music less than ten minutes per day.[5] Most of the elective-extracurricular music activities are usually on a twice-a-week basis. Some schools allow for a significant amount of individualized learning activity.

Personnel Responsible for Music Instruction

Music specialists and consultants are teachers who are certified in the area of music. They majored in music in college and then took methods courses and student teaching experience that qualified them for certification as music teachers in the elementary schools. Clearly, music specialists are strong in subject matter preparation. They are not usually assigned to just one school, but, like the instrumental music teachers, often travel among two or more buildings. They are responsible for only one subject: music. This has its advantages and disadvantages, as will be pointed out shortly.

The difference, if any, between music specialists and music consultants is the implication that consultants are more likely to spend their time helping classroom teachers to teach music. Actually, many people use the terms *specialist* and *consultant* interchangeably. The problem for consultants is that their advice is not requested nearly enough, except by a few teachers who are already strong in music. Teachers who are weak in music appear not to want to draw attention to that fact and, consequently, do not call on the consultant. Consultants have no administrative authority, so they cannot require that their ideas be implemented. In some cases, a consultant is responsible for a number of schools, which makes it difficult to have much personal contact with the classroom teachers. Written curriculum guides and memos must take the place of personal contacts. Sometimes consultants organize in-service instruction for teachers in a building or district. These sessions not only help the teachers to teach music better, but they also aid in improving communication and coordination among the different types of teachers.

Music supervisors are more likely to work with music specialists as administrators in the subject area of music, although the term *supervisor* is sometimes used as a synonym for *consultant*.

Classroom teachers hold a college degree in elementary education. They take about two music courses in their undergraduate preparation, so they have a quite limited training in music. Usually they are responsible for most of the instruction their students receive in school; the curricular areas for which they are not always responsible include physical education, art, and music.

They enjoy some advantages over music specialists in the teaching of music. They know the students in their classrooms better, and they can be more flexible about working music into the classroom routine. If ten o'clock is the best time to study the music of cowboys, then it can take place at that time. If the study of cowboy music is to be led by a music specialist, it will have to wait until the specialist's scheduled time. Furthermore, classroom teachers can integrate subject matter better since they teach most of the subjects.

Classroom teachers are clearly at a disadvantage in terms of their knowledge and ability in music. Activities that require on-the-spot musical judgments are not easy for most classroom teachers. Although they may know their twenty-five or thirty students well, they have little concept of the entire music program as it applies to other grade levels. This situation, along with the limited preparation in music, prompted the recommendation by the Teacher Education Commission of the MENC that music in the elementary schools be taught by music specialists.[6] However, the *Teacher Education in Music: Final Report* goes on to say, "Even when there is a specialist assigned to a school, there will be times when the classroom teacher must take some responsibility for classroom musical experiences."[7]

Over the years the music education profession has wavered in its opinion about the role of classroom teachers in teaching music. In the 1940s and 1950s a large portion of the profession promoted the idea of music teaching by classroom teachers. The 1960s saw a trend toward subject matter emphasis and a corresponding movement away from what was termed the "self-contained classroom," and so the profession retreated from the view that the classroom teacher could and should do much music teaching.

The change of attention to the subject matter content was not the only reason for less emphasis on music teaching by classroom teachers. Music educators began to realize that classroom teachers have a difficult time preparing for all the subjects they teach. Usually the subjects put off to last by classroom teachers are those that are considered "special," such as music. Also, music educators became more realistic about what could be expected of classroom teachers, who generally have little preparation in music. They realized that it is nearly impossible for classroom teachers to plan and carry out a coordinated program of music instruction from grades 1 to 6.

Sometimes curriculum guides for school districts specify a minimum amount of instructional time for music. Although this looks good "on paper," that amount of time may be much greater than the amount of time actually given to music teaching. Unless principals and curriculum directors make clear that the district regards music as important in the education of children and commends the music program to the classroom teachers, an anemic music program usually exists when left entirely to classroom teachers.

Although classroom teachers may not carry the brunt of the music instruction in a school system, they are still important to the success of the program in the elementary schools for the following reasons. First, there are simply not enough specialists teaching to take care of all the music instruction that is needed; classroom teachers must take up the slack, if indeed it is to be taken up.

Second, the attitude of classroom teachers toward music is important to the success of the program, even when they don't actually teach the music themselves. All teachers, whether they realize it or not, serve as behavior models for students. Research studies by Albert Bandura and others indicate that children imitate the examples set by adults, especially teachers.[8] Therefore, elementary school students are influenced by the attitude their teachers take toward music. Children are quick to detect how their teacher feels about a subject. When a music specialist visits the classroom, a lack of interest or support from the classroom teacher can undercut what the specialist is trying to accomplish. Some classroom teachers welcome the arrival of the specialist as a break time and hurry off as fast as possible to the teachers' lounge, while sometimes others say with dismay, "It's not time for music *again*, is it?" Occasionally classroom teachers turn over unruly classes to music specialists with words such as, "They're really climbing the walls today. Lots of luck!"

Third, classroom teachers can follow up the efforts of music specialists in many ways. For example, they can have the children review a song on a day when the specialist is not in the building, hear the rest of a recording that was begun during the music lesson, and practice reading pitch or rhythm patterns. Children benefit from limited amounts of daily work in skill areas such as reading or singing, and classroom teachers are the only persons who can provide daily practice. Such follow-up is vital because, as was pointed out earlier, even when music specialists are responsible for the music instruction, the amount of time for music is quite limited.

Combination Arrangements for Instruction

It is difficult to secure up-to-date and accurate figures on who is responsible for music instruction in the elementary schools. There are many variations from state to state and district to district, and some confusion about the terminology for designating the roles of teachers. One national survey from the National Education Association presents these data:

> The practice reported by . . . about 40 percent [of the schools] was to have the classroom teacher teach music with help from a music specialist. . . . The elementary-school classroom teacher had to teach music on his/her own in almost as large a percentage of schools in grades 1, 2, and 3, but in grades 4, 5, and 6, the teacher carried the full responsibility for music in less than a third of the schools. Music specialists alone did the teaching in about one fifth of the schools in grades 4–6, and in 12 to 15 percent of the schools in grades 1–3.[9]

A combination arrangement involving both music specialists and classroom teachers eliminates the disadvantages of relying entirely on either type of teacher. Music specialists can contribute their subject matter knowledge and skills, and the classroom teachers provide schedule flexibility and familiarity with the particular group of students.

Content of Classroom Instruction

The material taught in music classes in the elementary classrooms is general in nature. A wide variety of topics and activities is included, and none in much depth because of the limited amount of time available. Basically students learn about music and its constituent parts (melody, rhythm, timbre, form, and so on) by becoming involved in the basic musical processes (performing, creating, and analyzing). The traditional division of the elementary school music program was into the activities associated with the basic musical processes: singing, playing instruments, rhythmic movement, creating, and reading as a part of the process of performing, and listening as the activity associated with analyzing.

The actual content included under the various classifications can be best observed in the graded music series books available for use in the elementary schools. Three publishers currently market attractive series of music books: Holt, Rinehart & Winston, Macmillan Publishing Company, and Silver Burdett Company. The books contain many similarities, although there are a number of subtle and perhaps significant differences among them. They are filled with color illustrations, and their content is carefully prepared with the help of expert consultants to ensure accuracy. Each music series includes a teacher's edition for each grade level and a set of recordings of all the music presented in each book.

Traditionally the books were largely songbooks, but as the nature of the elementary music program has expanded, so has the variety of material in the books. The second grade books typically contain about seventy songs, of which about two thirds are folk songs. In addition, there are listening sections, charts, sound pieces, parts for classroom instruments such as autoharp, evaluation materials, ideas from the Orff and Kodály programs, the presentations of styles in music and the other arts, and suggestions for mainstreaming handicapped children. Fifth grade books contain more songs, including part songs, and present more advanced material similar to what is contained in the second grade books.

Although certainly not required for teaching music, the music series books are helpful. They are a good starting place for ideas and materials from which a teacher can build. They offer these benefits:

1. They are a source of songs and other musical activities, so a teacher is spared the effort of searching out material and ideas.

2. They provide a minimum or "bedrock" course of study in music. Often the content of the books is organized around topics or units, and in this way a sequence of instruction is provided.

3. The teacher's edition of each book suggests teaching procedures. Reference material is included, and the songs and learning activities are thoroughly indexed. Colored inks and other techniques are used to make the information for the teacher clear and concise.

4. Simple piano accompaniments are provided for most of the songs.

5. Ideas for incorporating classroom instruments and orchestral instruments into accompaniments are provided.

6. Pronunciation guides for all foreign language songs are included. Translations are also provided, if they are not already contained in the verses of the song.

7. The recorded performances are of a high quality. The instrumentalists hired to perform on the recordings are among the top people available. The rules of the American Federation of Musicians make it no more expensive to hire the best than to hire less able performers. The quality of the singing, often done by children, is also excellent. These performances provide a good model of singing for the children to copy. The musical arrangements of the songs on the recordings are tasteful, interesting, and quite authentic, with folk instruments used when appropriate.

8. They offer suggestions for extending the learning activities into other arts and other academic areas, including help for handicapped students. For teachers with the special musical approaches devised by Carl Orff and Zoltán Kodály (see Chapter Seven), there are recommendations for incorporating those teaching techniques into the music instruction.

To provide a better idea of what the teacher's editions are like, two pages are reproduced here—one from the second grade book published by Macmillan and the other from the fifth grade book published by Holt, Rinehart & Winston.

On the page from *The Spectrum of Music* by Macmillan (page 86) the suggestions for the teacher are printed next to the song. Since many of the users of the book are classroom teachers, curriculum information is provided in the yellow band (not visible here), as well as a phonetic pronunciation of the text. Other information is provided at the top of the page, including the key and starting note, the availability of an accompaniment, and the place in the record album where the recording can be located and other information about the recording. Cues for the teacher are printed on a reproduction of the students' page in red ink, which is not in color here, and ideas for extending the learnings are also given along with suggestions as to what to observe about the students' responses.

The page from Holt, Rinehart & Winston's *The Music Book* (page 87) also includes the page from the student book and questions for the teacher to ask, as well as teaching procedures. In addition, there is a suggested instrumental accompaniment for classroom instruments and another part for band instruments. A recording is available with an accordion, trumpet, clarinet, and tuba, but there is no piano accompaniment for this song.

Key: **F**
Starting Tone: **C** (5, sol)
Piano Accompaniment on page **P.A. 35**

RECORDING 2, SIDE B, BAND 1
Accompaniment: French horn, flute, oboe, clarinet, 2 bassoons
Form: Introduction, 1 verse
Voice: Children's choir

IDENTIFYING RHYTHM PATTERNS

Purpose: To identify short-long duration patterns.

Materials: Textbook, eye patches, sashes, cardboard swords, boxes decorated as treasure chests.

Motivation: Ask children to tell what they know about pirates. Read a pirate story. Show pictures of pirates, their ships, and a flag with skull and cross-bones.

Exploration: Have the children:

1. Dress using eye patches, sashes, and swords, and pretend to be pirates. Practice saying "Yo ho!"

2. Listen to the song. Become familiar with the words and the melody.

3. Sing the "Yo ho!" patterns initially. After repeated hearings sing the whole song.

4. Dramatize the song.

5. Find the number of times the "Yo ho!" pattern appears in the song. [4 times near the beginning; 5 times near the end of the song]

6. Reinforce the pattern with a short-long hand gesture, perhaps thrust upward.

7. Visually reinforce the pattern by charting the two different "Yo ho!" patterns.

    Yo ho!   Yo ho!

Extension: Play the patterns on the resonator bells. Find the short-long pattern in "Ach ja!" p. 73.

Desired Responses: The children should correctly identify the short-long patterns in the song. They should be able to play the pattern correctly.

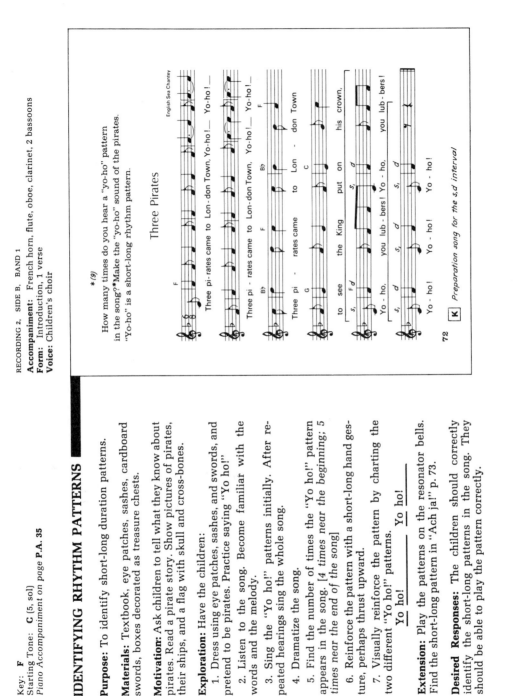

*(9)

How many times do you hear a "yo-ho" pattern in the song?*Make the "yo-ho" sound of the pirates. "Yo-ho" is a short-long rhythm pattern.

Three Pirates

English Sea Chantey

Three pi-rates came to Lon-don Town, Yo-ho!__ Yo-ho!__

Three pi-rates came to Lon-don Town, Yo-ho!__ Yo-ho!__

Three pi - rates came to Lon - don Town

to see the King put on his crown,

Yo-ho, you lub-bers! Yo - ho, you lub-bers!

Yo-ho! Yo-ho! Yo-ho!

72 **K** *Preparation song for the s,d interval*

Curriculum Correlation In the song "Three Pirates," have the children find the word "lubbers." Ask them what they think this word means. [*Awkward or inexperienced sailors*] Ask them for a word that rhymes with lubbers. [*Rubbers*]

From Mary Val Marsh et al., *The Spectrum of Music, Book 2* (New York: Macmillan, 1980). Used by permission.

Music Alone Shall Live

Key: F **Start:** A (3)

No piano accompaniment

Record 7 Side B Band 1
Voices: children's choir.
Accompaniment: trumpet, accordion, clarinet, tuba.

LEARNING OBJECTIVES

By **singing** and **playing**, the student will continue to develop the concepts of **Pitch** and **Expressive Whole**.

MATERIALS

- Soprano glockenspiel or resonator bells (G, A, Bb, C, D); bass xylophone (C, F) or piano

GETTING STARTED

Help the students learn the melody for "Music Alone Shall Live." Discover that the rhythm of the melody alternates between even (♩ ♩ ♩) and uneven (♩. ♪ ♩) patterns. Observe that Phrases 1 and 3 have the same melody. Sing with scale numbers; sing with words.

PROCESS

1. Read instructions at the top of the pupils' page. Discuss the meaning of the word **ensemble** (several people performing together).

   What will help us sing expressively? (Voice quality, tempo, dynamics, articulation, and phrasing.) Practice singing with attention to the expressive elements:

   - **phrasing:** Sing each phrase with a single breath so that the thought is carried along smoothly.
   - **tempo:** Sing in an allegro tempo (see page 34).
   - **dynamics:** Begin piano, and create a gradual crescendo throughout the entire song.
   - **articulation:** Sing in a legato style, connecting the tones smoothly.

   When the students know the song well, perform it as a two- or three-part round.

   Invite the students who are interested to practice the instrumental parts given at the bottom of the page. Add these parts to the ensemble. *Can we put everything together? voices singing in round and instruments? How should we begin?* The students may plan a sequence for their performance, such as,

   - begin with the bass xylophone and glockenspiel introduction;
   - voices enter in unison after four measures;
   - after the entire song is sung, continue with an instrumental interlude of four measures;
   - voices perform as a round;
   - end with instrumental coda.

EXTEND

Divide the class into small groups. Each group is to plan its own performance. Some students who study orchestral instruments may add the following parts.

Each group should perform for the rest of the class. *Did the performers listen carefully to each other as they performed?*

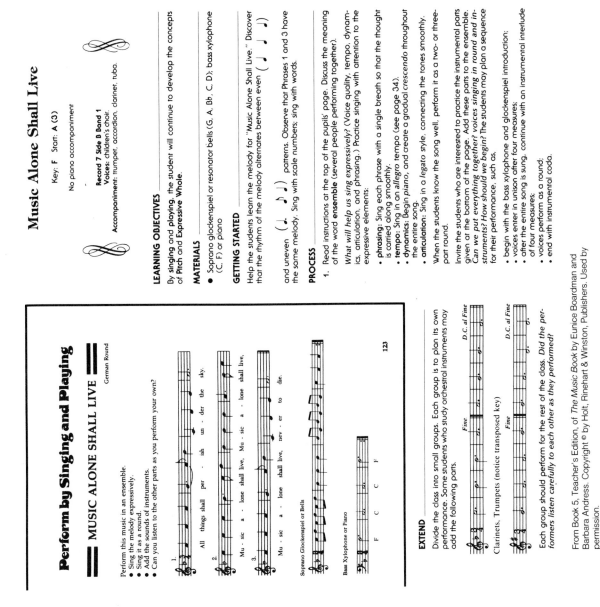

Perform by Singing and Playing

MUSIC ALONE SHALL LIVE

German Round

Perform this music in an ensemble.
- Sing the melody expressively.
- Sing it as a round.
- Add the sounds of instruments.
- Can you listen to the other parts as you perform your own?

All things shall per - ish un - der the sky.

Mu - sic a - lone shall live, Mu - sic a - lone shall live,

Mu - sic a - lone shall live, nev - er to die.

Soprano Glockenspiel or Bells

Bass Xylophone or Piano

F   C   C   F

123

Clarinets, Trumpets (notice transposed key)

Fine   D.C. al Fine

Fine   D.C. al Fine

From Book 5, Teacher's Edition, of *The Music Book* by Eunice Boardman and Barbara Andress. Copyright © by Holt, Rinehart & Winston, Publishers. Used by permission.

*N*o national pattern exists for schools containing grades 5 or 6 through 9. There are middle schools composed of grades 6–8 or 5–8, and junior high schools consisting of grades 7–8 or 7–9. In a few cases there still exist "elementary" schools containing grades 1–8. In fact, traditionally some states had two school systems, one for grades 1–8 and another for grades 9–12. Each system had its own superintendent, salary schedule, and school board. Under this arrangement some music teachers held contracts from two districts (with two slightly different rates of pay) when they taught in both the elementary and high school systems. This division has largely disappeared now, however.

General Music

American music education has an enviable record in terms of producing outstanding performing groups at the secondary school level, especially bands, but its accomplishments in the teaching of most students in its secondary schools are not very impressive. Part of the reason for this discrepancy between performance and nonperformnace courses lies in the interest music teachers have shown in the two areas. Some teachers consider the general music class as a feeder program for high school organizations. Others see it as a recreational period in which it doesn't matter much if the students learn anything. Many teachers of general music would rather be directing high school groups, and they simply have not given general music classes much attention and thought. As a result, quite a number of junior high-middle schools have reduced or eliminated general music. In the twelve years from the early 1960s to the early 1970s, when school enrollments were increasing significantly, enrollments in general music fell by over 5 percent.[10] Although a few music educators have worked hard to make general music the heart of music education for students in junior high-middle schools, they have not been able to reverse the long-term downward trend nationally.

Most of the elementary school music instruction is required of all students, but it is quite different in the secondary schools. At about the seventh grade level, give or take a grade level, the required program is discontinued. Sometimes music in the seventh grade may be a "semi-elective," so that a student is permitted to choose three courses out of four options. Usually students who elect a music organization, especially instrumental music, are no longer in the general music program, which means that many of the more interested and able students are not in general music. Some schools group the students homogeneously according to academic ability, and this grouping carries over into music. Others have classes composed entirely of girls or boys. (The arrangement makes it easier to meet the special musical needs and interests of each sex.)

In some school systems the general music course in the junior high-middle school is the first instruction in music the students receive from a music specialist. In other school systems the students have a strong background in music because of the elementary school experiences.

When general music is taught, it may be every other day for a year or for a semester; or it may be every day for six, nine, or eighteen weeks. The size of such classes varies also. Often they are the same size as other academic classes, but in some cases they contain sixty or more students.

The content of the general music classes at this level differs somewhat from music instruction at the elementary level in terms of the attention given the various aspects of music instruction. Although some singing and other music-making activities are continued, more time and effort is devoted to listening and analyzing. There are at least two reasons for the increased emphasis on listening in general music classes. One is that many of the boys are undergoing a change of voice, and singing is not as easy or satisfying during this transition. A second and more important reason is that after the students finish their education, the main contact most of them will have with music will be as listeners, not as singers or instrumentalists. Therefore, music teachers need to help students to improve their skill in listening to music. Suggestions for aiding students in listening are presented in books on music methods, several of which are recommended at the conclusion of this chapter.

Although listening should receive more attention in junior high school general music classes, singing and other types of music making should still be continued. As is pointed out in Chapter Four, singing and playing instruments can contribute much to the students' sensitivity awareness in music. General music should not become a class in which students only listen to and discuss music.

Elective Courses

In addition to the general music classes for most of the seventh grade students, specific courses are offered on an elective basis. These electives include band, choral groups, orchestra, and a host of extracurricular activities. The figure on page 90 shows the nature of the music program at the three levels found in America schools.

The most recent national data on the elective and general music courses in the secondary schools are as follows:[11]

Course	Students enrolled
Band	1,677,710
Orchestra	193,087
Instrumental ensembles	79,612

Instrumental classes	289,389	
Chorus	1,281,690	
Choir	417,452	
Glee Club	203,542	Total secondary school
Vocal ensembles	79,229	enrollment: 18,577,234
General music	1,632,665	
Appreciation	192,086	
Theory	64,777	
Total	6,111,239	

Although the exactness of the various figures may be questioned, they offer a good general idea of the situation in the early 1970s. Several important conclusions can be drawn from these data: (1) The enrollment in high school music courses is heavily in band and choral music. (2) Band enrollment is about nine times larger than that for orchestra, reflecting the fact that only about one high school in four

Music Program

	Required	Elective	Selective
Elementary School	General Music	Choral Groups Instrumental Study	
Middle School/ Junior High School	General Music	Choral Groups Instrumental Classes Beginning Intermediate	Choir Band Jazz Band Orchestra
Senior High School		Applied Music Appreciation Fine Arts Theory Choral Groups Voice Classes	Choir Band Jazz Band Orchestra
Extracurricular (after school, no credit)		Music Clubs Small Ensembles Musical Shows Pep Band Jazz Band Marching Band Auxiliary Units	

offers orchestra. (3) If general music (largely a junior high school subject) is removed from the totals, the enrollment in appreciation and theory courses make up only 5.73 percent of all the music enrollments, leaving 94.27 percent in performance groups. Clearly, the music curriculum at the high school level is overwhelmingly in performing organizations. (4) The enrollment in humanities and fine arts courses, courses much discussed and promoted since the 1960s, is so small that the 1972–1973 National Center for Educational Statistics study did not give it a separate category but instead lumped it in the totals for English and social studies.

Although performing groups dominate the music program in America's high schools, music educators should not forget about theory, appreciation, and fine arts courses. They should do what they reasonably can to bring the performance and nonperformance aspects of the program into a better balance. Often this balance can be helped by seeing to it that some nonperformance courses are offered in the school curriculum and then promoting them among the students. If teachers have the opportunity to teach such a course, they should devote as much effort to the course as they do their top performing groups. Finally, music educators should try to educate the school administration and community about the values of nonperformance courses in the music program.

Some historical background is needed to understand why secondary school music has become so performance-oriented. The great leap forward in secondary school enrollments occurred between the years 1910 and 1940. During that period a person's chances of attending high school increased from one in ten to three in four.[12] This increase meant that many of the students going to high school were not college-bound, so a greater variety of courses was needed in the curriculum. Also, attitudes changed somewhat about the values of studying subjects other than the traditional academic ones. Because school music at the secondary level expanded rapidly, there were few teachers trained to teach music at the secondary school level. Therefore, schools often turned to professional musicians, a trend that was greatly boosted by the unemployment of the early 1930s. These former professional musicians, naturally, worked with their performing groups in much the same way as a director of a professional organization. The period when the band or choir met was called a "rehearsal," and the purpose of the band or choir was to present polished and perfected performances. The teacher was designated the "director," a term more familiar to professional musicians. So music became the only curricular area in which "directors" conducted "rehearsals" instead of teachers teaching classes.

Many of the professional musicians who entered the teaching field made valuable contributions to music education. Even today the limited opportunities for making a living as a performer have turned many persons toward teaching in the schools. Common interests bind the professional musicians and music educators together, and the teaching profession needs capable and sensitive musicians. What should be realized, however, is that whatever is good for a professional organization is not always right for a school performing group. Because the two groups exist for different purposes, they should be approached somewhat differently.

There are several good reasons for continuing performing groups in the secondary school curriculum. One is that students learn by doing and experiencing. Students who go through the effort of learning their parts and rehearsing with the group know a musical work much more thoroughly than students who only listened to it. Many a student who had an initial lack of interest in a piece of music has ended up liking it after working on it and learning what it offers musically.

Another point in favor of performing groups is that they are well suited to meeting teenage needs for recognition and activity. In most of their other school courses the students sit passively. Music is one area in which they can truly participate. Preparing music for a performance motivates them, as well as offers them a chance for some recognition.

A third point in favor of performing groups is that they are well established in the school curriculum. One should be careful about criticizing success. Teachers are trained in teaching performing groups, and materials are available. Before discarding such achievements, something of greater value should be found to replace them.

What appears to be needed in the future is (1) a building up of the nonperformance courses and (2) an evolution (not a revolution) toward more educationally valid performing groups. Ways of increasing the amount and type of learning in performing groups, which are beyond the scope of this book, are presented in the author's *Teaching Music in the Secondary Schools.*

Types of Performing Groups

Not all secondary school students can profit equally from music instruction. Students want and need music that is suited to their abilities and interests. When enough enrollment permits, groups at different levels of ability should be offered. There can be a choir for the more interested and talented students, and a chorus for the less able and interested. The same idea holds true for instrumental groups. Such an arrangement is consistent with the democratic tenet of equal opportunity. Teachers should guard against slighting the less talented group. The education given students in a chorus is just as important as the education given the students in the top choir; only the level at which the learning takes place is different.

Small Ensembles. A weakness of music education at the secondary school level is its lopsided emphasis on large ensembles. Most music educators realize that performing in small ensembles is a valuable experience for students. They gain independence by being the only performer on a part, and small ensemble work engenders interest and good musicianship. In addition, there is a rich literature for combinations involving strings and groups such as woodwind quintets and brass ensembles.

At least three factors discourage small ensembles in the schools. To begin with, it is hard to work up much public enthusiasm for a woodwind quintet or horn trio, which is not true for bands or choral groups. Second, the time that teachers can devote to small ensembles is limited. Their schedules are filled with classes and large ensemble rehearsals. Few school systems can afford to hire a teacher for classes of four or five students. Third, the amount of time available to students for small ensembles is limited. Very few students have time in their school schedules for more than one music class per day, and that class usually is a large ensemble. Most small ensembles are formed for purposes of performing at a contest, and they meet only a few times with a teacher.

These problems do not erase the fact that small ensemble experience is highly desirable. Music teachers should encourage and plan for it as much as possible. Some teachers arrange for several small ensembles to rehearse at the same time in adjacent rooms so that they can circulate among the groups. In some situations the better performers can form an ensemble. Because they learn their parts more quickly than the other students, they can be excused from large ensemble rehearsal once or twice a week to rehearse small ensemble music.

Orchestras. For a variety of reasons orchestras have been far surpassed in enrollment by bands. Today only one secondary school in four offers strings, while virtually all offer band.[13] This is a most unfortunate situation, for two reasons. First, the orchestral literature is vastly richer than that for bands. Very few of the "name" composers throughout music history have written for bands. Except for some contemporary works, bands must play pieces written strictly for the educational market or transcriptions, which are not usually as effective as the original works. The wind band is slowly acquring some good contemporary literature of its own, and possibly in fifty years the problem of good literature will not be so serious. Second, the playing opportunities after high school for interested amateurs lie overwhelmingly in orchestras, which use only a limited number of winds. The existence of over 1400 community orchestras was mentioned earlier in this book, and most of them would like to have more string players.

When speaking candidly, many band directors give three reasons for not offering string instruction: (1) It might take potentially good players away from the band. The result would be two mediocre groups instead of one good organization. (2) There is no one competent enough to teach strings in the district. (3) The band director has no time for any more classes. The first reason may have some truth to it in school districts with enrollments of less than 1000 for grades 7 through 12. However, some small districts have a good band and a good orchestra. The excuse of a lack of string teaching ability is not valid. Band directors who are clarinet players do not hesitate teaching brass instruments, at least at the beginning and intermediate levels.

The matter of teacher time must be faced. It is not possible to get something for nothing. Fortunately, string instruments cost about the same as wind instruments, and often they can be rented from music merchants, in which cases an investment by the school district is not required. During the first year or two in which a string program is started, only a small amount of additional teacher time is needed. When the program reaches to all grades, the program adds about one-fourth to one-third as much instructional time as the winds require.

Marching Bands.   The marching band has commendable features. It is good public relations for the music department. Many people see the band only at a football game or street parade, and that is their only contact with the school music program. Its members achieve recognition, school spirit is fostered, and good feelings are generated all around as the colorful groups parade by. What could anyone have against something that gives so many people harmless enjoyment and impresses them favorably with the school music program?

The problem is that in some communities the marching band has dominated the music program in the school district; in some high schools the marching band has become the entire music program. In such instances the result is a narrow music education for a small number of students and just about no music education for the vast majority of the students.

The problem has been intensified over the past decade in many places because of the growth of marching band contests and the increasing popularity of the corps style of marching. Aside from its technical features, such as style of step, corps style bands usually learn only one show each year, and they perform this show for every appearance. Clearly this one show provides the students with a very restricted musical experience. Many of the appearances are at marching band contests, with some bands entering five or more contests each fall. The evaluation of bands at these contests is based largely on nonmusical factors, and a correlation has been observed by many people between the size of the group (band members and auxiliary units) and the ratings received. One study of high school bands uncovered the fact that many students liked the competition and potential recognition but realized that they learned much more in a concert band. Even many of the directors of successful contest bands freely admitted that the experience has little to do with educating students in music.[14] The values claimed for the marching activity, both at contests and at football games, were the promotion of the band and character building and recognition for the students—reasons that hark back to the topic of the nonmusical values of music discussed in Chapter Three.

What can music educators who teach bands do about the situation? In most American communities today the marching band is so much a part of the scene that it is unrealistic to suggest that it be discontinued, and probably that would not be a good idea anyway. Teachers can begin by bringing the attention devoted to the marching band into proportion with that given other aspects of the music program. In some cases this adjustment may mean reducing (over a period of a couple of years) the number of marching appearances or contests entered. It may mean simplifying the marching shows in terms of the routines the students are expected to learn. Truthfully, most football fans cannot tell the difference between a complicated and a simple band show (or maybe they don't care). A third action that will make the teachers' lives a little easier is to have someone else oversee the auxiliary units—flag bearers, rifle corps, pom-pom unit, and so on. Other teachers or people in the community can work with these groups, and music teachers will have more time for teaching music, which is what they were trained to do.

Jazz Bands and Swing Choirs. Should "specialized" performing groups such as jazz bands, madrigal singers, and swing choirs be included in the secondary school curriculum on the same basis as band, orchestra, choir, and general music? Certainly such groups should be offered when possible, but in most cases they should be operated as adjuncts to the larger groups. That is, jazz band membership should be made available only to the members of the concert band or to those who have been members for two or more years. If this condition is not made, a student's musical education is limited by his or her premature selection of one specialized area before becoming educated to some degree about a larger world of music.

In some schools such specialized groups have received most of the attention of the teacher and the public, and the larger group has been neglected. For example, one prestigious suburban high school let its concert band deteriorate noticeably while a steel band was receiving most of the director's attention.

Music teachers in many states are certified for all school grades.

Even when not certified for all levels, they should realize that they are a part of a large and varied program of instruction. If music is to be solidly in the schools, it needs to be a coordinated and planned effort from kindergarten through grade 12. Both the students and music teachers will benefit when this is done.

Questions

1. (a) What are the advantages and disadvantages of having music specialists be responsible for all the music instruction in elementary schools?

   (b) What are the advantages and disadvantages of having classroom teachers be responsible for all of the music instruction in elementary schools?

2. Consider the goals for general music on pages 75–77. Are these goals too ambitious? Too simple? Are some of these goals not very important? Are there some goals that should added?

3. How has the emphasis on performing groups in the high schools aided and improved music education? In what ways has it been detrimental to music education?

4. Why are strings and orchestra an important part of the school music curriculum?

Projects

1. Find out the arrangements for music instruction in the elementary school of a particular school district. Gather the following information:

   (a) Who teaches music?

   (b) How much time for music does each classroom receive each week?

   (c) Is a curriculum guide or other information on teaching music available?

2. Examine and compare two or three different sets of music series books for use in the elementary and junior high schools. Compare especially the teacher's editions, record albums, and other materials such as charts or tapes. In the teacher's editions, look for:

   (a) the amount and quality of the indexing

   (b) outline of units or minimum program

   (c) teaching suggestions, both general and specific

   (d) piano accompaniments

3. Examine the program of music instruction in the secondary schools of a school district. Gather information on the following:

(a) What classes are offered?

(b) Whether the courses are required, semi-elective, or elective

(c) If elective, what percentage of the students take various classes?

(d) What courses of study are available?

Suggested Readings

Bessom, Malcolm, Alphonse M. Tatarunis, and Samuel L. Forcucci. *Teaching Music in Today's Secondary Schools*. 2nd. ed. New York: Holt, Rinehart & Winston, 1980. Chapter 3.

Edelstein, Stefán and others. *Creating Curriculum in Music*. Menlo Park, Calif.: Addison-Wesley, 1980.

Hoffer, Charles. *Teaching Music in the Secondary Schools*. 3rd ed. Belmont, Calif.: Wadsworth, 1983. Chapters 7–13.

Hoffer, Charles and Marjorie L. Hoffer. *Teaching Music in the Elementary Classroom*. New York: Harcourt Brace Jovanovich, 1982. Chapters 4–19.

Mark, Michael L. *Contemporary Music Education*. New York: Schirmer Books, 1978.

Metz, Donald. *Teaching General Music in Grades 6–9*. Columbus, Ohio: Charles E. Merrill, 1980. Chapter 2.

Peter, G. David and Robert F. Miller. *Music Teaching and Learning*. New York: Longman, 1982. Chapter 2.

The School Music Program: Description & Standards. Reston, Va.: Music Educators National Conference, 1974.

Swanson, Bessie. *Music in the Education of Children*. 4th ed. Belmont, Calif.: Wadsworth, 1981.

Swanson, Fredrick J. *Music Teaching in the Junior High and Middle School*. New York: Appleton-Century-Crofts, 1973. Chapters 4 and 5.

References

[1] Karl D. Ernst and Charles L. Gary, eds., *Music in General Education* (Reston, Va.: Music Educators National Conference, 1965).

[2] *The School Music Program : Description & Standards* (Reston, Va.: Music Educators National Conference, 1974).

[3] Ernst and Gary, pp. 4–8. Copyright © 1965 by Music Educators National Conference. Used by permission.

[4] *The School Music Program*, p. 9.

[5] M. Barbara Amen, "The Effect of Selected Factors on the Time Spent Teaching Music by Elementary Classroom Teachers" (Ph.D. diss., Indiana University, 1982), p. 63.

[6]Robert H. Klotman, ed., *Teacher Education in Music: Final Report* (Reston, Va.: Music Educators National Conference, 1972), p. 20.

[7]Ibid.

[8]Albert Bandura and F.J. McDonald, "Influence of Social Reinforcement and the Behavior of Models in Shaping Children's Moral Judgments," *Journal of Abnormal and Social Psychology*, 67 (1963), pp. 274–281.

[9]*Music and Art in the Public Schools*, Research Monograph 1963-M3 (Washington, D.C.: National Education Association, 1963), p. 12.

[10]Logan C. Osterndorf and Paul J. Horn, *Course Offerings, Enrollments, and Curriculum Practices in Public Secondary Schools, 1972–73* (Washington, D.C.: U.S. Government Printing Office, 1976) (NCES 77-153), pp. 214–219.

[11]Ibid.

[12]*Digest of Educational Statistics*, Department of Health, Education, and Welfare (Washington, D.C.: U.S. Government Printing Office, 1970), p. 49.

[13]Osterndorf and Horn. Op. cit.

[14]George L. Rogers, "Attitudes of High School Band Directors, Band Members, Parents, and Principals toward Marching Band Contests" (D.M.E. diss. Indiana University, 1982), p. 83.

Contemporary American Curriculum Developments

A CERTAIN AMOUNT of ferment and change is always present in a field as diverse and large as music education. Usually several trends or changes are happening. Many of these changes are the result of music educators seeking to improve their profession, while others are reactions to events outside of the profession. This chapter examines some of the more contemporary and significant topics in American music education. It offers no final solutions to the complex problems that are being discussed; nor does it try to promote or discourage any particular effort for the improvement of music education.

Seminars, Commissions, and Projects

It is traditional when writing about recent developments in music education to organize the presentation according to the major seminars, symposiums, commissions, and projects that have met and published reports over the past twenty years. This is a logical way to cover the subject, but it does have some weaknesses.

One weakness is that the recommendations of such efforts are considered apart from the larger picture that may have strongly influenced the recommendation in the first place. Most events and actions in life have complex causes; they are not the result of just one thing. For example, although the Tanglewood Symposium in 1967 did increase the attention given the topic of music education for minority students in the urban areas of the United States, a host of other events also contributed to a greater awareness of the problems and opportunities of the cities and minorities. The Watts riot in Los Angeles occurred in 1964 and the 1967 Detroit riot happened during the Tanglewood Symposium, the "War on Poverty" had been declared national policy by President Johnson two years earlier, the civil rights movement was in full swing, the music of blacks and other minorities was beginning to receive the attention it deserved, minorities were voting in greater numbers and becoming a much larger percentage of the school population in several major cities, and so on.

Discussing music education in terms of projects or meetings tends to leave the impression that the report or project caused certain actions to be taken, which is the second limitation of the "seminar-by-symposium" approach. As Charles Leonhard points out in his delightfully candid evaluation of the influence of the 1963 Yale Seminar on Music Education, "The notion that the results of the deliberations of the Yale group or any other group can shake the world was and is absurd. . . . The residue of their deliberations appearing in the inevitable report may stir up some controversy among the few people who read and take such reports seriously, but to expect any such report to have any profound effect on practice is bootless and naive."[1]

A third weakness of the seminar approach is the increasing number of years since most of these events took place. The time period for most of the major seminars and projects in music education was the decade of the 1960s with its newly available federal funds for education. It is now two decades since most of these events took place. Some of the circumstances are unchanged over the years, but others are different. Whether meetings and projects taking place two decades ago are still "contemporary" depends on how one defines the word, but in any case they cannot be considered current or up to the minute.

The pointing out of the limitations of seminars and projects should not leave the impression that they were a waste of time and money. They were worth the modest (modest in terms of other governmental expenditures, at least) sums they cost. They focused attention on topics and offered suggestions for interested people to consider. What is being maintained here is that they were not the watershed events that sometimes has been assumed.

Contemporary Topics

*E*ach of the following topics could consume an entire chapter, which would obviously make for a very long book. Instead they are introduced, and it is hoped that readers will be motivated to explore further on their own those that are of special interest to them. Clearly many of the topics are interrelated, and one affects another. They are presented here in no special order.

Contemporary Music

Music education in America has a long tradition of using large amounts of music written for school use. Most of this music was, and often still is, composed by people who are not "name" composers. Neither was much of the music studied in the schools a part of the currently popular music, and not even much folk music was used until the past twenty-five years. By the end of the 1950s a number of musicians and educators were becoming increasingly concerned about the heavy domination in America's classrooms of music in the "common practice" style of the eighteenth and nineteenth centuries.

The most significant effort to update music in the schools was the Young Composers Project, which began in 1957 with a grant from the Ford Foundation. The idea was to place ten young (under thirty-five) composers as composers-in-residence in school systems with strong music programs. The hope was that the young composer would learn about the opportunities and challenges of writing for school groups and that in return the school and community would benefit and its interest in contemporary music would be increased. The first year of operation for the project was 1959, and by 1962 thirty-one composers had been placed in school systems. In many ways the response to the program was good, but the composers reported that many music teachers were poorly prepared to deal with contemporary idioms. Therefore, in 1962 the project was increased to become one of the Ford Foundation's ten major programs. The MENC submitted a proposal to the foundation for what was to become the Contemporary Music Project (CMP), and the idea was funded in the amount of $1,380,000. The purposes of the project were as follows:

1. To increase the emphasis on the creative aspect of music in the public schools;

2. To create a solid foundation or environment in the music education profession for the acceptance, through understanding, of the contemporary music idiom;

3. To reduce the compartmentalization that now exists between the profession of music composition and music education for the benefit of composers and music educators alike;

4. To cultivate taste and discrimination on the part of music educators and students regarding the quality of contemporary music used in schools; and

5. To discover, when possible, creative talent among students.[2]

The practice of placing composers in the schools continued, but the CMP added to that effort by establishing workshops and seminars at various colleges throughout the United States to educate teachers about contemporary music through analyzing, performing, and creating music. Six pilot projects were also established in the schools. Following the Northwestern University seminar in 1965, six regional institutes for Music in Contemporary Education, involving thirty-six educational institutions, were formed. In 1968 the Ford Foundation gave another $1,340,000 to the MENC, which contributed $250,000, for a five-year extension of the program. Some modest changes were made in the composer project, and twenty-one teachers were given grants to write curriculum materials using the methods and music from the CMP. The CMP ended in 1973.

During its final ten years the CMP devoted much of its attention to the skills and knowledge required to deal with all types of music. Its approach was a process-centered one that included three components: performing, organizing, and describing. This manner of teaching was often referred to as the "common elements approach." Through this approach, the CMP maintained, the compartmentalization in the music profession could be greatly reduced. No longer, for example, would the trumpet or voice teacher in the studio be concerned only with the performance of a musical work, but would also point out its theoretical and historical aspects.

Although it may not have met all its goals, the CMP clearly had an impact on the music education profession. Many music teachers are now more conscious of the need to teach and use some twentieth-century music. The elementary school music series books described in the previous chapter now contain a good representation of the various types of contemporary music, and publishers have brought out more contemporary materials for use by school groups.

Certain difficulties, however, still persist for music teachers with regard to teaching contemporary music. One problem is the several different types of contemporary music. There are types as different in style as those of John Cage, Milton Babbitt, Anton Webern, George Crumb, Hans Werner Henze, and so on. There is not just one but several contemporary idioms, and it is virtually impossible to cover all types in the time usually available for music instruction in the schools.

Second, technical problems make many contemporary works beyond the ability of many school groups. It is possible to find a few good twentieth-century works that are within the capabilities of many high school groups, but teachers have to make an effort to locate such music. One source for such music, by the way, is the library of music written by the composers in the Young Composers Project.

A third factor discouraging some teachers from teaching more contemporary music is that it does not find favor with much of the public and many students. Sometimes a contemporary work that the group has worked hard on is greeted coolly by the listeners.

In spite of these facts, music teachers should teach a proportionate share of contemporary music, for the reasons cited in Chapter Four about using a representative sample of music. It is a topic of importance to all music teachers.

Creativity

Somewhat related to the interest in contemporary music is the increasing amount of attention given creative activities in school music classes. This interest can be traced back to the increasing value contemporary American society places on individuality and creativity, as well as to the interest of music teachers in the topic. One can hardly pick up a magazine or educational journal without seeing something encouraging creative efforts in matters ranging from how one dresses to methods of teaching.

Not only has there been more interest in recent years in creative efforts in music classes, the form these efforts have taken has been broadened. When the topic was mentioned in the elementary music series books and methods books forty years ago, it was usually a description of how a class could compose a song together. Today individual efforts in creating music are emphasized, and they include sound pieces, works of electronic music, ostinato accompaniments, improvising phrases, and short songs. The music series books offer suggestions for creating music with tape-recorded sounds or with sounds located around the classroom and for creating or improvising simple parts on classroom instruments. Theory classes at the high school level also often contain a number of creative activities.

This trend toward more creativity has been helped by the availability of relatively inexpensive tape recorders and moderately priced tone synthesizers. Students can gather sounds on the cassette recorders that many of them own, and then those sounds can be transcribed to a reel-to-reel recorder for manipulation. Most schools own several tape recorders, so no extra expenditure of money is needed for equipment. Only a decade ago the idea of an affordable home computer seemed as unlikely as affordable tone synthesizers. Today both pieces of equipment are realities. They offer a whole new range of possibilities for creating music.

The exploration of sound and creativity in the schools was fostered to some degree by the Manhattanville Music Curriculum Program (MMCP). The program was funded by grants from the U.S. Office of Education and was named for Manhattanville College of the Sacred Heart in Purchase, New York, where it began in 1965. At first it was an exploratory program to locate and identify innovative and experimental music programs throughout the United States. Ninety-two programs were studied, fifteen of them in depth. The portion of the MMCP for which it is best known today began in 1966 and consisted of three phases spread over three years. The first phase studied how students learn, curriculum, and classroom procedures. The second phase was a refinement and synthesis of the information gained in the first phase into a course of study. The third phase consisted of field testing and refinements, as well as plans for teacher training and assessment. The project ended before the assessment could be conducted.

The MMCP took the solipsistic view that only what the student figures out for himself or herself is really learned. As Ronald B. Thomas, MMCP director, wrote: "We must stop pretending that we have the sacrosanct perspective and the duty to inflict it, in *our* terms, on captive students. Real education is not a study about things; it is experience *inside* things."[3] The MMCP program attempted to have children learn to hear music the way a composer does—that is, to perceive music without having first to interpret it cognitively. The children were to think in the medium of music and to study music as a whole to experience all aspects of music. Students were asked to compose, perform, conduct, listen, and not to stand back and consider music reverently.[4] A music lab was advocated as the needed physical setup for achieving these goals, and individual or small group activities were the means. Learning in the MMCP view is essentially problem solving; each problem solved leads to a new synthesis and increasing insight into music.

The field tests of the program in phase three revealed that some modifications were called for and that teacher in-service training was needed. The MMCP personnel had four concerns about the music teachers who were involved in the field trials:

1. Teachers did not know enough about music to work with students creatively.
2. Teachers found it difficult to consider goals other than skill achievement and performance.
3. Many teachers were method-oriented and found it difficult to work in a new framework.
4. Many teachers had not personally experienced creative accomplishment and were therefore not secure in an atmosphere of creativity.[5]

The teacher reeducation program devised by the MMCP required from sixty to ninety hours of instruction.

For some of the reasons cited, many music teachers have found the MMCP program difficult to establish in their schools. In addition, its requirement of a music lab and a sizable amount of teacher time also greatly inhibited its adoption. The program was sometimes difficult to explain to parents and administrators; the sounds emanating from the music lab sounded to an outsider more like noise instead of music. The fact that the MMCP felt that so much of the existing music instruction in the schools was wrongheaded raises the question of who was "out of step" with whom—most of the music education profession or the MMCP? Perhaps both were to some extent.

Enriching Rehearsals

The Final Report of the Yale Seminar on Music Education contains this observation about students in school performing organizations: "Even in students who are potentially gifted and intellectually capable, creativity and agility of musical thought and judgment are left almost entirely undeveloped, while fingers and lips are drilled to considerable speed and accuracy. . . . A society that prized creativity, originality, and individualism seems to have known best how to produce the musical technician, follower, and teammate."[6] A similar thought is expressed in a more direct style by Jack Mercer, an experienced school band director who traveled around the United States and interviewed 222 band directors. His report contains several important points:

> Somewhere between multiple performances and the purpose of performing groups must arise a philosophical question: Is performance total music education? . . .

> The original interview questionnaire asked each director to describe his course of study and curriculum for band. The question was dropped after talking with the first fifty directors because in each case the director interpreted the question to mean, "What rehearsal techniques do you use?" and proceeded to give me a detailed account of the procedures he used to warm up and tune the band.

> If I had asked a teacher of mathematics or social studies or science to describe the curriculum of his department, there would have been no confusion. . . .

> . . . the content of the course of study is fortuitous, depending almost entirely upon whether it is football season or concert season; upon the whim of the director; and upon the required numbers on the contest list for a particular year. For these directors, the goal of musical training is to present a polished musical performance. . . .

> This procedure is so familiar to each of us reared in the tradition of music-making that the spontaneous response is likely to be, "You didn't have to travel 17,000 miles to discover that." Yet, I *did* have to travel 17,000 miles to discover the obvious because I, too, have been living from performance to performance for over twenty years. The scores needed for the next halftime or concert have been the curriculum for my band. . . .

> Under the present system, many students who have had four years of high school band with over 720 hours of rehearsals will still be musical illiterates. . . . Students with four years of band are only slightly better prepared to listen to music and enjoy a symphony concert than the 80 percent of their peers who receive no music education at all in high school. And it is probable that this situation holds true in choral and orchestral classes as well."[7]

Several attempts have been made to improve the quality and scope of what students in performing organizations learn. Although they were not commercially successful, several worthwhile books were published for use in the rehearsal of secondary school performing groups: the *Performing Music with Understanding* books published by Wadsworth Publishing Company and the *Comprehensive Musicianship* books developed by the Hawaii Curriculum Project and marketed by Addison-Wesley.[8] These books presented practical but different ways in which more than performance skills could be learned in rehearsals. The idea is not to make the band or choral group into an academic class, but rather to integrate the learning of information about music with its performance. Pieces of music become the vehicles for learning basic information about music theory, literature, and other aspects of music, as well as being music to perform.

The idea of including a group's understanding of music and aural skills as a part of a contest rating has been suggested in several states and tried in at least one state, Indiana.[9] In that trial a test lasting for about thirty minutes was devised to determine the students' basic information about music and their ability to recognize aspects of the music aurally. Questions such as "What is the V or dominant chord in the key of G?" were asked, and the tape included examples in which students identified instruments or whether a work was contrapuntal or homophonic (although those terms were not used). During the field trial period the results were not made public and did not affect a group's rating; only the director was informed of his or her students' scores. The idea behind the musicianship test was to encourage directors to devote some time to teaching something in addition to performing. The incorporation of the test in the final contest rating and the fact that the results would be made public would provide them with quite a bit of motivation to do that kind of teaching. However, the contest association did not permit making such results public or having them included in the rating, so the idea was not tried a second year.

The situation still remains, however. Most members of school performing groups understand little about the music they play or sing. This is unfortunate because with a little extra effort on the part of their directors they could learn a great deal about music. These students can perform the music as well as study it, which is quite an advantage. It is also unfortunate because, as the enrollment figures in Chapter Five indicate, very few of the members of performing groups take any other music course while in high school.

Youth Music

The attention given in the late 1960s and early 1970s to the topic of youth or popular music in the curriculum had a number of causes. One cause was the unusually large proportion of the population who were teenagers. The "baby boom" of children born following World War II entered the secondary schools and then college. Another cause is the youth orientation of American society, in which looking and thinking young is highly valued. A third reason was that teenagers became a commercially viable market for products such as clothes, movies, and music. The popular music and movie markets are now heavily the youth market.[10] A fourth reason was the turmoil and questioning of values encouraged by the Vietnam conflict. A fifth cause was the fragmentation of American society according to age. At one time in America parents, children, and grandparents all lived together in the same household on a farm or in a small town, but that is rarely true today. Each age group often associates largely with others of its own age group. A sixth reason was the rapid rate of social change in the twentieth century. For example, the first automobiles appeared on roads about the turn of the century, and by 1969 a man had walked on the moon. All this change has led to a situation in which, as anthropologist Margaret Mead has pointed out, young children easily accept ideas that their elders are still struggling with.[11] Music has not been exempt from all these sociological influences.

There are also some social psychological reasons for teenagers having a music that they consider their own, just as their parents before them did. They want some music (and clothing styles and slang words) that they know but their elders don't. That contributes to feelings of competence, which is a necessary and valuable part of growing up, and serves to identify them with their age groups. The music of the big bands or the Beatles is not the music of teenagers today. Any teenager who dances the waltz or fox trot at a social function would be considered as an eccentric by his or her peers.

The Tanglewood Symposium was organized in 1967 by the MENC and funded with a grant from the Presser Foundation to explore the broad topic of "Music in a Democratic Society." The topic of the symposium made it logical for it to consider the matter of youth or popular music. One of its pronouncements was the following:

> Music of all periods, styles, forms, and cultures belongs in the curriculum. The musical repertory should be expanded to involve music of our time in its rich variety, including currently popular teenage music and avant-garde music, American folk music, and the music of other cultures.[12]

What the Tanglewood Symposium did was to declare publicly and, in a sense, to place a seal of approval on something that had been evolving in music education for a number of years prior to 1967. Although little was said about it, many junior high general music teachers had for years been including units on jazz and Broadway musicals in their classes and stage bands existed in many high schools. Some popular music was standard fare with marching bands, and concert bands and choral groups also performed some popular music. The question was not "Should some popular music be included in the curriculum?" but rather "How much popular music should be included, and how should it be taught?"

Some music educators have worried—not without justification in a number of school situations—that the content of many music courses would become heavy with popular music and that art music would be nearly abandoned. Others have no such worries; they consider art music to be an out-of-date product from eighteenth- and nineteenth-century Europe. Most teachers hold views somewhere between these extremes. They teach and use popular music to a reasonable extent. Such music is a good way to gain the interest of students, and musical information can be taught with it. One can gain listening skills regardless of the music heard, and can learn about certain techniques such as ostinato, syncopation, and improvisation in several different types of music. Popular music is taught as music without any value judgment being offered by the teacher. Publishers of music books and other materials appear to have adopted this attitude. They freely include popular material alongside art and folk music.

Individualized Learning and Open Education

Good teachers have for many decades been treating students as individuals by putting them in different reading groups, giving them extra help in a subject, and letting them work on individual projects.* However, in the last two decades the amount of attention given to meeting individual needs and styles of learning has been increasing. Individualizing learning and open education have in common their concern for treating students as individuals. However, they can differ in several major respects.

Individualized learning often refers to the rate at which the students are expected to learn the material and sometimes to the way in which it is learned. For example, the teacher may decide that a student needs extra work on reading music. So extra individual work—perhaps a unit in programmed style—is prescribed. In this example, the teacher decided what the pupil needed and how the perceived deficiency should be overcome.

Open education is a more comprehensive concept, and it is also somewhat harder to define. In fact, many advocates of open education say that the term cannot and should not be defined. As Roland Barth points out: "Open education does not exist. It does not lie out there . . . awaiting discovery and description. . . . Those who are most carefully and persistently trying to capture the essential nature of open education are, by doing so, *creating* it. For this reason, there is and will always be disagreement about what open education is."[13] If it is possible at all to pin down what open education is, it can be identified by certain characteristics:

1. The teacher's role is seen as an "enabler" or "facilitator" in the learning process, not as the source of information. The teacher does not transmit subject matter content to the students but rather organizes, encourages, and works with the individual students so that

---

*In fairness it should be mentioned that there have been, and still are, teachers who do none of these things.

they can learn through their own efforts. The teacher is not central to the process, but rather is somewhere outside of it.

2. Usually the means of learning are informal and often appear to be play, not work.

3. The individual student selects the manner in which the topic will be studied and sometimes the topic that will be studied.

4. The motivation comes from the students' natural and individual interests, not extrinsically from something that the teacher does or provides.

5. The topics the student works on may or may not be of his or her choosing. Advocates of open education are fuzzy and sometimes contradictory on this point. As one reads about open education, it is easy to get the impression that usually the students learn what they want to learn. However, statements such as this one are encountered: "This does not mean that children learn only what they want to learn. Open educators must be extremely perceptive about where children's interests can lead them."[14]

6. The classroom does not have a formal arrangement of furniture. Instead the space is used flexibly with movable screens and "interest areas." Many learning activities take place outside of the classroom.

7. Evaluation is in terms of the objectives set by the students and teacher jointly, not in terms of traditional learning. In fact, the results of the commonly used achievement tests are rejected because they are not considered valid for students involved in open education.

Since there is no clear definition of open education, it is not possible to give categorical answers about what happens to music instruction in such a setting. It is reassuring to know that most of the proponents of open education give strong verbal support to the inclusion of the arts in the school curriculum. The nature of what students learn and do in conjunction with music, however, may be different from the traditional music instruction, as best that can be determined. Open education may possess some or all of these features:

1. Be individually oriented. There is little teaching of a class of students the same thing in the same way at the same time. Nor is there a course of study that students are to learn. Instead students develop and pursue their own ideas, with guidance from the teacher, about what they will study.

2. Attempt to relate what the student is learning in music with other activities in the classroom. The idea is to have music be an integral part of the school day.

3. Contain little formality. Each child or small group of children works in its own way.

4. Give less attention to performing music and more to individual exploring and creating, as well as listening.

5. Include in the physical facilities provision for individual work through interest centers and equipment for listening with headphones and creating music.

Few educators oppose the idea of students learning on a self-directed, self-motivated basis. Clearly, when a person is studying what he or she is interested in, more learning takes place. Questions arise, however, about those areas that a person may not happen to like and, therefore, does not choose to study. How many of us, if we had been left to our own inclinations, would have learned the multiplication tables, England's location on a map, or the notes on the bass staff? It seems that there are some topics that we learned because someone said we needed to learn them. No one advocates ramming useless information down the throats of uninterested students, but the idea of allowing the entire curriculum to depend on the individual interests is hard to defend.

The limitations of time and money work against large amounts of individual instruction, which is clearly not the way any teacher would like it but something that must be faced. If a music specialist in the elementary schools sees each room of thirty children for thirty minutes twice a week, one does not have to be much of a mathematician to compute that the teacher can allot only two minutes per week to each student. It would take an extremely able and dedicated teacher to organize much in two minutes with a student.

What seems to be needed is for music teachers to implement some of the open classroom philosophy while keeping in mind (1) the practical limits of time and facilities and (2) the success of such efforts with the group of students. Treat students as individuals and with respect? Absolutely. Consider their interests and abilities? Positively. Recognize that there are limitations to how fully these desirable goals can be carried out? Definitely. Individualized learning and open education are good ideas—if not carried to excess.

Combined Arts

The past two decades have witnessed increasing interest in relating music to the other fine arts, and to some extent to the entire curriculum. There are two general ways in which music and other subject matter areas may be related or integrated. One is to combine them into a course for study, while the other is to bring the arts into other areas of the curriculum. Both of these approaches merit further explanation.

The idea of combining arts into a course exists in many colleges but is not often found in secondary schools, as was pointed out in Chapter

Five. Sometimes such a course consists of the various arts—usually two- and three-dimensional art, literature, and music—and sometimes includes theater and dance. The average three-credit college course meets three hours a week for fifteen or sixteen weeks. When five subjects are divided into forty-eight or less class meetings, that leaves only nine or so classes for each art, which certainly isn't much time. If the course is enlarged in scope by adding philosophical and historical ideas, thereby making it a humanities course, the amount of time for each subject is reduced further. What these time limitations mean is that, at best, such courses can be only introductory to further study in each art.

Time is not the only obstacle, however. How many teachers are truly competent to teach four or five different arts? There are a few—very few. Often the solution to the instructor problem is to form a committee of several arts teachers, which is never an easy undertaking. Not only do several compatible teachers need to be found, but they need to have time to meet together for planning. In some cases the committee falls back on a let's-each-take-a-turn approach in which the time is simply divided up among them.

Another problem with combined arts courses is the temptation to draw false parallels among the arts. For example, the fact that the word *rhythm* is found in both music and painting does not mean that it refers to the same thing. Rhythm in music evolves through time, while rhythm in painting is a repeated pattern or shape that is perceived within a millisecond. A musical rhythm cannot take up physical space; a visual rhythm cannot be represented in a span of time. Looking for a parallel that does not exist is confusing to the students and takes their attention away from the qualities they should notice.

The points about the limitations of time, the question of who should teach, and the danger of false parallels are not offered here to leave the impression that fine arts courses should be avoided. Rather the point is that one should not enter into them without carefully considering the obstacles that need to be overcome to make the course a success. Such courses require extra effort on the part of the faculty members involved because the number of books and amount of other material for such courses are very limited. Furthermore, the students, administration, and other faculty members may not have a clear understanding of what the combined course is trying to accomplish. The goals need to be precisely stated in terms that nonmusicians can understand.

Combined arts instruction does not happen very often in the elementary schools, probably because the level of study in any of the arts in the elementary school is not at a level that is conducive for such combinations. One interesting approach was developed in a graded series of elementary school books under the title *Self-Expression and Conduct*.[15] The books are organized around the concepts of truth, beauty, love, justice, and faith, which are studied through art, dance, drama, music, and language. The arts are included whenever they can aid the development of the humanistic concepts presented in the books. Few music teachers would be satisfied with the coverage of music in these books, but they are an excellent extension if there already is an effective music program.

An approach to integrating the arts in elementary and middle schools that is more suited to that level is the idea of infusing the rest of the curriculum with the arts. Although the idea had been explored previously, including a program called CUE (Culture Understanding and Enrichment) in New York in the mid-1960s, a major effort that promoted this idea was the IMPACT (Interdisciplinary Model Program in the Arts for Children and Teachers) project of the early 1970s. The project was the joint effort of the four arts education associations: MENC; National Art Education Association; American Theater Association; and the Dance Division of the American Association of Health, Physical Education, and Recreation. Later other organizations joined in the effort. Five broad objectives were listed for IMPACT:

1. To reconstruct the educational program and administrative climate of the school in an effort to achieve parity between the arts and other instructional areas and between the affective and cognitive learning provided in the total school program.

2. To develop educational programs of high artistic quality in each art area, that is, the visual arts, music, dance, and drama, in each of the participating schools.

3. To conduct inservice programs, including summer institutes, workshops, demonstrations, and other similar activities, for the training of teachers, administrators, and other school personnel in the implementation of programs exemplifying high aesthetic and artistic quality into the school program.

4. To develop ways to integrate the arts into all aspects of the school curriculum as a means of enhancing and improving the quality and quantity of aesthetic education offered in the schools, and as a principal means for expanding the base for affective learning experiences in the total school program.

5. To invite a number of outstanding artists, performers, and educators into the school system to enhance the quality of the art experiences of children.[16]

The IMPACT program was implemented in five locations throughout the United States and was tried for two years. When the project concluded in 1972, the general consensus among those who worked in it was that the idea was successful. The best objective news for music teachers from the IMPACT trials was the academic test scores, which indicated that the students' academic work appeared to improve with the introduction of the arts program. School attendance also improved.

The successor to the IMPACT project was the Arts in General Education (AGE) program promoted by the JDR III Fund, which gave a group of nine states funds to form the "Coalition for Arts in General Education." Not only were funds from the JDR III Fund used, seven or eight different grant programs of the federal government were tapped, including Artists in the Schools, Aid to Handicapped, and Title III.[17] The objectives of the AGE programs were similar to those of IMPACT. Each state was allowed quite a bit of latitude in developing and operating its plans for enriching the curriculum through the arts. Most states designated demonstration sites that were to serve as models for the other schools in the state. The states differed in how well they carried out their plans; some were reasonably successful, as IMPACT had been, but others never seemed to get going.

Part of the problem in evaluating the success of the AGE program is determining what new and different things teachers did as a result of the AGE. Many of them already utilized the arts to some extent, and often these activities were continued but now credited to AGE. One example can serve to indicate the type of learning that the JDR III Fund personnel hoped to see happen. The students were studying the angles in mathematics. The teacher enriched and made more vivid this lesson by having the students form acute and obtuse angles through physical movements.[18] In this way, mathematics and dance were integrated, presumably to the benefit of both subjects.

Music for All Students

Back in 1923 the Music Supervisors National Conference adopted the slogan "Music for Every Child—Every Child *for* Music." Like most slogans that are no longer in vogue, it strikes one today as a bit quaint. However, no one can argue with it as a desirable goal for music education. Unfortunately, over the years that goal was only partially achieved. By the beginning of the 1960s it was becoming increasingly clear that music education as it then existed was not reaching a sizable number of students, especially minority and culturally disadvantaged students in the large cities.

The 1967 Tanglewood Symposium was the first major attempt of the music education profession to speak to this situation. As was mentioned earlier in this chapter, the factors that encouraged a hard look at urban education and the students it tried to serve existed before the symposium met. The statements issued by the Tanglewood Symposium did, however, focus attention on the fact that music education was not reaching many students. Article 7 of the Tanglewood Declaration reads: "The music education profession must contribute its skills, proficiencies, and insights toward assisting in the solution of urgent social problems as in the 'inner city' or other areas with culturally deprived individuals."[19]

The question of what music to teach culturally disadvantaged students is as complex as American society itself. Some of the factors to consider are sociological, some are the feelings of racial pride (ethnicity), some involve curriculum decisions, others are matters of methods, and some of them have to do with economics. A thorough exploration of this topic is tempting for an author, but it would move beyond the scope of this book and an introductory course for future music teachers. All that can be begun here is a discussion of a few matters about making music for every child more of a reality.

American culture is a mixture of types of music, foods, styles of speech, manner of dress, and value systems. It is, to use the sociological term, *pluralistic*. This is the result of America's large and diverse size—both in terms of geography and population, the varied backgrounds of its peoples, and its great tolerance of differences and preferences among individuals and groups of people.

The expressed ideal of American society was for many years that of the great "melting pot" in which all people were blended into a unified nation. To a high degree that has happened, especially for the immigrants from Europe who came to America before World War I. However, for several other large ethnic groups that blending (the sociological term is *integration*, not to be confused with school integration) has occurred only to a limited extent. However, it has taken place in the United States more than in any other large nation and more than in many smaller countries.

To music teachers the existence of a pluralistic society means that there is not now, and will not be in the foreseeable future, one kind of music for all. Rather, there are a number of musical subcultures and a very small core of music that most people know. To realize how small that core of commonly known music is, try naming songs that you can be quite sure most Americans know well enough to sing together without previous rehearsal. After "America" and "The Star-Spangled Banner" the list begins to consist of songs from which people know only phrases. The common listening repertoire is not much larger either, except for the few weeks a popular song is at the top of the charts.

For music teachers the pluralism of American culture means trying to meet the need for "diversity within unity," which are two contradictory goals. A society and its music need some elements (the more, the stronger the society is) that are held in common among its members, just as they need to speak the same language to function well together. Yet there exists the wide variety of ethnic and social backgrounds and interests that students bring to school with them. Much of the culture of the subgroups is deeply felt, and pride is rightfully taken in it. Music teachers should not want to lose the richness and variety that the music of the Chicanos, blacks, or American Indians offer, just as they should not want to lose the music of the German,

English, or Italian immigrants of a century ago. For this reason, the guideline of representative selection presented in Chapter Four is especially important. All students should learn something about the music of all the groups that make up American society. Black children should learn some songs in the Appalachian mountain folk heritage, and white Anglo-Saxon children should learn some music in the black heritage, and so on. No group should become provincial and exclusive in its knowledge of music.

Music teachers should attempt to convey to their students an attitude of respect toward the music of all peoples. Each music has qualities that make it interesting and worth knowing. Teachers should never pit one type of music against another; that is not education, but rather indoctrination. Students and teachers should realize that the music of Spanish-speaking Americans is as expressive and interesting to them as black music is for blacks and Beethoven piano concertos are to some musicians. It is fine to take pride in the music of one's culture or subculture, but that pride should not mean looking down on any music that is different. Music education needs to be inclusive (drawing in as much of the world of music as possible), not exclusive (rejecting or avoiding portions that a teacher or students do not happen to know or like).

Music for Special Learners

If the goal of music for all children is to be achieved, students with handicaps must be included in music instruction. Fortunately, almost all students can learn to enjoy music and to participate in it to some extent. For some handicapped students music can be particularly valuable because they can use it to compensate for their limitations.

The past two decades have seen a greatly increased interest in providing educational opportunities for handicapped students. Although for a hundred years many states had a few special state schools for the deaf or blind, these efforts did not involve most of the handicapped students. By the 1960s and early 1970s many communities and states had established regulations and provisions for educating handicapped students. Even with those efforts, however, by the time federal law PL 94-142 was passed in 1975 only about half of the eight million handicapped children in the United States were being given some education, and one million were receiving no schooling at all. Therefore, the mandates of the federal law, as specified in the *Federal Register* in 1977, required a significantly increased effort on the part of public school systems to increase the amount of education for special learners. Naturally these changes have affected music instruction.

The U.S. Department of Education identifies handicapped students in seven categories: mentally retarded, physically handicapped, visually impaired, hearing impaired, speech impaired, learning disabled, and emotionally disturbed. The identifying of a child's handicap can be difficult because there may be no obvious characteristics of the problem or because there are multiple handicaps. However, even if identified accurately, the classification is of limited value to teachers. As Sona Nocera points out: "The medical profession most often labels by etiology, or the cause of the disability. The psychology profession most often labels by the dysfunction itself. Although these terms may be meaningful to *those* professions, they do not provide much insight that will enhance the *educational* management of children."[20]

The 1975 federal law mandates a "free appropriate public education" for all handicapped students. The law also specifies that students be placed in the "least restrictive environment" and "to the maximum extent appropriate, handicapped children . . . are educated with children who are not handicapped."[21] In other words, when possible, handicapped students are to be *mainstreamed* with normal students. The only exception is allowed "where a handicapped child is so disruptive in a regular classroom that the education of other students is significantly impaired, the needs of the handicapped child cannot be met in that environment. Therefore, regular placement would not be appropriate for his or her needs."[22]

The basic goal of music instruction for handicapped students is the same as it is for all students: to teach them to be sensitive to music, knowledgeable about it, and somewhat skilled in its performance. With handicapped students the nonmusical benefits of music assume greater importance. This emphasis shows up more in terms of the way something is taught than it does in what is taught. Furthermore, handicapped students learn music in much the same way that other students learn it: they begin with the same fundamental experiences and proceed through the same essential sequence of learning.

When adjustments in the program are needed, they usually involve the *rate of learning* and in some cases the *scope of what* is learned. The handicapped student may take much longer to accomplish the same amount as the nonhandicapped student. Nor can every handicapped student accomplish every task. Clearly, blind students cannot read music, but they can be taught Braille notation. Children who cannot walk will not be able to march with the music, but they can keep the beat in other ways. Mentally retarded children may never be able to understand some points about music, but most of them are able to sing and play simple instruments.

Usually music teachers do not teach a group consisting only of handicapped students; generally they are integrated with the other students. Unless informed about which students have handicaps (which should be a regular procedure), several weeks or months might pass before a music teacher discovers that a child has a handicap. Also, children with different handicaps are often in the same classroom. One student may be sight impaired, while another is learning disabled, and so on. Such differences complicate any adjustments in teaching procedures for a particular type of handicapped student.

The job of teaching music to handicapped students is not easy. Even with good support services in terms of counseling and materials, the responsibility falls largely on the teacher, who needs to be informed, patient, understanding, and inventive. When all is said and done, a positive attitude on the part of the teacher may be the most important factor in teaching handicapped students. If the teacher sees such students as a challenge rather than a burden, the music experience can be interesting and useful for both the teacher and the students.

As the opening sentence of this chapter says, plenty of changes have been taking place in American music education. Future teachers need to know about these trends because they are going to work with music education as it will be ten and twenty years from now. The changes occurring over the past twenty or so years offer a glimpse of what the profession is becoming, just as the material in Chapter Five offered a broad picture of what music education is today.

Questions

1. The CMP was started because a number of people believed that not enough contemporary music was being studied in the schools. Think back on your school music experiences. Was a proportionate amount of attention given to contemporary music? What factors encouraged or discouraged the use of such music?

2. Think back to the rehearsals you attended while in high school. Was any attempt made to teach you more than how to perform the music? If so, how was it done? What were the results? If not, think of instances where more than performance skills could have been taught.

3. What factors in a school situation should affect the amount of popular music used in a course: age and/or background of the students, the topic being taught, the interests of the teacher, or the availability of other music courses in the school?

4. What aspects of music can be learned best individually? What aspects almost always require that they be studied in a group situation?

5. What are the theoretical and practical reasons for combining instruction in the arts into one course?

6. Consider the example of the students moving through various angles, as described on page 113. What are the advantages of this for

the teaching of dance? For mathematics? What are the weaknesses of such a teaching procedure?

7. Should music teachers attempt to develop a more unified American culture? If so, what could they do to accomplish this?

8. What are the advantages for handicapped students of mainstreaming? What are the advantages for nonhandicapped students of mainstreaming?

Projects

1. Examine a couple of the books in the music series books described in Chapter Five. Compute the amount of coverage they provide of the various musical subcultures in American society. Also notice how such music is presented.

2. While observing classes in the schools, ask the teacher to let you know which students are handicapped. Notice how they respond in music class and what special techniques the teacher uses to help them learn.

3. Study some curriculum materials developed for one of these areas: youth music, creativity, enrichment with the arts, or individualized instruction. Prepare a short report on the nature and content of the materials.

References

[1] Charles Leonhard, "Was the Yale Seminar Worthwhile?" Council for Research in Music Education Bulletin, no. 60 (Fall 1979), pp. 63–64.

[2] "Contemporary Music Project in Perspective," *Music Educators Journal*, 59, no. 9 (May 1973), p. 34.

[3] Ronald B. Thomas, "Rethinking the Curriculum," *Music Educators Journal*, 56, no. 6 (February 1970), p. 70.

[4] Ronald B. Thomas, "Learning Music Unconventionally—Manhattanville Music Curriculum Program," *Music Educators Journal*, 54, no. 9 (May 1968), p. 64.

[5] Michael L. Mark, *Contemporary Music Education* (New York: Schirmer Books, 1978), p. 110.

[6] Claude V. Palisca, *Music in Our Schools: A Search for Improvement*, Report of the Yale Seminar on Music Education (Washington, D.C.: U.S. Government Printing Office, OE-33033, Bulletin 1964, no. 28), p. 5.

[7] R. Jack Mercer, "Is the Curriculum the Score—or More?" *Music Educators Journal*, 58, no. 6 (February 1972), pp. 52–53.

[8] Charles R. Hoffer and Donald K. Anderson, *Performing Music with Understanding* (two books) (Belmont, Calif.: Wadsworth, 1970 and 1971). Bret Heisinger,

Comprehensive Musicianship through Band Performance (two books), (Honolulu: University of Hawaii, 1973 and 1974). Malcolm Tait, *Comprehensive Musicianship through Choral Performance* (two books) and Vernon R. Read, *Comprehensive Musicianship through Orchestral Performance* (two books).

[9]Charles R. Hoffer, "The Music Contest Steps Off in a New Direction," *Music Educators Journal*, 62, no. 5 (January 1976), pp. 67–69. See also: Charles R. Hoffer, "The Development of a Musicianship Test for Students in High School Performing Organizations," Bulletin of the Council for Research in Music Education, no. 50 (Spring 1977), pp. 37–41.

[10]*The Consumer Behavior of Children and Teenagers: An Annotated Bibliography* (New York: American Marketing Association, 1969), pp. 3–6.

[11]Margaret Mead, *The School in American Culture* (Cambridge, Mass.: Harvard University Press, 1951), pp. 33–34.

[12]Robert A. Choate, ed., *Documentary Report of the Tanglewood Symposium* (Reston, Va.: Music Educators National Conference, 1968), p. 139.

[13]Roland S. Barth, "First We Start with Some Different Assumptions," *Music Educators Journal*, 60, no. 8 (April 1974), p. 25.

[14]Mark, p. 263.

[15]Paul Brandwein and others, *Self-Expression and Conduct: The Humanities* (New York: Harcourt Brace Jovanovich, 1974).

[16]David Boyle, ed., *Arts IMPACT, Guide to Programs* (Washington, D.C.: National Endowment for the Arts, 1973), pp. 2–3.

[17]Laura Brodian, "An Examination and Analysis of Comprehensive Statewide 'Arts in Education' Plans and Programs in Nine States" (D.M.E. diss., Indiana University, 1982), pp. 165–166.

[18]Gene Wenner, "Arts in the Mainstream of Education," *Music Educators Journal*, 62, no. 8 (April 1976), p. 35.

[19]Choate, p. 139.

[20]Sona D. Nocera, *Reaching the Special Learner through Music* (Morristown, N.J.: Silver Burdett Company, 1979), p. 3.

[21]*Federal Register*, vol. 42, no. 163 (121a.550), August 23, 1977, p. 42497.

[22]Analysis of the regulators for Section 504 of the Rehabilitation Act of 1973; ibid.

C H A P T E R   S E V E N

AMERICA HAS A LONG TRADITION of adopting artistic ideas from other countries. For example, furniture makers during the eighteenth century adopted stylistic ideas from the Orient, resulting in what is called today "Chinese Chippendale." Until well into the twentieth century painters and composers felt that a period of study in Europe was a prerequisite to a successful career. However, Americans were not so quick to adopt ideas about education from other countries. Until the past few decades educators felt that America's great experiment in universal education had little to learn from the educational practices of other countries. In fact, after the end of World War II it seemed as if many other countries were adopting American educational ideas as fast as they could. Even today, many educators show little interest in educational developments overseas.

Music educators are different in this respect, perhaps as a result of their artistic heritage. Beginning in the 1960s they have shown interest in three significant approaches or "methods" from other countries: the Orff *Schulwerk* from Germany, the Kodály concept of music education from Hungary, and the Talent Education program of Suzuki in Japan. Also there has been renewed interest in the methods of the Swiss music educator Jaques-Dalcroze. The reason for the interest of American music teachers in these four programs is not hard to pinpoint: each has produced highly impressive results with its students. It is the results, not clever promotional schemes, that have attracted the attention of music teachers.

While these four approaches are certainly not the only innovative or different ones to be found in other countries, they are the ones that have come to the attention of American music educators. Prospective music teachers should be familiar with the main features of each of them.

Dalcroze Approach

Development and Background

Emile Jaques-Dalcroze (1865–1950) began teaching music shortly before the turn of the century. Music study at that time was divided into segmented courses such as harmony, sight singing, form and analysis, and so on. Jaques-Dalcroze* noticed many students knew music only in an intellectual way:

> When he asked his students to write down chords during their harmony classes he discovered that they were not really hearing what they had written, and that for most of them harmony was simply a matter of mathematics. It became clear to him that the traditional method of training musicians concentrated on the intellect to the detriment of the senses, and failed to give students a valid *experience* of the basic elements of music sufficiently early in their studies.[1]

To remedy this condition, he first developed singing with syllables (*solfège*).

He also noticed that students had trouble performing rhythmic patterns but had no problem with rhythmic motor activities such as walking. From these observations he concluded that people instinctively have musical rhythm but do not transfer these instincts to music. He started experimenting with this idea by having students walk to music in different tempos. Slowly more parts of the body were asked to respond to music. In this way he developed an approach for learning music that has three main parts: (1) *eurhythmics*—the rhythmic response to music; (2) solfège—singing with syllables; and (3) improvisation. A Dalcroze lesson should incorporate and integrate these three activities. Intensive listening is also essential in all Dalcroze instruction.

The idea of responding physically to music was revolutionary in Geneva in 1902. (The students in Jaques-Dalcroze's classes were barefooted and wore comfortable clothing!) He soon left the Geneva Conservatory and opened his own studio and continued to experiment. Later a group of Geneva businessmen set up a school for him in Hellerau, Germany. The school included a number of buildings and a theater. Between 1910 and 1914 interest in his method grew greatly. Among the famous people who attended his classes were the English playwright George Bernard Shaw, the Polish patriot and pianist Paderewski, Rachmaninoff, and dancers like Martha Graham and Ted Shawn. The outbreak of World War I in 1914 caused him to leave Germany and to establish the Institut Jaques-Dalcroze in Geneva, which is now a part of the Conservatory of Music.

Although Jaques-Dalcroze felt that his method could not be understood only by reading about it, he did write down some of his exercises. In *Rhythm, Music and Education* he presents a list of twenty-two kinds of exercise for each of the three branches of his approach under these headings: "Rhythmic Movement," "Solfège or Aural Training,"

---

*For some reason, his approach is often referred to by only the second half of his name.

and "Piano Improvisation." The approach depends almost entirely on personal instruction, however. As one writer explained:

> M. Jaques-Dalcroze will only issue a certificate authorizing a pupil to teach after he has himself tested the capacity of the would-be teacher; and since comparatively few of these authorized teachers have come to America (in 1924 there were eleven in the United States), the spread of the method here is necessarily slow.[2]

Jaques-Dalcroze also demonstrated an interest in working with exceptional students, both those who were especially able and those with handicaps. He taught blind students for awhile and devised special exercises for them.

The Dalcroze approach was introduced in the United States in about 1915. The public schools could not provide time or space for it to be taught in its authentic form—the way Jaques-Dalcroze wanted it taught. However, some teachers adapted his procedures, and in other cases teachers were influenced by the approach without being aware of it. The use of "walking" and "running" as designations for quarter and eighth notes is one common example in the elementary schools. By the 1930s a number of college music schools or physical education departments were requiring courses in *eurhythmics,* the term often used for Dalcroze-like instruction. The interest in it seemed to level off at that point and then decline. A modest renewal of interest in it has taken place since 1970. About twenty colleges offer some instruction in the approach, with four of them giving a Dalcroze certificate.

Characteristics of the Dalcroze Approach

1. A physical response to music is basic to the Dalcroze approach, and it somewhat dominates the early lessons. This portion is the one for which it is best known and is called *eurhythmics*—a word derived from the Greek, meaning "good rhythm or flow." The purpose of the movement is to create rhythmic sensitivity in the students by making them feel musical rhythm in their entire bodies. Musical concepts are also reinforced through physical movements. Sometimes the students begin with a representation of an idea, such as something getting louder. The bodily movement to represent the idea, which should be one familiar in life, is tried first without music. For example, it might consist of walking with the steps becoming more and more energetic. Next the student listens to music in which a crescendo is easily heard. Then the movement is synchronized with the music. The term *crescendo* may follow the experience of the idea through bodily movement, and later the musical symbol for it may be presented. In more advanced classes students may use the idea in notation and improvisation.

The physical movements are not predetermined, but rather are the spontaneous products of each individual. Therefore, great differences are usually seen in the responses of a group of students to the same music. However, the students do learn a "grammar of gestures" in a way similar to that of a conductor. The movements are always to be expressive of what the student hears and feels about the music. The classes usually involve some group interaction, as well as individual response. Although some ballet dancers studied with Jaques-Dalcroze, he insisted that he was a teacher of music, not dance. There are, however, many consonant ideas between modern dance training and eurhythmics.

Three rhythmic exercises are cited here from an adaptation of Jaques-Dalcroze's book to give a clearer idea of the type of activity that takes place in the classes.

Exercise 1. Following the Music, Expressing Tempo and Tone Quality

The teacher at the piano improvises music to which the pupils march (usually in a circle) beating the time with their arms (3/4, 5/8, 12/8, etc.) as an orchestra leader conducts, and stepping with their feet the note values (that is, quarter notes are indicated by normal steps, eighth notes by running steps, half notes by a step and a bend of the leg, a dotted eighth and a sixteenth by a skip, etc.). The teacher varies the expression of the playing, now increasing or decreasing the intensity of tone, now playing more slowly or more quickly; and the pupils "follow the music" literally, reproducing in their movements the exact pattern and structure of her improvisation.

Exercise 6. Phrasing

Everyone knows that music, like speech, is broken up into phrases. A singer pauses to take a fresh breath at the beginning of a new phrase. In movement a new phrase may be indicated in several ways: such as a change of direction of the march on the part of the whole group, or by a change from one arm to another on the part of the individual. This is an exercise in ear-training, in attention and in the creation of new ways of expressing the beginning of a phrase, that is, improvisation.

Exercise 9. Independence of Control

This exercise is one in polyrhythm, the pupil expressing several rhythms at the same time. He may perhaps beat three-four time with the left arm and four-four with the right at the same time walking twelve-eight with the feet. There are many variations of this though in the beginning pupils find it sufficiently difficult to beat two with one arm and three with the other, especially since each arm must "remember," so to speak, the accent which falls on the first beat of its own measure. Another form of this exercise is to have the pupils march one measure while beating time for another; as three with the arms and four with the feet. These are worked out mathematically at first but soon the pupils learn to keep in their muscular and mental consciousnesses the pulse of the two rhythms simultaneously.[3]

2. The second main branch of the Dalcroze approach is solfège, in which the familiar pitch syllables are used, but *do* is always C, *di* is C#, and so on. Jaques-Dalcroze thought that solfège singing developed the ability to listen to and remember tonal patterns. Singing and hand positions for designating the level of pitches of the scale are used in learning solfège, and these activities precede experience with notation.

Much emphasis is placed on inner hearing—the ability to imagine music in the mind. Students in Dalcroze classes sing intervals and songs with syllables. Some of the measures in the song are sung aloud, and others are sung silently in the mind.

> A melody would be placed on the blackboard with some empty measures which the student would be expected to fill in, improvising, as he sang the melody for the first time.

> Another exercise involved writing a melody on the blackboard and as the students sang it through, each phrase was erased upon completion of this initial singing. A student would then be asked to sing the entire melody by memory.[4]

Reading music and working with notation is a part of solfège training, but only after a solid foundation of experiences with music has been built. Notation is always related to sound. For example, tones may be played on the piano, and the young students identify them by standing beside cards laid on the floor containing the numbers 1 through 8. Rhythm may initially be notated by marking patterns on large sheets of paper with dots and dashes to represent the various lengths of notes or rests.

3. Improvising is the third main branch of the Dalcroze approach to musical training. It is an integral part of eurhythmics and solfège activities. Jaques-Dalcroze believed that each student should have the experience of expressing his or her own musical ideas.

Improvisation is begun on percussion instruments or with the voice. Sometimes a child is given one measure to which he or she improvises a response, all the while maintaining the basic beat. Spoken commands or signals are given while improvisation is going on. This practice makes the students listen carefully and encourages skill development. For example, while the students are executing a rhythmic pattern with their feet, they may be asked to do a contrasting pattern with their arms. Or, four pitches are given, maybe D, E, F#, and G#. As the teacher plays the harmonic background on the piano, each student takes a turn singing an improvised pattern lasting for two measures and using two of the four pitches.

After the students have successfully improvised with their voices and on percussion instruments, they begin to improvise on the piano. Improvising at the piano is stressed for advanced students and teachers.

Orff *Schulwerk*

Development and Background

Carl Orff (1895–1982) was a recognized contemporary composer. His best-known works are *Carmina Burana* and *Catulli Carmina*. He began the *Schulwerk* (which in German simply means "school work") with Dorothea Günther in Munich in 1924. At the time, education in Europe was heavily influenced by Jaques-Dalcroze, and there were numerous schools for gymnastics and dance. What made *Schulwerk* different was that its main interest was in music. The school grew and in due course had an ensemble of dancers and an orchestra, with the players and dancers being interchangeable. The group toured Europe and attracted much favorable attention.

During World War II the school was destroyed and the instruments lost. Orff did not renew his educational activities until 1948, when he was asked by the Bavarian radio to present a program of music for children. The request caused him to rethink his views on music education. The earlier school with Günther had been for teenagers, but now Orff realized that the educational process should start much earlier with young children.

> I began to see things in the right perspective. "Elemental" was the password, applicable to music itself, to the instruments, to forms of speech and movement. What does it mean? The Latin word *elementarius*, from which it is derived, means "pertaining to the elements, primeval, basic." What, then, is elemental music? Never music alone, but music connected with movement, dance, and speech—not to be listened to, meaningful only in active participation. Elemental music is pre-intellectual, it lacks great form, it contents itself with simple sequential structures, ostinatos, and miniature rondos. It is earthy, natural, almost a physical activity.[5]

The reborn *Schulwerk* was a success, and what started as a single broadcast was continued for five years. Between 1950 and 1954 the five basic volumes of *Schulwerk* music were published. Regular courses in *Schulwerk* were started in 1949 at the Mozarteum in Salzburg, Austria, under the direction of Gunild Keetman. The Orff Institute was established in Salzburg in 1963.

Although five books of Orff's music for children are available, he intended them to serve only as models for what the children can do. In no sense do they constitute a course of study or standard repertoire. The emphasis on improvising has also discouraged the use of music notation. The main purpose of writing music down is to retain a piece once it has been worked out.

Schulwerk does not have a set course of study; "those who look for a method or ready-made system are rather uncomfortable with *Schulwerk*," Orff has stated.[6] The lack of an established set of procedures leads to quite different actions and results under the heading of Orff *Schulwerk*. Orff himself has commented on the situation in these words, "Unfortunately, it [*Schulwerk*] has often been misinterpreted, exploited, and falsified to the point of caricature."[7]

Orff's interest in "elemental" music may strike many readers as a bit unusual. It derives from a theory about human development that states that children's musical development roughly corresponds to the development of music. According to this theory, rhythm preceded melody, and melody preceded harmony. Whether one finds this theory agreeable or not, it is not necessary to adopt it in order to teach aspects of *Schulwerk*.

Orff's ideas have been studied by many American music educators. By 1980 about two thirds of the elementary music specialists in the United States had participated in workshops on *Schulwerk*, with nearly one fourth of these teachers having four or more weeks of special training in it.[8] Several trial programs were conducted in school districts around the United States in the 1960s and 1970s. *Schulwerk* has also been adapted for use with handicapped and exceptional children.

Characteristics of *Schulwerk*

1. Speech rhythms are an important part of the early instruction in *Schulwerk*. The children chant out rhymes, calls, and traditional sayings in a vigorous rhythmic fashion. For instance, short phrases for chanting can be derived from the pattern of the students' names[9] as in the following example:

Meter and accent are also introduced in speech patterns. The students sometimes chant a phrase or sentence in canon—a spoken round. As

the children become more adept at speech patterns, they are introduced through them to phrasing, dynamics, and styles such as legato and staccato; simple forms such as rondo can also be introduced through speech patterns. Speech patterns are often combined with patterns of body rhythms: clapping; snapping the fingers; and *patschen* (thigh slaps), which are characteristic in *Schulwerk*. A pattern of clapping and thigh slapping can become a theme, for example, and it can be varied, repeated, performed antiphonally, or become the theme for a rondo.

2. Singing experiences follow the speech pattern work, which adheres to Orff's idea that melody follows rhythm. Singing at the early stages contains many short phrases sung back and forth between teacher and students and between students. Usually the singing is accompanied by instruments and/or body rhythms.

The first interval learned is *sol-mi*, the descending minor third. Unlike the Dalcroze method, however, the syllables are movable, not fixed. Words are usually added to these simple two-note phrases, as in this example:

"No. 8" from Carl Orff and Gunild Keetman, *Music for Children, Volume I: Pentatonic*, English adaption by Doreen Hall and Arnold Waltzer (Mainz: B. Schott's Sohne, 1960), p. 92. Used by permission of European American Distributors Corporation, sole U.S. agent for B. Schott's Sohne.

The intervals are introduced in a certain sequence. After *sol* and *mi* comes *la*, then *re*, and then *do*, which completes a pentatonic scale. The major and minor scales are taught, but not until later. Orff favors the pentatonic scale because he thinks it is more natural. Also, half steps with their strong melodic tendencies are avoided when improvising, a topic that will be mentioned shortly.

3. Movement is an important part of *Schulwerk* as conceived by Orff, but it is not utilized as much in American adaptations of it. Orff's views about the value and purpose of bodily movement are similar to those of Jaques-Dalcroze. The natural, untrained actions of children are the basis for movement. Running, skipping, hopping, and other physical movements are part of the students' musical development. Generally the movements are free and individual, and are intended to express the music.

4. Improvisation is central to *Schulwerk*, and it is found in all its activities—speech, movement, singing, and instrument playing. The initial efforts in improvising are highly structured. As in the Dalcroze eurhythmics, the child is given a limited number of pitches to use in creating a short melodic or rhythmic fragment of a specified length. Often these first efforts involve only *sol* and *mi* for one or two measures. As the students gain experience in improvising, more pitches are added and the patterns are made longer and more complex. Many times short introductions and codas are added to pieces, and many pieces employ an ostinato.

5. Instrument playing is an important aspect of *Schulwerk*. Not just any instrument is acceptable in the program. Orff wanted the children's ears to become accustomed to the sound of good instruments. Furthermore, he wanted the instruments to be easy to play, and he favored those that had a "primitive appeal." So he had simple mallet instruments constructed that are capable of carrying the melody: xylophones, metallophones, and glockenspiels in various sizes. Later, instruments such as flutes and gambas were added. Some percussion were also used. After the original instruments were mostly destroyed in World War II, Orff worked with Klauss Becker, who developed the Studio 49 instruments found in many Orff classes today and shown in the picture on page 130. Not only do these instruments have a good tone quality and come in several sizes, they are useful in improvising because any unneeded bars can be removed temporarily so that they will not be struck accidently by the student. The piano is not used for most works. *Schulwerk* instruments are not considered toys, but rather as an important means for making music. Most of the playing is done from memory or is improvised, which frees the student from the demand to read music.

6. The reading of music comes only after several years of training. Even then its main function is to preserve improvisations and arrangements.

7. Orff's music, and the music used and created in *Schulwerk*, has a strong folklike character. It contains short, energetic melodic ideas, many ostinatos, simple harmonies, and at times an almost primitive quality.

Kodály Approach

Development and Background

Like Orff, Zoltán Kodály (1882–1967) was a recognized composer. *Háry János* is his best-known work, but he has many successful compositions. He was a friend and colleague of Béla Bartók, and he worked with him on studying and collecting Hungarian folk songs. He was also greatly interested in the music education of children. "No one is too great to write for children," he wrote. "Quite the op-

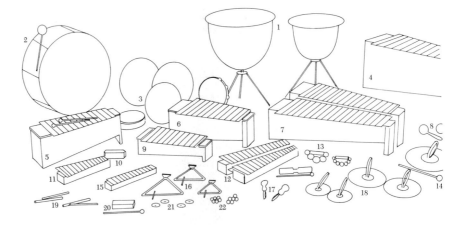

1	Kettle drums	9	Soprano xylophone	17	Castanets
2	Bass drum	10	Box rattle	18	Hanging cymbals
3	Tambours (hand drum)	11	Alto glockenspeil	19	Claves
4	Bass xylophone	12	Alto-soprano glockenspeil	20	Wood block
5	Alto metallophone	13	Bell spray	21	Finger cymbal
6	Alto xylophone	14	Felt head beater	22	Sleigh bells
7	Alto-soprano xylophone	15	Soprano glockenspeil		
8	Gourd	16	Triangles		

posite—one should strive to be worthy of this task."[9] Living up to his word, Kodály composed about twenty books of music for school students. They begin with very simple material for preschool children and continue through four-part works of great difficulty. In addition, he guided his native Hungary in the establishment of an exemplary program of music education in its schools.

World War II and the Nazi occupation of Hungary delayed the implementation of Kodály's educational ideas until after 1945. A new educational system was being established, and in spite of its political limitations, the situation provided an unusual opportunity to design a new music program. Education in Hungary is state controlled and has a heritage of strict academic training, so it was possible to institute a strong national program. Today most children in the elementary schools of Hungary receive two forty-five-minute periods of music each week. Through the fourth grade music is taught by classroom teachers, who have had much more collegiate training in music than their American counterparts. From grades 5 through 8 music is taught by specialists.

The portion of Hungary's music education program that has especially impressed foreign observers is the 130 "Music Primary Schools" or "Singing Schools." These schools are similar to other elementary schools, except for one important difference: the students receive one hour of music instruction each day from a music specialist. Parents make application to these schools on behalf of their children, who are then selected on the basis of musical tests.[10] Therefore, the Singing Schools are not typical elementary schools. A carefully devised course of study in music is followed rigorously in these schools. The overall plan for the presentation of topics in grade 1 appears on page 132. The curriculum prescribes the sequence of instruction and the textbooks provide a minimum amount of material. Each teacher then develops at the beginning of the year a syllabus that states when the material will be studied during the year. Some activities are left up to the teacher's interest and abilities. Some music teachers in Hungary are more capable than others, a situation that is true of every country.

The Singing School program began to attract international attention after presentations by Hungarian music educators at conferences of the International Society of Music Education in 1958, 1961, and especially 1964, when Kodály himself addressed the conference. Since the mid-1960s American music educators have traveled to Hungary to observe or study the program, and a number of Hungarian music teachers have taught in the United States. By 1980 nearly half of the elementary music specialists in the United States had taken workshops in the Kodály approach, and over 12 percent had had more than four weeks of training in it.[11]

Kodály's manual for Hungarian teachers has been translated into English, and much of the music he wrote for children is available in the United States. Several American music educators have developed materials based on Kodály's ideas. One of the first to do this was Mary Helen Richards; Lorna Zemke, Denise Bacon, Lois Chosky and others have followed. Some Kodály techniques are also included in the music series books.

First Grade Curriculum of the Hungarian Singing-Music Primary Schools (1978)

I. Musical Materials

   Singing
      45–50 rhymes, children's game songs, composed songs, patrotic songs (required material indicated)
      Kodály, 333 *Singing Exercises* (selections as appropriate)
      Kodály, *Pentatonic Music, Vol. I* (selections)
   Music Listening
      Performances by the teacher of children's and folk songs
      Recordings (or live performances) of significant portions of
         Bartók, *For Children*
         Kodály, *Children's and Women's Choruses*
         L. Mozart, *Children's Symphony*
         Kodály, *Pentatonic Music, Vol I.*
      Recordings of folk instruments and field recordings of folk music performances

II. Musical Knowledge and Skills

   Steady beat
   Melodic rhythm
   Quarter note
   Paired eighth notes
   Quarter rest
   Half note
   Half rest
   Duple meter (simple)
   Bar line
   Double bar line
   Repeat sign
   Extended pentatonic scale notes (*so mi la do re la, so, do'*) with solfège, handsigns, staff placement, reading, and writing in the solfège system
   Perception and discrimination of different timbres: vocal/instrumental, child's/adult's, male/female, piano/recorder/metallofon
   Musical ensembles (chorus/orchestra)
   Dynamics: fast, slow, moderate
   Motives from children's songs
   Repetition
   Ostinato
   Playing of simpler pentatonic motives on the recorder

III. Distribution of class time

   Required material: approximately 85 classes

Supplementary material: approximately 43 classes
Of this: 60% singing activities
10% listening activities
30% cognitive activities

IV. Behavorial objectives (corresponding to above material)

Characteristics of the Kodály Program

1. Kodály saw as the purpose of music education the creation of a musically literate population. "Is it imaginable that anybody who is unable to read words can acquire a literary culture or knowledge of any kind? Equally, no musical knowledge of any kind can be acquired without the reading of music."[12] This interest in understanding notation is in contrast to Orff and Jaques-Dalcroze, and it led Kodály to several techniques for teaching children to be literate musicians.

Before developing the Singing School program, Kodály made an intensive study of the existing systems of teaching music in many countries. From England he adopted two techniques. One was a system of hand signs developed about a century earlier by John Curwen. The other, which is closely related to the hand signs, is the use of the *sol-fa* or movable *do* pitch syllables. In movable *do* the tonic note in major is always *do*. Therefore, the syllables represent relative pitch relationships, not fixed pitches as they do in solfège. The hand positions, which are a form of of kinesthetic reinforcement of the relative pitch, were altered slightly by Kodály. They are shown on page 134. Kodály also adopted Curwen's idea of abbreviating the syllable names to only the first letter. These letters are not intended to replace standard pitch names; their purpose is to aid in learning pitch relationships.

The pitch syllables are presented in an order similar to that used in Orff's *Schulwerk*: *sol, mi, la, do, re,* and then later in second grade (third grade in the nonmusic primary schools) *fa* and *ti*. In later years *fi, si,* and *ta* are added, and music that modulates is sung with these syllables. During the primary years of instruction much of the music sung is pentatonic. Kodály found that children tend to sing the fourth slightly sharp and the seventh slightly flat, and that the pentatonic scale eliminates these problems. Also, the pentatonic scale is strongly rooted in Hungarian folk music.

2. The learning of patterns and motives is an important aspect of the Kodály approach. For the most part, they are derived from the music the students are singing. The more common patterns are practiced persistently, and the students are made aware of them. In this way the students' sense of syntax for music is aided.

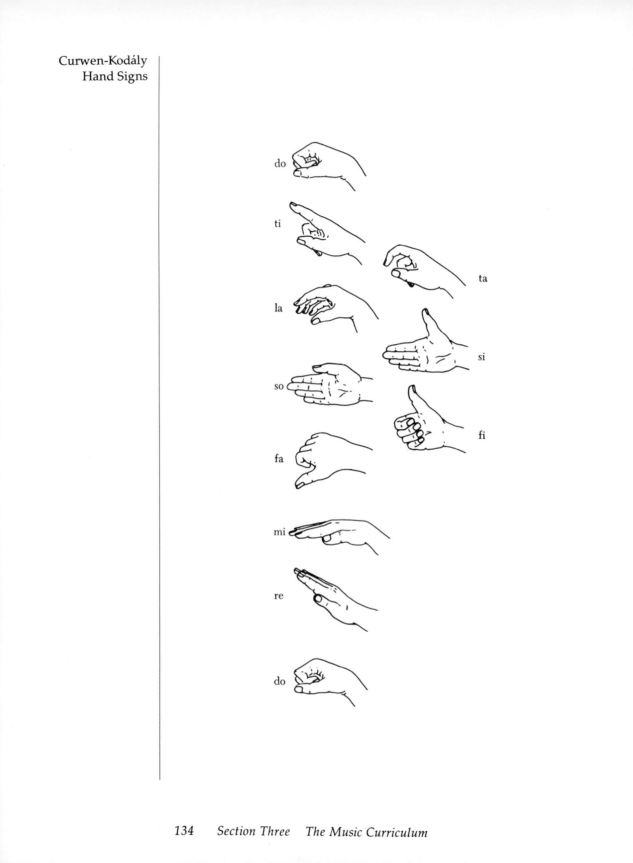

3. Rhythm patterns are also taught by relating them to the material being sung. Rhythmic values are represented visually by a vertical line or stem for a quarter note and by a pair of vertical lines joined together at the top by a brace or ligature for an eighth note, as in the following example:

Rhythmic syllables are often said to the note values: "ta" for a quarter note and "ti" (pronounced "tee") for each eighth. Half notes are said "Ta-a," dotted half notes "ta-a-a," and whole notes "ta-a-a-a."

Initially the notes are presented pictorially with the size of the notes adjusted to give the children an indication of the length of the note.

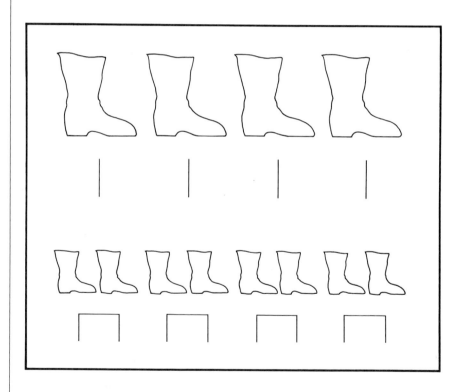

4. Music in the Kodály program is largely taught through singing. Kodály was a strong believer in using the voice: "Only the human

voice, which is a possession of everyone, and at the same time the most beautiful of all instruments, can serve as the basis for a general musical culture."[13] Recorder playing is introduced in second or third grade after a solid foundation has been laid through singing. Little enthusiasm is expressed for the piano. Since Hungary is not a wealthy country, there aren't many pianos in the schools anyway.

5. One of the reasons Kodály so strongly favored unaccompanied singing was his wish to have children develop an accurate sense of pitch and the ability to hear music in their minds. Hungarian school students do sing in a far more polished manner than their American counterparts. Their intonation seems impeccable, and their vocal timbre pure and light.

Many activities are designed to develop inner hearing. In addition to listening carefully to intonation in both unison and part singing, the students sing music silently in their minds. A song is sung aloud until the teacher signals silence, at which time the students continue it in their minds. Singing aloud is resumed upon another signal from the teacher. Sometimes the students read a short song silently. After they have memorized it, the music is covered up or erased, and they sing it aloud.

6. Kodály was firmly convinced that music instruction should start at an early age, well before the children enter elementary school.

> Obviously, all reasonable pedagogy has to start from the first spontaneous utterances of the child, rhythmic-melodic expressions with repeated simple phrases which slowly give way to more complex structures. Since children learn most easily between the ages of three and six, the kindergartens would be able to accomplish much more in music if they would observe this pedagogic principle.[14]

This belief in the importance of the initial efforts in learning music is the opposite of that of many American music teachers, who devote much of their attention to the performing groups in the secondary schools. Kodály points out that without a solid foundation in the early years, the results later on will be stunted.

7. The music used for the first several years of the curriculum consists largely of Hungarian folk songs. The association of the Kodály method with its folk and nationalistic roots is something that is often overlooked by foreigners. Hungary is a rather small nation with a population about the size of Ohio. Several times in its past it has experienced long occupations by outsiders—Turks, Austrians, Germans, and now Russians. Two things make it possible for Hungarians to retain their national identity under such circumstances: their language (which is most closely related to Finnish) and their music. Therefore, a knowledge of music is especially significant to Hungarians. It is impossible to know how much this feeling of nationalism influenced

Kodály when he developed the program following World War II. In one sense it doesn't matter, because his ideas clearly have proved that they have validity without any nationalistic associations.

His views on the value of folk music are clear.

> I dare say we may attribute this [successful] result mostly to the folk song, which is our chief material. Folk songs offer such a rich variety of moods and perspective, that the child grows in human consciousness and feels more and more at home in his country....

> To become international we first have to belong to one distinct people and to speak its language properly, not in gibberish. To understand other people, we must first understand ourselves. And nothing will accomplish this better than a thorough knowledge of one's native folk songs.[15]

8. The Kodály program strongly emphasizes music of a high quality. No commercial popular music is found in the program. "In art," Kodály has written, "bad taste is a real spiritual illness. It is the duty of the school to offer protection against this plague.... The goal is: To educate children in such a way that they find music indispensable to life ... of course good artistic music."[16]

Suzuki Talent Education

Development and Background

With the work of Shinichi Suzuki* (b. 1898), this chapter shifts from vocal-general music to instrumental music. Suzuki's views on teaching the violin are heavily laced with the belief that musical talent is a product of one's upbringing. "All human beings are born with great potentialities," Suzuki has said, "and each individual has within himself, the capacity for developing to a very high level."[17] The belief in the universal nature of music talent led to the inclusion of "Talent Education" in the name of the program.

Suzuki's father owned a violin factory, and he learned about violins and how to play them as a boy. His study also included eight years in Berlin in the 1920s. Before World War II he formed a string quartet of himself and three brothers and did some teaching. After the war he started teaching young people to play the violin. His accomplishments as a teacher become first known in the United States in 1958 at a meeting of the American String Teachers Association at Oberlin College, when a film of 750 Japanese children playing Bach's Concerto for Two Violins was shown. A year later John Kendall trav-

---

*In Japan the family name is first, but Americans and Europeans refer to the second of the two names out of habit.

eled to Japan to observe Suzuki at work, and he made a second trip in 1962. In 1964 the American String Teachers Association presented Suzuki and ten of his students, who ranged in age from ten to fourteen, at the MENC national convention in Philadelphia. The impact on the audience was electric. Few of the teachers in the audience had ever heard young students play so musically and so well. Following that appearance, hundreds of workshops on the method have been held, and Suzuki has made several more trips to the United States with his students. For several reasons that will become apparent shortly, the impact of the Suzuki approach in the public schools has been somewhat limited, but his ideas have certainly been influential.

Characteristics of Suzuki Talent Education

1. Suzuki strongly favors beginning instruction at an early age; in fact, the younger, the better. Violin instruction in the Talent Education program usually begins at three years of age but it can begin earlier. He favors playing good recordings for children while they are still in the crib, and for several weeks before the first lesson the parents every day play the recordings of the violin pieces the child will study later. Then the child attends a few lessons and watches and listens to what is going on; this is followed by being given an instrument.

It should be pointed out that string instruments, unlike many other instruments, can be adjusted in size, which facilitates working with young children. Many of Suzuki's youngest pupils begin on a 1/16th-sized violin. As they grow larger, they are given larger instruments until they play a full-sized violin.

2. The method of learning is rote imitation. The student hears something and attempts to imitate it. Suzuki believes that music is learned in much the same way that language is learned. He has pointed out, "All children in the world show their splendid capacities by speaking and understanding their mother language, thus displaying the original power of the human mind."[18]

The imitating of an aural model is an aspect of Suzuki's pedagogy that seems to be often overlooked. Not only does it help the students to play musically and without the mechanical qualities often associated with beginning instrument study, it appears to guide students over technical problems, even those for which they have had no specific instruction.

3. All the music the student performs is memorized. The technical matters of playing music on the the instrument are learned first, and then the student may begin looking at notation. Of course, reading by three-year-old children is out of the question because their eye muscles have not developed sufficiently to allow them to focus on objects the size of music and printed material. The parents use the books and follow the music to help the child practice, however.

When reading is introduced after some years of study, the process is one of following the notation of a work that the student already knows. In this way, the logic of music notation is more easily understood because it is a process of visualizing what has already been learned.

4. Whatever is learned by the students is learned thoroughly. For example, while the students are playing a work such as the Vivaldi A Minor Concerto, the teacher may direct them to do knee bends or walk up and down stairs. Sometimes a group of students is divided in half. One half plays while the other half follows along silently, ready to pick up the music on a moment's notice without causing a break in the flow. The entire work is performed alternating between the two groups with no interruptions.

5. One of the parents, usually the mother, attends the lessons and learns the violin along with the child. Suzuki wants the parents involved in order to impress the child with the importance of the activity, and also so that they can help in guiding the home practicing.

6. The lessons are private and rather short, especially for the younger students. If a child yawns, the lesson is concluded. The students and teacher stand throughout the lesson. This helps maintain a better position and also contributes to better attention. The room is kept free from distractions because Suzuki wants the student to concentrate on playing the violin. Often other children observe a lesson and perhaps join in the playing of one number.

7. All students, regardless of ability, learn the same sequence of music. Some students may go through it faster than others, but all study the same works in the same order. Therefore, all Suzuki students have the same repertoire, which makes it easy to combine them for large group performances without prior rehearsals. The materials almost completely lack etudes and scales, which used to be dear to the hearts of many instrumental music teachers. Instead, shifting, vibrato, bowing, and so on are dealt with in relation to their appearance in works of music; technical exercises are drawn from the setting in the music. Suzuki avoids what he terms "manufactured material" before advanced levels are achieved.

8. The ten manuals or books contain carefully selected music, much of it by Bach, Handel, and Vivaldi. Recordings are available for the works in the first five or six volumes, and recordings made by artist violinists are used for the other works, which are standard concert pieces.

9. Cooperation, not competition, is fostered among the students. Students of all levels of advancement play together, and older students help the younger students. An attitude of mutual respect is maintained among parents, teachers, and students.

Suzuki-like instruction is available from private teachers in a number of communities in the United States, and a number of programs have been functioning for over fifteen years. Also, adaptations of Suzuki's ideas for teaching the violin have been made, with his approval and at his school in Japan, for the cello and the piano. The only concession to size on the piano is the use of a box to raise the height of the pedals for the small children. America is not Japan, of course, and a number of cultural factors make some of Suzuki's ideas difficult to carry out here. Nevertheless, some students who have started in Suzuki-like programs in this country have succeeded very well.

Foreign Methods in American Schools

*M*usic teachers who are professional about their work are constantly examining and considering new teaching ideas. One source of fresh ideas is the successful methods from other countries. However, as successful as many of these methods are in their native land, American music educators should keep several facts in mind about adopting or adapting them.

It is not possible to pick up an educational program from Hungary or Japan or any other country (except maybe Canada) and drop it down intact in Bloomington, Illinois, Indiana, or Minnesota. Why? Because there are significant musical, educational, and cultural differences between each country and the United States. A musical difference, for example, can be found in the use of 6/8 meter. Many children's songs in America ("Pop Goes the Weasel," "When Johnny Comes Marching Home," and others) are in 6/8, but it is not so common in Hungary. In that country the introduction of 6/8 meter is held off until the fourth grade level, which would not be sensible in America. On the other hand, the pentatonic scale is found frequently in Hungarian folk music but is rather rare in American folk music. If the music program is to be based on folk music, as Kodály strongly suggests, then in America much less use will have to made of the pentatonic scale.

There are also important educational differences among the countries of the world. For example, schools in most European countries have a shorter school day than American schools but do not offer extracurricular activities or provide lunches. The one or two hours that this makes available to European school students can be used in a variety of ways, one of which is music study at a community music school. Therefore, much less music, especially instrumental music, is taught during the school day in most European schools. In some countries the secondary schools are either academic or trade schools; the comprehensive high school that is the ideal in the United States does not exist in most countries (and in many places in the United States, but that is another topic). The nature of these schools, then, differs from that of most American secondary schools.

American music educators also need to keep in mind that *Schulwerk* and Suzuki violin instruction are almost never taught in the public schools of the countries with which they are associated. They were designed for and are taught in private schools that charge the students a tuition. Dalcroze eurhythmics are taught in some public school systems in Swiss cities, but seldom in the schools of other countries. Even the Kodály program is basically for a special type of school that is very different from the average American elementary school.

There are also cultural differences among nations, some of which are subtle and difficult to describe in a few sentences. An example of such differences is the willingness to work. In 1971 Eric Mitchell, an Australian piano teacher, spent over a year traveling around the world observing piano students. One of the interesting facts that his research uncovered was that American and Western European students practiced their piano lessons about eighty hours per year, while students in Japan and Hungary practiced around 300 hours per year, and those in the Soviet Union practiced about 560 hours each year. The effect of the differing amounts of practice could have been predicted: the students who practiced more hours usually played better.[19] American students are apparently less able to tolerate routine activity than students in many other countries. Also, school in America is not viewed, at least not by most students, as a place where one does hard work. Nor are teachers in the United States treated with the unquestioning respect that their colleagues in most other countries enjoy, which has both its good and bad points.

An additional incident can illustrate further the depth of cultural differences among nations. While observing Suzuki's work in Japan, John Kendall talked with a sixteen-year-old boy about studying violin. Although he planned to become an engineer someday, the young man was faithfully practicing his violin a couple of hours each day. The high school he attended did not have an orchestra for him to play in, and community orchestras are rare in Japan, so Kendall realized that the boy had no place to play the violin with others, and probably would not in the future. Why then, Kendall asked, was he working so diligently at the violin? "Because it is good for my soul," was the young man's response.[20] It is indeed difficult to imagine a similar response from a sixteen-year-old American student!

Although it may be difficult to transplant a music teaching approach that works well in Germany or Japan to the United States, it is quite easy to adopt some techniques from a method. Kodály himself adopted the hand signs from the Englishman Curwen, and they can rather easily be adopted by American music teachers. The same is true of some techniques from each of the methods described in this chapter. However, there is much more to each of these methods than their techniques. Jaques-Dalcroze, Orff, Kodály, and Suzuki each have more to offer the world than a few teaching "recipes," gimmicks, or teaching procedures. Just having students put on leotards and move to music does not mean that one is teaching eurhythmics, any more than playing an ostinato on a metallophone means that one is following the Orff method. Although the methods contain the features listed in this chapter, there is much more to them than those features.

American music educators need to be careful when adapting any approach from another country. Such adaptations should be undertaken only after a thorough knowledge of the particular method has been acquired. Thomas Huxley was correct when he wrote, "A little knowledge is dangerous."[21] A misuse of a teaching method may do more harm than good, to say nothing of being a distortion of the original.

Questions

1. What are the similarities among two or more of the four approaches discussed in this chapter? What are the significant differences among them?

2. What ideas from Jaques-Dalcroze, Orff, Kodály, or Suzuki might American music educators adapt or adopt?

3. What are the advantages and disadvantages of solfège (fixed *do*) in contrast to movable *do* in teaching children music?

4. Should American music teachers confine instruction in the primary grades largely to pentatonic songs? Why, or why not?

Projects

1. Select one of the four approaches discussed in the chapter and examine some of the materials developed for it. Compare and contrast their features with those of similar materials developed in America.

2. Compare the sequence of topics in the Kodály approach listed on page 132 with that presented in one of the graded music series books published in the United States.

References

[1] Jack Dobbs, "Some Great Music Educators: Emile Jaques-Dalcroze," *Music Teacher*, 47, no. 8 (August 1968), p. 13.

[2] Jo Pennington, *The Importance of Being Rhythmic: A Study of the Principles of Dalcroze Eurhythmics Applied to General Education and to the Arts of Music, Dancing, and Acting.* Based on and adapted from *Rhythm, Music and Education* by E. Jaques-Dalcroze; with an introduction by Walter Damrosch (New York: G. P. Putnam's Sons, 1925), p. 8.

[3] Ibid., pp. 14–26.

[4] Arthur F. Becknell, "A History of the Development of Dalcroze Eurhythmics in the United States and Its Influence on the Public School Music Program" (Ph.D. diss., University of Michigan, 1970), p. 13 as cited in Beth Landis and Polly Carder, *The Eclectic Curriculum in American Music Education: Contributions of Dalcroze, Kodály, and Orff* (Reston, Va.: Music Educators National Conference, 1972), p. 26.

[5] Carl Orff, "The Schulwerk—Its Origins and Aims," trans. Arnold Walter in Landis and Carder, p. 158.

[6] Ibid., p. 152.

[7] Ibid., pp. 152–153.

[8] Charles R. Hoffer, "How Widely Are Kodály and Orff Approaches Used?" *Music Educators Journal*, 67, no. 6 (February 1981), pp. 46–47.

[9] Egon Kraus, "Zoltán Kodály's Legacy to Music Education," in Landis and Carder, p. 124.

[10] Landis and Carder, p. 64.

[11] Hoffer, pp. 46–47.

[12] Zoltán Kodály, *Visszatekintes* (published by Zenemukiado, 1964). Quoted in Helga Szabo, *The Kodály Concept of Music Education.* English edition by Geoffrey Russell-Smith (London: Boosey and Hawkes, 1969), p. 10.

[13] Kraus, p. 126.

[14] Kodály, p. 141.

[15] Ibid., p. 143.

[16] Kraus, p. 129.

[17] John Kendall, *Talent Education and Suzuki* (Reston, Va.: Music Educators National Conference, 1966), p. 9.

[18] Ibid., p. 9.

[19] Eric Mitchell, "A Report on Methods and Standards Investigated in the U.S.A., Hungary, the U.S.S.R., and Japan. Comparisons with Australia and Recommendations," unpublished report, 1972, p. 56.

[20] Conversation with John Kendall, St. Louis, Mo., April 1965.

[21] Thomas Henry Huxley, *On Elemental Instruction in Physiology* as quoted in John Bartlett, *Bartlett's Familiar Quotations*, 14th ed., ed. Emily Morison Beck (Boston: Little, Brown, 1968), p. 725.

C H A P T E R E I G H T

HELGA GEIGER HAS just started her new job at Westport High School. As she goes to her mailbox in the office, the principal says to her, "Oh, Helga, better get your concert dates set on the school calendar by next week, because we want to get the thing run off by then." Helga checks last year's school calendar and sets dates for programs at approximately the same times for the coming school year. As she plans for her next day's classes, she wonders, "Just how will the music I'm teaching now be related to the concert I've set in May—or in December, for that matter. I haven't even decided what to do—I've merely set a date for a program." After another moment she wonders, "Really, why am I having public performances in the first place? Why particularly in December and May? Should I have more or none at all? What kind of programs should I present?"

Reasons for Performances

$\mathcal{T}$o begin to answer Helga Geiger's questions, one must return to the issues raised in Chapter Three. The goals of music education are crucial in deciding why there are performances and what they should be like. Certainly they should not be the "be-all and end-all" of school music, although they have been so regarded by many teachers. Performances do contribute to the music education of students, but teachers should keep their priorities straight. Students in school music groups give performances because they have learned; they should not learn *only* to give performances.

Some teachers think of school programs as being much the same as professional concerts or recitals. Such thinking is not logical. Professional musicians perform because that is their chosen work and because they get paid to do so. Any educational or psychological values accruing to them are largely irrelevant. It is the opposite with school students. Their pay is an occasional free meal. The educational benefits, which will be mentioned shortly, are paramount. Both school and professional musicians wish to give musically creditable performances, of course. This goal is the main objective of professional musicians, but it is only one of several desirable outcomes for school groups.

A distinction is being drawn in this discussion between the performing of music, such as singing songs or playing works on the piano. The making of music is vital to the art of music, because music is inert dots and marks on paper until someone brings it to life through performing it. Performances for an audience are a somewhat different matter. *If done properly*, they are definitely of value to school groups, as is pointed out in the next section.

Performances can benefit school musicians in a number of ways.

1. They provide a definite goal toward which to work. Learning is satisfying for most students, but they are more strongly motivated when they have something concrete to work for.

2. Student motivation is helped by the presence of definite goals. It is only human to work harder at something you know will be observed.

3. Performances can educate the audience about music and the school curriculum. The performance is in a sense a report about what is going on in the music class.

4. Social and psychological values accrue to the students from participating in performances. Teenagers achieve recognition for their accomplishments as performers, and they gain poise and self-confidence from appearing before an audience.

5. Group consciousness is aided by performance.

6. Performances benefit the school and community. The pep rally is peppier when a band is present, and the civic ceremony is more impressive when young people contribute music to it.

Guidelines for Performances

A careless or poorly managed performance can reduce the benefits just mentioned. What can be done to achieve quality performances, without detracting from the music education of the students?

First, *performances should be an outgrowth of actual school work.* Education should not be interrupted to prepare something for a performance.

Second, *performances should present music of the best quality appropriate for the occasion.* The marching band and concert choir perform under very different circumstances. The type of music suitable for one is not necessarily suitable for the other. Each, however, should present music of quality that is suitable for the occasion.

Third, *performances should receive proper preparation.* It is impossible to spell out specifically how much time is required to prepare a program. There are too many variables—the ability of the group, the length of the program, the difficulty and newness of the music, and the efficiency and standards of the teacher. Fortunately, if the performance is an outgrowth of class activity, time for preparation and time for learning the subject are no longer distinct and separate. For this reason, except when special circumstances prevail, all preparation should take place in the regular class periods for curricular groups. Such preparation also includes routine matters such as publicity, tickets, and equipment.

Fourth, *performances by any one group should not be so numerous that they interfere with the total education of the students.* The precise number cannot be indicated for the reasons discussed under preparation time. However, when the curriculum of a choral or instrumental group becomes merely preparation for one performance after another, the number is excessive. Time should be allowed to study music, as well as to perform it. Without such learning a band or choral group ceases to be an educational organization and has gone into the entertainment business.

Fifth, *performances should adhere to acceptable moral and ethical standards.* The vast amount of music available makes it easy for school music teachers to avoid musical productions that cast students in morally undesirable roles or in situations that are inappropriate to their age and experience. As an influential social institution, the school should promote the best aspects of civilization and personal conduct. With so much to teach and so little time to teach it, the schools cannot afford to do less.

Sixth, *performances should include all students who study music in performing classes.* The temptation, of course, is to concentrate on the most talented students, because they present a more favorable picture of what is being done in music. This situation occurs when a chorus of seventy-five presents a musical built around two or three principals and five or six minor roles. The other sixty-five students sing a few simple chorus parts, make scenery, assist with makeup, and pull the curtain. The principal performers sometimes get an inflated opinion of their abilities and contributions. This is not to say that talented students should not be given additional opportunities, but they should not be given special attention to the detriment of the others. For example, teaching a solo number should take place in private sessions, not during class while the rest of the students sit watching.

Seventh, *performances should be planned to receive optimum responses from the audience.* Unless the audience generally feels good about the program they have heard, the social or psychological values will be reduced for the student musicians. The success of the performance affects future students as well as present members of the group. When the performance is well received, not only are more students motivated to enroll in music courses, which in turn increases the effectiveness of performing classes, but there is also better support and understanding on the part of the school administration and public.

Eighth, *performances should be viewed in proper perspective by students and teacher.* If a concert is an outgrowth of class work, then it should be treated as such. Some teachers believe that by whipping up fervor in the name of the almighty performance, they will achieve the optimum effort from the students. Unfortunately, they usually achieve the optimum effort plus tension and fear. Certainly this is a misuse of performance. A month's work is not ruined because of a missed entrance in a concert; a month's work can only be lost in the classroom. Teachers should not get the cart before the horse here. Their primary concern should be the musical education of students, not the presentation of flawless performances.

Planning for Successful Performances

The education of the students and the interest of the audience are not necessarily contradictory propositions. In fact, imaginative teachers can combine the two. Less successful teachers see good music education and a high degree of audience enjoyment as irreconcilable, and they proceed either to ignore the listeners or to forget about music education for the sake of audience amusement.

If performances by school groups are to achieve their goal of being both educationally valid and successful in the eyes of the audience, then teachers should keep in mind two points. One is the need for informality. Elementary and secondary school students are not collegiate or professional musicians, and music teachers need not present concerts that pretend they are. They have personality, imagination, and genuine audience appeal, if these attributes are not snuffed out in a stiff atmosphere. There is no reason why teachers cannot offer a few comments about the music during the program, no reason why there cannot be informative notes in the printed program, and no reason why a class activity other than performance cannot be shown to the audience. Music teachers sometimes overlook the fact that people are curious about simple things: how a French horn player who has been resting for several measures knows when to come in, how the singers find which pitch in a chord to start on, and what a conductor does to indicate loud and soft.

The second point is the age of the students. Younger students should be presented with greater informality. A seventh grade class can present a number or two using water glasses it has tuned to study the intervals of the scale and tuning, or it may sing a simple unison folk song with Autoharp accompaniment. A senior high school group, however, should present more polished performances and more sophisticated music, simply because that is the level at which it studies music.

School Assemblies

With the exception of the marching and pep bands, school groups perform mostly for school assemblies and public programs at school. In a number of schools, however, assemblies have been largely abandoned because the auditorium holds only half of the student body at a time or because student behavior has become too unruly.

In secondary schools that still present assemblies or convocations, music teachers are presented with both an opportunity and a challenge. The opportunity is the chance to show the students what the group has accomplished and in the process to encourage interest in the group. Such performances can greatly influence student opinions about music and may determine whether or not some of them will enroll in a music course in the future. The challenge comes from the fact that the audience at an assembly is volatile and responsive. Therefore the type of music presented and the way it is presented must be carefully thought out ahead of the performance. The program should inform the students about music and give something to listen for in each work, and yet it should also give them something to applaud. One teacher planned one number each year that was designed to appeal to students in the assembly situation. The assembly program must "move"; "dead spots" in it are deadly.

Informal Programs

So far the discussion of music presentations has centered on the band, orchestra, or choral organization, each of which is a performance-oriented class. These are not the only groups, however, that appear before the public. General music classes, frequently in combination with other sections of the same course, may perform once or twice a year. In addition, performing organizations make informal appearances, such as a Parents' Night. On these occasions audience interest is achieved by showing the learning activities of the class. Students can play portions of recordings they have studied and offer explanatory comments; they can display the music notebooks they have compiled; they can describe current class projects. The Autoharp can be used to accompany songs, and part singing can demonstrate the use of changing voices.

With performances of this type, attempts at a formal presentation are out of character. The appeal to the audience lies in the personalities of the students and their responses to the music. Instead of entitling a performance "Spring Concert by West Middle School," teachers might call it "Music at West" or "Invitation to Music at West Middle School." People appreciate an unassuming program appropriate to the age and nature of the students.

Programs Outside of School

School groups are often invited to perform for community organizations. It may become necessary for the teacher to apportion the number of such appearances so that the educational purpose of the music group does not suffer. If refusals for performances around the community are necessary, they are usually best handled through a policy statement on out-of-school appearances drawn up by the music teachers, student officers, and school administration. In this way the onus does not fall on an individual teacher, and the matter receives the attention of more than one person.

Two special considerations should be given to performances away from school. First, they must not infringe on areas that properly belong to professional musicians. The Code of Ethics states that school music groups may perform at educational, nonprofit, noncommercial functions, as well as at benefit performances for charitable organizations, nonprofit educational broadcasts and telecasts, and civic events that do not usurp the rights and privileges of local professional musicians. Performances by school groups at other civic programs are permissible only if they are mutually agreed on by the school authorities and official representatives of the local musicians' union. Professional musicians have in their province such events as community concerts and community-centered activities and other nonschool activities, and functions furthering private or public enterprise, partisan or fraternal organizations. The Code says further:

> Statements that funds are not available for the employment of professional musicians, or that if the talents of the amateur musical organizations cannot be had, other musicians cannot or will not be employed, or that the amateur musicians are to play without remuneration of any kind, are all immaterial.

The second consideration is the place of performance. If it is impossible for the group to practice in the new location, the teacher should at least see the surroundings beforehand. Some teachers have had the unfortunate experience of agreeing to sing for the Rotary Club only to find that the Rotary meets in a room that is too small to hold both the singers and the Rotarians. If a piano is needed, the position and quality should be determined ahead of time.

There is much that could be said here about how teachers should handle public performances. Planning programs, making the performances more attractive, and managing the business aspects such as publicity, programs, and tickets could be discussed, but such topics are beyond the scope of an introductory textbook. They are covered in methods textbooks such as *Teaching Music in the Secondary Schools*. For now, prospective teachers need only to become acquainted with some of the issues regarding the purpose and value of performances. The decisions that teachers make on these matters have an important effect on the nature of their teaching, especially at the secondary school level. Performances are an important aspect of the music curriculum.

Questions

1. What do these performance-related incidents reveal about the teacher's understanding of music education?

(a) Ruth Farnham has five sections of eighth grade general music. For a PTA program on music, she chose the best twenty-five girls from the five classes to sing. "After all," she says, "there are a lot of kids in those classes who have precious little ability."

(b) Eric Holm is rehearsing his high school band. The first horn bobbles a note. "If you do that in the concert," Eric says sternly, "I'll clobber your grade, so help me. The audience cannot excuse mistakes."

(c) Lynne Hardesty wants the performance of the latest Broadway musical to be as nearly professional as possible. As a result, her singers rehearse only that music for three months in preparation for the performance.

2. Suppose you are asked to have your students provide fifteen minutes of after-dinner music at a service club luncheon. The performance is strictly for entertainment. Should you not accept the engagement? Why or why not?

3. Which performances are acceptable under the Code of Ethics with the American Federation of Musicians?

(a) an appearance by the band at a Memorial Day observance

(b) a performance in connection with the opening of a new Sears store

(c) a performance at the swearing-in ceremony of city officials

(d) an airport appearance by the band when the national vice-presidential candidate comes to town

(e) a performance by the school stage band at a dance held in a private club paid for by a group of families

(f) a performance by the choir at a hospital benefit dinner

4. Should the group learn different music for a school assembly, an evening concert, and a performance at noon for a service club? Why or why not?

4 | The Process of Teaching

ALTHOUGH AN INTRODUCTORY COURSE does not delve deeply into the matter of how music is taught, some general and basic information about the methods of teaching music is useful. This is true because basic principles and guidelines apply to any type of music teaching at any level. Also, specific teaching procedures can be derived from general principles. For example, if teachers understand the principles of how the human mind retains information, they can apply this understanding to their teaching. Although one could make up a number of rules about how to help students retain what they have learned ("Review all factual material that has been taught within one half hour of presentation"), such a specific procedure is not very adaptable and may be forgotten more easily than a general understanding. For this reason, Chapter Nine deals with principles and guidelines of the teaching-learning process in music.

There are basic guidelines to consider in handling student behavior, somewhat as there are guidelines for other aspects of teaching. This topic, which is of concern to many prospective and beginning teachers, is covered in Chapter Ten.

CHAPTER NINE

BELOW IS A true-false quiz containing some common-sense beliefs about learning music. It can be an interesting springboard to a comparison between what everyone "knows" about teaching and what research into the learning process reveals. The answers to the questions are disclosed at various points in the chapter. Prior to reading the chapter, you may wish to try your luck at the quiz.

T F 1. There is one best way to teach a new work to a group, and the prospective teacher should learn and use that method.

T F 2. In learning new music, a performing group should first get the notes right and then work on interpretation.

T F 3. Students learn better when they understand the reason for what they are doing.

T F 4. Children in elementary school can learn the basic points of a subject if it is properly structured for them by a teacher.

T F 5. The most effective way to correct the performance of a particular rhythmic figure is for the teacher to tell the students how to do it.

T F 6. Thinking, especially in solving difficult mental problems, is a skill that is developed through practice in much the same way that physical exercise builds muscles.

T F 7. General ideas are usually remembered better than particular facts.

T F 8. If you want to learn to play a Mozart sonata, you will get better results if you practice it for two hours on each of the last two days before your lesson than if you work on it for thirty minutes for the six days preceding your lesson.

T F 9. If a performing group cannot get a passage right, the students should go over it again and again until they can do it correctly.

T F 10. Because people remember so little of what they learn in school, teachers should concentrate on seeing that the students enjoy music, whether learning takes place or not.

Although there is a little truth in each of the ten items on the quiz, seven are false. Which are correct and which are incorrect is not the point at this moment. What matters now is that each answer calls for an assumption about how music is best learned. Just as teachers reveal their beliefs about the purposes of school through their actions (see Chapter Three), teachers make decisions based on their fundamental beliefs about learning, whether they realize it or not. These basic principles have a strong bearing on what happens in music classes.

Virtually all students enrolled in teacher education programs are required to take a course in educational psychology, which is intended to provide basic information about the learning process. For one reason or another many music education majors do not gain such information from the course. One reason may be that the points are not applied specifically to teaching music, something that this chapter will do. Whatever the reasons, an understanding of how students learn is essential in becoming a good teacher.

Types of Learning

*L*earning is a many-sided word. It can refer to kinesthetic or psychomotor skills, as when a violinist learns to shift from first to third position. Learning also refers to memorizing information, such as the fact that A above middle C vibrates 440 times each second or that Mozart was a composer of the Classical period. Learning may also mean problem solving. For example, a student may have studied some impressionistic music and its phrasing. When presented with a work by Debussy that is unknown to him or her, the student is able to phrase it properly. Finally, a person has learned a piece of music when he or she can listen to it with understanding or play it and convey its aesthetic intent.

For these reasons there is no one correct way to teach music. The answer to question 1 is "false." The appropriate method depends on the situation, the students, and what the teacher wants the group to learn.

Recognizing the fact that learning involves different areas of human activity, Benjamin Bloom and others have developed hierarchies or taxonomies (a word referring to classifying something according to comprehensiveness) for two types of learning, or what they call "domains." The domain of information and understanding, which is called the *cognitive domain*, was devised first. The *affective domain*, which involves feelings and attitudes, came some years later. Although Bloom and his colleagues recognized the area of physical skills, or what is termed the *psychomotor domain*, they did not attempt to develop a taxonomy for it. Elizabeth Simpson has constructed a widely accepted taxonomy for this domain. Such taxonomies are useful to teachers because they offer a better understanding of educational objectives and the comprehensiveness of test items.

The taxonomies for the three domains are presented later in this chapter in conjunction with the discussion of each type of learning.

Maturation

Over the last two decades psychology has shown renewed interest in the topic of student maturation or readiness. This interest in the topic is due largely to the influence of one man: Jean Piaget. Piaget spent most of his long life observing the growth and development processes of children, with his own children being his main subjects for a number of years. While he did not engage in an extensive program of experimental research, studies conducted by others dealing with music and other areas have tended to support his findings.[1] Although he saw cognitive growth as a continuum, Piaget divided it into four stages: the *sensorimotor* stage covers the years from birth to two; the *intuitive* or *preoperational* stage spans approximately the ages from two to seven; the *concrete operations* stage lasts from about age seven to eleven; and the *formal operations* stage includes the years from eleven to sixteen.

The sensorimotor stage consists of activity based primarily on immediate experiences through the senses. For example, when infants are hungry or their diapers are wet, they cry. It does little good to tell them that food or a diaper change will happen in a minute. Objects are watched only when present, but when they are absent, the sensorimotor child thinks an object no longer exists.

The preoperational stage sees children freed from a dependence on immediate sensory information. Their capacity to store images (words and language, for example) expands greatly. While the average two-year-old understands and uses about 200 or 300 words, the average five-year-old understands about 2000, which is an enormous percentage increase.[2] Preoperational children use these words on an intuitive level, with little concern about the consequences of what they say. During this stage they consider "bathroom" language to be the height of funniness, and they tend to talk *at* rather than *with* others. They have active imaginations, sometimes including make-believe playmates.

Preoperational thinking is best revealed in Piaget's experiment of pouring the identical amount of water into two vessels, one tall and thin and the other wide and short. The child intuitively says that there is more water in the taller glass; it looks taller, and why worry about it being thinner? It does no good to tell a child at this stage about the "real" reasons why the amount of water is the same. The results would be a parroting back of the reasoning but with no understanding of the point. Such thinking leads to curious versions of songs or prayers, such as the young boy who said part of the Lord's Prayer, "Give us this day our jellied bread."

The concrete operations stage is of more direct practical interest to school teachers because it encompasses most of the elementary school years. Children who are this age become logical in a concrete, literal sense. Activities can now have rules, and skills and specific activities can be successfully taught. When abstractions are encountered, they are translated into concrete terms. Even the way work is done becomes established in specific terms. More than one parent, in trying to help a child with homework, has been told, "But that's not the way the teacher wants us to do it!" The children's sense of humor at this stage is also concrete. One researcher reported the following story as the most popular with children at this stage. A mother loses her child named Heine. She asks a policeman, "Have you seen my Heine?"[3] Usually the children start laughing so hard while telling it that they never get to the last word. At least it is an improvement over "poop face" and similar humor in the preoperational stage.

The formal operations stage more or less coincides with adolescence. Over these years children can begin dealing, sometimes erratically, with logical and rational abstractions. Symbolic meanings can be understood and implications drawn. In other words, thinking begins to assume adult qualities.

These general stages should be considered in making decisions about teaching music. For example, the concrete operations stage is especially suitable for beginning skill activities such as playing instruments and reading music, but it is not a good one for conceptualizing about types or styles of music. The choice of song material should be influenced by the concreteness of the text, as well as the length of the song and its pitch range. After reviewing the pertinent research, Marilyn Zimmerman reports that the various aspects of music seem to call for this order of study:

> From this discussion of research findings pertaining to perception, it can be concluded that the perception of musical stimuli follows a developmental sequence. Loudness discrimination develops first, with pitch and rhythm discrimination developing somewhat concurrently. The latter discriminative abilities improve with the increasing attention span and the improvement of the memory function. Because perception of loudness develops without formal training, instruction can focus on methods of improving pitch and rhythm discrimination.
>
> Perception of simultaneous sounds or harmony seems to be the last to develop, possibly because of the perceptual centration phenomenon. Studies with American, English, and French children were consistent in the finding that a rapid development in melodic perception occurs between ages six and eight, with age eight marking the beginning of a critical period for the development of harmonic perception.[4]

The age of the students is only one factor to consider with regard to readiness. Other matters make a significant difference, especially the children's previous experience and training in music. Because of their previous education in music, some children in the second grade can do tasks that some fifth graders cannot do. Also, the intelligence and the motivation of the students make a difference. In some music classes the students are selected, and this fact can greatly affect the level at which the group operates. The point is that not all students of the same stage operate in the same way.

Making decisions about the readiness of a class for a particular musical activity is a tricky matter that must be learned from experience. Some help is provided by the music series books, and some districts have curriculum guides that provide some ideas. Teachers should present material that is challenging to the students but yet not so difficult that it frustrates them. Beginning teachers should have two or three pieces of music of differing difficulty ready as backup in case the first choice seems not to be suitable. Most new teachers just out of college should incline toward having the tasks of music be on the easy side for the students during the first few weeks of school.

Cognitive Learning

As mentioned earlier, the cognitive domain includes the learning of factual information and the gaining of intellectual understandings. Here is an abbreviated version of the taxonomy for it as devised by Bloom, with a musical example for each level.[5]

1. *knowledge:* the ability to recall specific items of information without regard to the understanding of it (for example, naming notes on the bass clef)

2. *comprehension:* the ability to grasp the meaning of the material, including interpretation, translation, and prediction (for example, understanding the function of the tonic chord in tonal music)

3. *application:* the ability to use material in new situations (for example, finding the tonic chord in a number of different pieces of music)

4. *analysis:* the ability to divide material into component parts so that the underlying structure is understood (for example, describing the factors in a piece of music that characterize it as romantic in style)

5. *synthesis:* the ability to put parts together to form a new understanding through new structures or patterns (for example, the development of a new description of the effect of chromaticism in Wagner's music)

6. *evaluation:* the ability to judge the value of material for a given purpose (for example, the ranking of Wagner's music dramas in terms of their presentation of the characteristics of romanticism)

In addition to these six levels, Bloom and his associates divided each level into several subcategories. However, the particulars of each level in the taxonomy are not as significant as the general idea of the increasing comprehensiveness and complexity with each level. The taxonomy should not be interpreted to mean that the lower levels are of less value than the upper levels. Some knowledge and facts are needed, just as comprehension, analysis, and evaluation are needed. What teachers should avoid is emphasizing any one level while ignoring the others.

Ways of Cognitive Learning

Psychologists do not agree on how learning in the cognitive domain happens. Some psychologists, often referred to as "neobehaviorists," believe that a person learns one bit of information after another in response to various stimuli. Eventually these bits of learning add up to form larger ideas and concepts. Another group of psychologists, often designated as "cognitivists," believe that learning consists more of grasping the "large picture" in moments of insight and that isolated bits of information are rather useless. There are several reasons for these two differing viewpoints: too much theorizing and not enough practical research, different testing situations, and differing ideas about what learning is. In recent years psychologists and educators have realized that both positions have merit and that people actually learn in both ways. Individual items of information are examined, but at the same time a person's mental processes organize that information into a meaningful pattern.

For this reason music teachers should consider both approaches in sequencing material that is to be learned. If a song is being learned, the teacher should help the students understand its text and general mood. At the same time the teacher may need to correct a missed final consonant or an out-of-tune C sharp. Generally the answer to question 2 is "false." The right notes (particular items) and the proper interpretation (whole) are learned at about the same time. Certainly there should be no lengthy separation between them.

The issue of how students learn cognitive information is not the only topic of interest to educational psychologists, of course. Several other topics such as motivation, structure, sequence, reinforcement, and intuition have been studied, and the psychological insights that have been uncovered merit the attention of music educators.

Motivation

Teachers should build on the fact that most students have a built-in curiosity and desire to be competent in what they undertake. Although they may not act like it at times, they really do not want to be ignorant or to fail to learn. A number of researchers have observed this natural curiosity even among the higher animals. In one experiment a monkey worked at a complicated metal lock for ten straight hours. The experiment was terminated because the experimenter grew tired; the monkey was still going strong.[6] In another experiment the researcher made a small peephole in a screen to watch a monkey. The peephole, however, soon attracted the monkey's attention, and when the experimenter tried to see through the hole, all he saw was the eye of the monkey looking at him from the other side of the hole!

Students seem to be motivated the most when they are presented with a modest challenge. To use an analogy from the world of athletic competition, you would not find the high-jump bar set at 1 foot very challenging; nor would it be set at 6 feet. Such a height is near the world's record, and you realize that in no way can you jump that high, so you would not be motivated in trying this impossible task. Teachers should set the "height" of the task at a level just a bit higher than what the students have done previously. For example, a band that can play grade 4 music without undue effort should be challenged with a grade 5 work.

Learning and motivation are aided if the students understand the purpose of what they are doing. Therefore the answer to question 3 is "true." It is not enough for a teacher to expect students to learn "on faith." If the beginning violinists are told to maintain a straight left wrist, they should be shown how this practice helps them finger notes on the G string better, how it aids them in using the firm tip of the fingers on the strings, and how it allows for easier shifting to higher positions. The teacher of general music classes faces the same requirement. The class may have a project of filling twelve water glasses, one for each semitone. The teacher sees the point of this activity as an exercise in understanding pitch and tuning. The students need also to understand the purpose of the activity. It helps if the teacher can relate the water glass activity with singing in tune by saying, "Remember the water glasses we tuned yesterday? What happened when we got to a point where we needed just a little more or a little less water? We had to listen and work very carefully, didn't we? Listen to the pitch of your singing in the same careful way you did then."

Part of the process of challenging students is not only spelling out the objectives for what they are doing but also offering some criteria for learning. The more concrete and specific these objectives and criteria are, the better it is for the students. The objective may be the identification of songs from looking at the music, with the level of

successfully completing the activity being to get three out of five correct. Students at all ages appreciate such specific conditions.

Structure

Perhaps the most important obligation of teachers is to teach the basic and fundamental ideas—the structure—of the subject. Every area of the curriculum, music included, has its basic knowledge and way of thinking, as was pointed out in Chapter Four. Probably the most frequently cited view of Jerome Bruner, the noted psychologist, is the belief that any given subject or area of knowledge can be structured so that it can be transmitted to and understood by almost all students.[7] But this statement does not mean, for example, that an elementary school student can fully master the elements of tone row compositions. Rather it means that the basic ideas of tone row music can be learned *if* presented in a simple enough fashion. As a result of such teaching, a student would be able to discuss tone row music in a manner that a music theorist or composer would find recognizable. The answer to question 4 in the quiz is "true"; children can learn the fundamental ideas of a subject.

There is a certain progression in the way in which children acquire understandings. The first step in the sequence is in terms of action, which Bruner terms "enactive." The idea that actions and experiences are the basis for ideas and knowledge goes back at least as far as the seventeenth-century essayist John Locke:

> Let us then suppose the mind to be, as we say, white paper, void of all characters, without any ideas; how comes it to be so furnished? . . . To this I answer, in one word, from experience. . . . I find I am absolutely dependent upon experience for the ideas I can have and the manner in which I can have them.[8]

What this means is that students learn about the beat in music by feeling it, not by memorizing a definition of it. Therefore the answer to question 5 about the teaching of a rhythmic figure is "false." Talking about rhythm is not an effective way to teach it.

Two qualifications are necessary to make the experiences and actions effective. First, the experience must be of the right kind. A student can easily do the wrong thing—hold an instrument incorrectly, for instance. Second, the experience must be instructional. Not all learning experiences are equally instructional. Some require more time and effort than they may be worth. What is needed is to do significant activities correctly and not just to do something for the sake of activity.

Actions and experiences are especially important for children in

elementary school, but they are also valuable for teenagers and adults. For example, holding a string instrument is best accomplished with a few words and the teacher showing the student. In fact, much learning takes place through students mimicking a teacher or other students. Although rote imitation and mimicking have sometimes been looked down on because they are not particularly intellectual ways of doing things, the amount of learning that takes place that way is enormous. Everyone learns to talk, sing songs, and perform most bodily motions by copying others.

Several important music educators have realized this fact and have developed ways of teaching based on it. One is the noted violin teacher Shinichi Suzuki, whose pedagogical methods were discussed in Chapter Seven. Not only does this method present an aural model for students to copy in terms of phrasing, tone, and style, but it also appears to aid them in overcoming some of the technical problems encountered in playing. Hugh Tracey, an authority on African music, has described how time after time he has seen an African father teach his young son to drum by reaching around him from behind and guiding the boy's hands.[9]

The next step in Bruner's structure is the representation of ideas on a pictorial or "iconic" level. Teachers who use figures such as $\square \; \bigcirc \; \square$ to represent ABA form are using such a mode or representation.

The third and final step is symbol representation, which is primarily through language. Language makes for greater efficiency in acquiring information and also helps people to think more compactly.

As useful as language is, teachers should avoid overteaching by using more words or materials than are necessary for the students to learn. Concise summaries are more likely to be effective than are complex presentations, because complexity has a way of obscuring the main point. Good teaching (and textbook writing) should simplify and synthesize material to make it more easily understood.

Sequence

Teaching involves guiding learners through an appropriate sequence of activities related to learning the subject. The sequence in which the aspects of the topic are presented often determines whether or not the students will learn; they may successfully learn something when presented in one sequence and fail to learn if presented in a different sequence. Bruner feels that the sequence of progressing from activity to representation to symbolization is probably the best general sequence for learning. The progression in teaching music is probably one of moving from experience to symbolization, as is represented in the old dictum for learning to read music, "Ear it

before you eye it." Sequencing should also involve presenting challenges to the students. If learning is to continue, students need to be motivated throughout the process, not just given one motivational boost at the beginning.

Reinforcement

Most psychologists agree that reinforcement or feedback is required in learning, because students need to know how they are doing. Not only do they need to know this, they learn best when they are given feedback rather soon after the completion of the effort at learning. If such information is provided before the learning task is completed, it can confuse the learners; if it comes long after the task is done, the learners may find it of little value because they have gone on to other things.

Reinforcement should be given in terms the learners understand. For example, if a child is trying to tap out rhythmic patterns, the feedback of this active type of learning should not be given in verbal explanations. A tapped version of the correct pattern should be provided so it can be compared with what the student did.

The word *reinforcement* can call up thoughts of rewarding correct answers with pieces of candy, merit points, words of praise, or other types of extrinsic motivation. Sometimes rewards are given to reinforce learning, especially to encourage proper behavior in class under the rubric of "behavior modification," which is briefly described in Chapter Ten in conjunction with managing the classroom. The use of extrinsic rewards is usually successful under some short-term circumstances, but it is questionable over a long period of time. A student should not expect to be rewarded for each bit of learning in each subject year after year. (One could conceivably grow very tired of M and M's or begin not to believe the teacher's favorable comments.) Rather the goal of education is self-sufficiency in which the students are not dependent on reinforcement by teachers. The "reward" then becomes what is gained from the learning activity.

Intuition

There are times when teachers should challenge students to use their intuitive sense and make what is sometimes called a "perceptive leap" in attempting to discover a relationship or pattern. The elementary school music teacher might say: "The first section of the piece we just listened to was rather fast and somewhat loud; the third section was even more loud and just as fast. But the second section was quiet and smooth. Can you think of a reason why the composer might have made the second section different?" It is hoped that the students would come to a conclusion about the need for contrast in the music.

As valuable as these perceptive leaps and techniques of "discovery learning" are, they are not suitable for many learning situations. Such learning requires much time and skill on the part of the teacher. What seem to be most useful for student discovery are basic principles that account for important aspects of the subject. Asking students to assume the responsibility for some of what they learn requires teachers who are bright and flexible and who have a thorough knowledge of the subject. Such teaching also demands patience on the part of the teachers. When successful, however, the time and effort are well worth it in terms of what the students gain from the experience.

Part of the success of having students make perceptive leaps and discover things for themselves stems from the fact that it involves them in the learning process. When students are involved, they usually learn better. For example, two researchers reported a study in which fifth graders were taught Spanish.[10] One group of classes used teaching machines, a second group used a programmed textbook, and a third group was given traditional classroom instruction. The teaching machines were early models, and they broke down frequently. The more highly trained teachers put aside the machines and instructed the students in other ways. The teachers with less training told the students to fix the machines as best they could and continue. In some classes as much as a fourth of the time was spent repairing machines. Which group of students learned more Spanish—those with the capable teachers who were clever enough to move to other modes of instruction or those with less able teachers, who in effect said, "Fix it yourself and learn what you can?" Surprisingly, higher achievement was shown by the students who were given less help, a fact that was true at every IQ level. Similar results have been reported from studies in which students discovered principles in mathematics on their own.[11]

Other Aspects of Cognitive Learning

In addition to the basic points just presented, two other areas of cognitive learning merit some attention. These are the matter of transfer from one subject matter area to another and the factors that encourage students to remember what they have learned.

Transfer. Transfer occurs when something learned in one area is applied to another area. For example, the idea of transfer can be traced back to the ancient Greeks, who believed that one's mind was disciplined by schooling. They thought that the mind was like a muscle that must be exercised until it became strong; then it could learn just about any new material. This idea, sometimes called "formal discipline," went unchallenged until nearly the turn of the twentieth century. The results of research dating back to William James, E. L. Thorndike, and Charles Judd demonstrate that the automatic transfer does not happen to any great extent. Therefore the answer to question 6 is definitely "false."

What does research indicate about transfer? First, there is no such thing as *automatic* transfer. Second, transfer depends on the degree of similarity between the two areas involved. For example, studying the historical development of musical notation will not improve the students' understanding of Brahms's music, but studying Liszt's techniques of theme transformation will, because Brahms also uses theme transformation extensively.

Teachers can teach for a greater transfer of what is being taught. If the students play a particular rhythmic pattern by rote, they may not do much better on that pattern when it is encountered in another work. On the other hand, if teachers teach the students how to recognize aurally and visually the relationships among the note values, then what is learned has a greater chance of being applied to other situations.

Teachers should jog the students to think about other applications of what is being learned. One way to do so is by questioning. "How does the articulation in this piece compare with the articulation in the piece we just finished rehearsing?" "What kind of cadence occurs just before the tempo changes?" Too often students do not apply what they learned in music theory or literature classes to their performance of music. If they try to apply that knowledge to the music they perform, more of it will transfer.

Memory.   Remembering what has been learned is a major goal of education. Sometimes the importance of remembering is downgraded by saying that all students do is "regurgitate facts." However, without memory we would live only on a level of instinct and impulse. The real issue should not be the merits of remembering but rather the value of what the students are taught and asked to retain. This is, of course, a curricular question, dealing with what is taught, not the way it is taught.

There are several ways in which remembering can be encouraged. One is to present the material in its best light so that its usefulness is apparent. People on a sinking ship will remember a set of instructions about finding their lifeboat much better than will the jovial passengers just sailing out of the harbor. While teachers can scarcely make what they teach seem to be of lifesaving importance, they can help the students see where it fits into the subject in particular and life in general. When students understand the purpose of the material to be learned—which is suggested elsewhere in this chapter—they will remember better.

Although the use of examinations is occasionally criticized, studying material for a test does aid in remembering. A test provides students with an immediate reason for learning. The criticism directed at "learning to pass a test" would be better aimed at *what* the students are tested on rather than at the practice of giving examinations.

Teachers can also urge the students to concentrate on the ideas of the material, not on isolated, detailed information. Broad conceptual ideas are remembered best. A few years after having taken a course in chemistry, for example, most people will remember generally what atomic theory is but have forgotten the atomic weight of iron. The answer to question 7 is "true."

The quality of remembering is affected by the quality of the original learning experience. Often what is forgotten was never thoroughly learned in the first place. This fact does not justify going over the same material repeatedly, but it does suggest the need for adequate clarity and comprehension when something is first taught.

Remembering is aided by the impact with which something is learned. This is one reason for using films and other visual aids in teaching. The more vivid the experience, the better it will be remembered. For example, placing key words in a lesson on the chalkboard does make a difference. One general music teacher played a fanfare on the piano and then announced in stentorian tones, "Today we will study *syncopation*." If he does not overuse this gimmick, it will grab the attention of the class and contribute to remembering.

Memory is aided when the students recognize a pattern. Nonsense material is much less likely to be retained, probably because it doesn't fit into a pattern. A series of numbers such as 1 11 12 5 14 2 8 7 is more difficult to remember than a series such as 1 5 2 6 3 7 4 8.

Finally, remembering is aided by frequent review. Most of what is forgotten fades soon after it is learned, usually within an hour. Hermann Ebbinghaus conducted the classic studies of memory, and from his research he plotted a "curve of forgetting." His curve has been confirmed by other psychologists, especially Luh, whose name appears in Figure 9.1.[12] In practical terms the forgetting curve indicates that the students will retain more if there is review at the conclusion of the class, in the next meeting of the class, and every so often after that.

The forgetting curve does *not* say that people forget 60 percent of whatever they learn. It's not that simple! Remembering depends on what is taught, how it is taught, the interests and abilities of the students, and much more. So the answer to question 10 is "false." Not only are concepts retained, but with good teaching methods many details and specific skills can also be remembered.

Figure 6.1
Ebbinghaus curve of
forgetting

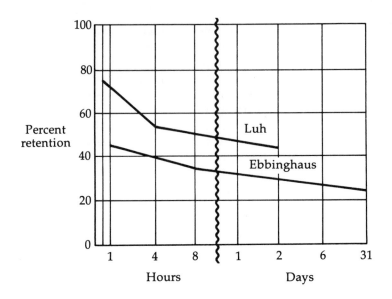

**Psychomotor
Learning**

*A*n area or domain that psychologists have not given as much attention to as they have the cognitive and affective domains is that of psychomotor or skill learning. And it is an important domain to music educators, because much of what they teach involves skills such as playing or singing music, reading music notation, and hearing and notating aspects of music. In terms of the amount of attention given the three domains in school music instruction, it probably surpasses the cognitive and affective domains.

A taxonomy for the psychomotor domain has been devised by Simpson and is as follows:[13]

1. *perception:* the awareness of the object and relationships through the use of the sense organs (for example, hearing and feeling the distance between the pitches of the major triad on the piano)

2. *set:* the readiness for an action (for example, learning the correct position for playing the cello)

3. *guided response:* the ability to execute an overt action under the guidance of a teacher (for example, playing the major scales on the piano during a lesson)

4. *mechanism:* the development of an automatic learned response (for example, when playing the piano, the maintaining of the Alberti bass pattern in the left hand while concentrating on the melody in the right hand)

5. *complex overt response:* the ability to execute a complex set of actions smoothly and efficiently (for example, playing a Beethoven piano sonata well)

6. *adaptation:* the ability to change the execution of actions to make them more suitable (for example, while playing piano in a piano trio, the adjusting of performance of the part to fit better with the other two players)

7. *origination:* the ability to develop new skills (for example, Franz Liszt's adapting the techniques he heard in Paganini's violin playing to piano compositions)

As with the taxonomies for the cognitive domain, the higher levels of the psychomotor taxonomy are marked by increasing complexity.

Psychomotor skills are especially interesting to teachers and psychologists for a number of reasons. One reason is the limited control of the mind over muscular functions. If the mind had to tell every muscle what to do for a simple action like walking, it would require several minutes to take one step. It has been calculated that 512 muscle settings are involved in striking just one key on the piano![14] It is apparent, therefore, that much of the control over the muscles in carrying out the skill tasks comes from lower orders of the nervous system. While the mind may occasionally intervene—and is needed to start the muscular process going—other parts of the nervous system largely guide the many muscles involved.

Exactly how the muscles and nerves operate in executing an action is not fully known. Therefore it is only partially clear how best to teach psychomotor learning. Some of the same guidelines that operated for learning in the cognitive and the affective domains seem to apply; for example, skills are learned in units or patterns, as they are in some cognitive learning.[15] But other guidelines from those domains do not apply. However, some guidelines for learning skills can be offered that appear to help.

Distributed Practice

Educational psychologists have found that it is far more efficient to learn a skill in numerous short sessions than it is to learn the same thing in a few long sessions. Some psychologists refer to this principle as "distributed effort," others as "distributed practice" or "spaced practice." In an experiment by Lyon the subjects learned stanzas of poetry.[16] When two stanzas were learned in one sitting, it required .38 of a minute per stanza. However, when one hundred stanzas were learned in one session, it took 3.85 minutes per stanza, ten times as long for each stanza! The significant figure here is the amount of time required per unit being learned. Many other experiments, ranging from juggling to addition, have reached the same conclusion.[17] So it is many times more efficient to practice an instrument for one hour each day of the week than it is to practice seven hours in one day. More learning takes place in the first ten minutes of practice than takes place in the next ten, and with each additional amount of study there is a corresponding reduction in the amount learned. The answer to question 8 is "false."

There are several other reasons for encouraging distributed effort in teaching. First, fatigue and boredom set in during long practice sessions, and the desire to improve is diminished. Second, mistakes are more likely to be repeated in a long session and become fixed in the response pattern. Third, forgetting is a learning experience since it shows what elements have been inadequately learned. If there are additional practice sessions, these weaknesses can be overcome. Fourth, a person tends to resist immediate repetition of an act, and this resistance continues as the repetition continues. Fifth, incorrect acts are forgotten more quickly than correct ones, and spaced practice allows incorrect responses to be dropped.[18]

Music teachers must realize that it is better to leave something unfinished and come back to it another day than it is to overwork it. Negative threats such as "We're going to stay on this until it's right" are not effective. On the other hand, distributed effort must not serve as a means of escape from hard work. Persistence is still vital to good teaching, but persistence should not be confused with dull repetitiousness. The answer to question 9 is "false."

The maximum amount of time that should be spent on any one activity varies with the amount of concentration required, the age of the students, and their interest in the activity. Students can work for about ten to twenty minutes on a piece of music or on a musical topic in the general music class. In a drill activity, which may require more concentration, the time should be shorter.

Singleness of Concentration

People can concentrate on only one muscle activity at a time. When concentrating, they let the remainder of their actions continue without conscious thought. The necessity for singleness of attention raises problems of priority when one considers all that is involved in making music. Tone, words, notes, and style are all present together, yet an individual can think about only one aspect at a time. The answer lies in emphasizing different phases of the music at different times and in forming good habits quickly so that they become automatic responses as soon as possible.

Developing good habits in making music is much like learning to drive a car. When a person first begins to drive, he or she must consciously think of each step: turn the ignition key, release the brake, set the transmission, step on the accelerator, turn the steering wheel. Eventually these actions become automatic; people can simultaneously drive and carry on a conversation.

Although the degree is exaggerated for illustration, young violinists are occasionally instructed something like this:

> Hold the violin under your chin so that it points halfway between straight front and straight to the side. Keep your left elbow well under the violin and your left wrist straight; hold the neck of the instrument between the thumb and the index finger, like this; turn the left hand so that the little finger is nearest you.
>
> Now, the bow is held in the right hand with the thumb curved a bit so it touches the angle between the stick and the frog; lean your hand inward so the stick crosses under the index finger at the middle joint; the little finger regulates the balance and is curved so only the tip touches the top of the stick. The wrist is flexible but not flabby; the muscles of the bow arm are relaxed, just tense enough to move the bow properly. Now the bow is drawn at a 90-degree angle to the strings. Don't let the angle change as you approach the tip. Remember, you *draw* the bow gently across the string—don't scrape or bounce it.

Then pointing to the music, the teacher says:

> The note on the second space of the treble staff is A.

If the student hasn't given up by now, the teacher may go on:

> There are four beats in a measure. You know what beats are, don't you? Each note of this kind, with no stem and not filled in, gets four beats. Now we can figure out all the other note values mathematically.

At least one thing can be said about this example of teaching, which violates the idea of experience as the basis for learning and can only bewilder most students: it is thorough.

Affective Learning

*T*he domain that includes the learning of attitudes and commitments is the affective domain. Bloom and his colleagues developed the following taxonomy for it:[19]

1. *receiving:* the willingness to pay attention (for example, being willing to listen to a musical work)

2. *responding:* the willingness to participate in an activity (for example, taking part in the singing of a song)

3. *valuing:* the placing of value on an object or activity (for example, buying a recording of a piece of music or checking it out of the record library)

4. *organization:* the bringing together of different values and resolving conflicts between them, and the building of a consistent value system (for example, a concern for the preserving of the music of other cultures, even though one does not fully understand or appreciate all other cultures)

5. *characterization by a value:* the maintenance of a system of values over a long period of time so that it is consistent, pervasive, and predictable (for example, consistently supporting music through attending music programs, buying recordings of music, and giving to the local symphony orchestra)

The main difference between this domain and the cognitive domain presented earlier in this chapter is the increasing attitude commitment rather than intellectual abstraction with each higher level.

Applying Psychological Principles

The findings of psychology do not provide music teachers with step-by-step recipes for successful teaching. Rather they supply the ground rules that teachers should follow. If teachers will evaluate their work according to these principles, their chances for effective teaching will be greatly improved. They can check their work out with questions such as these:

Was the lesson of reasonable difficulty for the students?

Did the students experience music or just hear words about it?

Were the aesthetic qualities of the music brought out?

Were the students involved in the learning activity?

Were the students given reasons for what they studied?

Did the students gain general understandings in addition to useful information?

Was the material presented in a way that encouraged remembering and transfer to other musical situations?

If the learning involved acquiring skills, was the effort distributed over a span of time? Was the students' attention focused on one aspect of the skill at a time?

Was the lesson presented so that it encouraged positive attitudes toward music?

These and other questions are also valuable in planning as well as in evaluation. When questions are based on solid psychological principles, they can guide teachers in how they should teach.

Questions

1. Arrange these cognitive activities in order from the most specific to the most comprehensive.

(a) deciding what features of a work make it more suitable for flute than violin

(b) knowing that Franz Schubert was born in 1797

(c) arranging an organ work for brass choir

(d) being able to explain that an art song is a musical setting of a text for solo singer and piano

2. Suppose that a band director wanted to teach the band about the form of a march.

(a) If he or she were a "neobehaviorist," what general steps might be followed?

(b) If he or she were a "cognitivist," what general steps might be followed?

3. What principles of learning are expressed in the old saying in teaching music, "Ear it before you eye it?"

4. Describe five ways in which teachers can increase the chances that the students will remember what they have learned.

5. How can teachers increase the chances that learning in one area might transfer to another?

6. Arrange these psychomotor activities in order from the simplest to the most complex.

(a) playing the violin with correct right- and left-hand position

(b) concentrating on the phrasing of a melody while playing all the notes correctly

(c) creating a new set of bowing exercises for violinists

(d) playing a violin etude with all the notes correct

7. What is the principle of "distributed effort" or "spaced practice?" In which domain of learning does it apply?

8. Arrange these affective activities in order from the least to the most commitment or interest.

(a) The general music class elects to attend a movie on a piano competition instead of one on stock car racing.

(b) The general music class members pay attention during a report on black spirituals and ask intelligent questions afterward.

(c) The general music class members stay in their places and stop talking while a record is played, but many of them look out the window or daydream while doing so.

(d) Some of the general music class members become so interested in music that they sign up for chorus in high school.

References

[1] Marilyn P. Zimmerman, *The Musical Characteristics of Children* (Reston, Va.: Music Educators National Conference, 1971), pp. 18–21.

[2] Richard C. Sprinthall and Norman A. Sprinthall, *Educational Psychology: A Developmental Approach* (Reading, Mass.: Addison-Wesley, 1977), p. 127.

[3] Martha Wolfenstein, *Children's Humor* (Bloomington: Indiana University Press, 1978), p. 83.

[4] Zimmerman, p. 10.

[5] Benjamin Bloom et al., *Taxonomy of Educational Objectives. Handbook I: Cognitive Domain* (New York: David McKay, 1956), pp. 201–207.

[6] S. B. Stolz, L. A. Wienckowskik, and B. S. Brown, "Behavior Modification: A Perspective on Critical Issues," *American Psychologist*, 30, no. 11 (1975), pp. 1027–1048.

[7] Jerome S. Bruner, *Toward a Theory of Instruction* (Cambridge, Mass.: Harvard University Press, 1966), p. 44.

[8] J. E. Russell, *The Philosophy of John Locke*, extracts from *The Essay Concerning Human Understanding* (New York: Holt, Rinehart & Winston, 1891), p. 35.

[9] Hugh Tracey, personal conversation (Mexico City, September 1975).

[10] Henry Clay Lindgren, *Educational Psychology in the Classroom*, 3rd ed. (New York: John Wiley, 1967), p. 388.

[11] Ibid., p. 271.

[12] Hermann Ebbinghaus, *Memory*, trans. H. A. Ruger and C. E. Bussenius (New York: Teachers College, Columbia University, 1913), pp. 68–75.

[13] Elizabeth Simpson, *The Classification of Educational Objectives, Psychomotor Domain*, Final Report, U.S. Office of Education Contract no. 5–85–104 (Urbana, Ill.: College of Education, University of Illinois, 1966).

[14] David LaBerge, "Perceptual and Motor Schemes in the Performance of Musical Pitch," in *Documentary Report of the Ann Arbor Symposium: Applications of Psychology to the Teaching of Music* (Reston, Va.: Music Educators National Conference, 1981), p. 184.

[15] Ibid., pp. 190–191.

[16] D. O. Lyon, "The Relation of Length of Material to Time Taken for Learning and the Optimum Distribution of Time," *Journal of Educational Psychology*, V (1914), pp. 85–91.

[17] See H. B. Reed, "Distributed Practice in Addition," *Journal of Educational Psy-*

chology, XXVI (1935), pp. 695–700. See also C. G. Knapp and W. R. Dixon, "Learning to Juggle. I. A Study to Determine the Effect of Two Different Distributions of Practice on Learning Efficiency," *Research Quarterly*, XXI (1950), pp. 331–336.

[18]Lee J. Cronbach, *Educational Psychology* (New York: Harcourt Brace Jovanovich, 1954), p. 368.

[19]Benjamin Bloom et al., *Taxonomy of Educational Objectives. Handbook II: Affective Domain* (New York: David McKay, 1964), pp. 176–185.

C H A P T E R　　　　　T E N

PROBABLY NO ASPECT of teaching is as much on the minds of future teachers as the matter of student behavior in class. In one study 3000 prospective teachers were asked, "What gives you the greatest concern or worry as you plan for your first teaching position?" Of these, 2480 answered, "Discipline."[1]

**Discipline and
Teaching**

*F*or some reason there is a tendency among prospective teachers (and some experienced teachers, too) to think of the teaching process and the handling of student discipline problems as two separate and distinct matters. Methods classes cover topics such as teaching students to perform music or write chords, but if they mention student behavior at all, they switch to discussing the means of keeping the students "in line." The teaching of music is approached in a positive tone, while the handling of classroom discipline is dealt with in a negative way. Such a view is unfortunate, and it tends to keep teachers from working at the correction of classroom conditions that encourage misbehavior.

Some educators are very willing to manipulate classroom situations so that students learn subject matter, but they think that managing a situation so that the students learn necessary social skills is somehow not quite right. Such a belief is hard to understand, because unless sufficient social skills are learned, very little learning of subject matter can take place. The two types of learning are very much interrelated.

Almost everyone believes that students ought to behave in school, but why? When all is said and done, the reason students need to behave is so that they can learn. It's just that simple. Yet students and teachers sometimes forget this basic fact. Students find it easy to fall into the habit of thinking that behaving in school is the teachers' idea. In other words, the focus of class behavior is diverted from creating a situation in which learning can take place to one in which students respond to teacher-created rules. And when that happens, often the response of the students is to make a game of violating those rules. This situation can be partly overcome if the class members get to help in the formulation of the class conduct guidelines. In that way they will understand them better and feel that they are fair.

Teachers should keep the reasons for classroom discipline in mind for their own sake, too. True, teaching is easier and more enjoyable when class behavior is good, but that is not the main purpose of good classroom discipline. A greater goal is involved here: student learning.

Developing Desirable Classroom Behavior

*H*ow do teachers, experienced or inexperienced, go about developing classroom situations in which students can learn and be productive? Here are some suggestions, which are offered in no special order.

Work on building a desire to learn in the students. What is pointed out in Chapter Nine about children's curiosity is true. However, is there enough curiosity to motivate students through the over one thousand hours of school each year, year after year? It appears that there isn't. Students may be curious and want to learn generally, but that does not mean they care about learning to play recorder in general music class in a particular week in February. And how can the students' desire to learn be increased? Start by making sure that your teaching follows the guidelines suggested in Chapter Nine. Well-taught classes in which the students see the point of what they are doing are much more likely to encourage students to learn. As might be expected, the more motivated the students are, the better their behavior will be.

Reward and reinforce the students in their learning and, equally important, *withhold reinforcement for undesirable behavior.* Rewards need not be tokens or pieces of candy, especially at the secondary school level. They can be words or looks of approval and the granting of activities and privileges. For example, music teachers in the elementary school usually find their students eager to play the instruments for accompanying songs. Teachers can reward those students who make a good effort in their singing and behave themselves by giving them the first chance to play an instrument. In the high school band an instrumentalist who wants to be the "class clown" has invalidated his or her chance to play first chair, even if that person is the best player in the section. The student in this instance should be told that a reward is being withheld because of undesirable behavior. An association needs to be formed in the students' minds between good behavior and favorable treatment.

One example of how reinforcement can be employed to improve the behavior of a class is reported in a study by Hall et al.[2] A seventh grade class was being rather disruptive—talking, throwing things, and so on—when it should have been working. It met daily for forty-five minutes: it had a five-minute break and then a forty-minute session. Observations of the class revealed that only 47 percent of the time were students behaving as they should. The teacher was approving of some aspect of behavior about six times per session and disapproving about twenty times during that time span. First, the teacher increased the amount of time given the school work and decreased the attention given misbehavior. Also, the amount of approval and disapproval were made about equal. The results were an increase in appropriate student behavior to about 65 percent, but the noise level remained high. Next, the teacher placed a chalk mark on the board when students disturbed the class, with each mark reducing the break time by ten seconds; twenty-four marks eliminated the break entirely. The appropriate behavior increased to about 76 percent and the noise level dropped.

The teacher then tried doing away with the chalk marks, but the class behavior became worse; studying decreased and the noise level increased. So the chalk marks were reinstated, and this time the rate of appropriate behavior increased to 81 percent, and it stayed there for the remainder of the study.

Among other things, the study demonstrated the fact that class management does not lie in adopting an either-or position regarding approval or disapproval. Both have their place, if used correctly. Teachers need to develop the right "mix" of approval-disapproval and seek the right amount of leadership, a point depicted in the cartoon on page 180.

Although the reinforcement of poor behavior is not intended by some teachers, it is unwittingly encouraged when they yell at or in some way give recognition to students who are doing something they shouldn't. Although the words do not compliment the misbehaving students, they are giving them some attention, which is seen by them as better than being ignored.

Work on correcting specific actions. It does not help when a teacher accuses students, for example, of having a "bad attitude." That is so broad a charge that the students would not know what to change—even if they wanted to. What are the actions of the student that indicate a "bad attitude?" Being late for class? Talking at the wrong times? Slouching instead of sitting up straight? Writing obscenities on the pages of the music? Refusing to take part in class? Particular actions can be changed; general or vaguely stated impressions cannot.

In many ways, working on specific behavior problems is similar to teaching subject matter. Objectives are stated, a teaching procedure enacted, and the results assessed according to observable actions.

"Accentuate the positive," to cite a line from an old popular song.[3] Teachers should spend as much time and effort trying to catch stu-

THE PROBLEM

The kids in your class are disrespectful and unmanageable . . .

THE WRONG APPROACH   THE MAD APPROACH

© 1971 by E.C. Publications, Inc. Reprinted by permission of MAD.

dents doing something right as they do in trying to catch them doing something wrong; they should be at least as quick to praise students for the good things they do as to criticize them for the undesirable things they do.

Some music teachers have been so well schooled in the goal of perfection that they find it hard to praise the less-than-perfect efforts of school students. These teachers should not give up their high standards, but they should be much more ready to be positive about what the students have achieved.

Devote more attention to the many students who are neither the best nor the worst in the class. The best students receive plenty of attention.

They play solos, answer questions in class correctly, get to sit in the first chairs of sections, and the like. Teachers enjoy having such students (and there is nothing wrong in that), and this pleasure is probably evident in the teachers' actions. The worst students often get a lot of attention, too, but in different ways. They get yelled at, kept in for recess or after school, have private conferences with teachers, and get special visits to the principal's or counselor's office. One of the ironies of teaching in the schools is the amount of effort teachers expend on the pupils who least want to learn. In the meantime, the large group of "average" students get the rather limited amount of the teachers' attention that is left over after the best and worst students have been taken care of. This situation is wrong; teachers should probably give priority to the majority of their students who are neither very good nor very bad.

Be consistent. It is difficult to do, but teachers should try to be consistent from day to day and from situation to situation in dealing with students. The same student actions should produce the same response from the teacher, regardless of who the student is or what the day is. For example, if two students on two different days forget to bring their instruments to school, they should be treated in the same way. Inconsistent teacher actions have an unsettling effect on the students, because they don't know what to expect.

> Marsha Martin was determined that there be no horseplay in chorus rehearsal. On Monday Jim Norton, a weak bass, was caught tossing a bit of paper at another bass. She immediately asked him to leave the room, and he was given an hour in the school's after-school "quiet room."
> On Wednesday Peter Ott, the only good tenor, was caught flipping a little piece of dried mud from off his shoe at another chorus member. Miss Martin just glowered at him and said, "Now look! Let's leave the horsing around to horses." Peter was given no penalties.

Mean what you say. Teachers who do not intend to follow up what they say should not say it in the first place. Students are quick, very quick, to discover idle threats. From the first day on teachers must mean what they say, or else they will be in for a long year.

> The chorus students at Webster High School soon discovered that Jana Movesian's threats didn't mean a thing. When they came into class, they stood around the room in small groups, talking and laughing. Some students sat down in the wrong seats. Finally, after shouting and pleading, she got the chorus seated. She then started to talk about the day's work.
> Some members of the chorus began to converse with one another, and Jana barked out, "If you people don't stop talking, I'm going to assign extra homework!" The talking stopped for a few moments, then started again. She raised her voice so that she could be heard above the sound of shuffling feet

and conversation. Finally after more admonitions to be quiet, the chorus started singing, almost ten minutes after the hour began.

A few students had not bothered to pick up their folders, and Jana noticed that they were just singing along without music. The song stopped. "Where's your folder?" she asked Joe Hinman.

"Guess I left it in my locker," Joe replied lazily.

"Listen, you people who forgot your folders," she said, "tomorrow I'm going to check each one personally for his folder. If you don't have a folder, I'm lowering your grade." The students weren't worried. She had made the same threat before but had never carried it out.

Involve the students in developing the guidelines for class behavior. Madsen and Madsen make these suggestions about developing guidelines:

1. Involve the class in making up the rules.
2. Keep the rules short and to the point.
3. Phrase rules, where possible, in a positive way. ("Sit quietly while working" instead of "Don't talk to your neighbors.")
4. Remind the class of the rules at times *other* than when someone has misbehaved.
5. Make different sets of rules for varied activities.
6. Let children know when different rules apply (work-play).
7. Post rules in a conspicuous place and review regularly.
8. Keep a sheet on your desk and record the number of times you review rules with the class.[4]

The suggestion about posting rules depends somewhat on the age of the students. It is more effective with younger students. The more mature groups in high school rather resent the idea that they need much instruction on behaving in class.

In the teaching of secondary school students, *be alert to whether the misbehavior is serious or just "pulling the teacher's leg."* Usually it is the latter. It is hard to put into words how you can tell, but with a little experience you can sense a certain look in the eyes and a lack of conviction in the voice of the students when they are just trying to get away with something, often for no other reason than to add a little zest to what they consider a humdrum day.

Do not be afraid that reprimanding a student will cause you to be disliked by the class. Inexperienced teachers are often reluctant to be effective in managing classrooms, partly for this reason. This worry is unjustified. If the students have participated in making the rules, the action of the group will support the teacher in maintaining order. The majority of the class wants the students who don't behave dealt with, because the majority feels that if they behave themselves, so should everyone else. Even the student who is being reprimanded seldom resents being put in line, although he or she is not overtly pleased at being singled out for misbehavior. Furthermore, teachers should remember that they will be seeing the students for many classes for a school year, so the students will have plenty of time to find out what a teacher is really like; they will not base their judgment on the handling of just one or two incidents.

Appeal to the students' desire to be adults. Encourage the formation of an association between maturity and proper behavior in class, which is what the teacher is trying to do in this example.

> Ray Johnson found that this reminder was effective with his students: "Look, you're big boys and girls now. You know the rules that we all worked out together for conduct in band. So do what you know is right. If you act like adults, you'll be treated as adults, and everything will be just fine. When you act like children, everyone, including me, will treat you as children. It's up to you. Now let's get to work on this music."

Remain calm and rational, even if things go badly. No matter how disgusted, disappointed, or exasperated you may become, do not lose your temper. You should be adult enough to avoid the trap of acting childish. Firm, clear, reasonable, and unemotional directives achieve control without harmful aftereffects. Also, by remaining uninvolved personally and emotionally, you will be better able to deal with the problem.

Finally, *make a distinction between disliking as a person the student who misbehaves and disapproving of the things he or she does.* Try to have the students realize that you make this distinction.

> Jim Baker found it necessary to penalize his principal second violin for persistently talking out of turn in rehearsal. "Look, Bill," Mr. Baker said, "personally I like you and you're a good fiddler. But in orchestra there are rules about talking and we all agreed on them. You seem to have trouble following them. I don't like this, and neither does the rest of the orchestra. Not only aren't you learning anything, but you're keeping the others from learning. So I think you'd better put in an hour after school. There are some bowings to mark in the violin parts. Why, I'd have to penalize my own mother if she talked as much as you do."

The position taken by the teacher in the example is a good one, for several reasons. First, it is direct and easily understood. Second, it separates the student as a person from his actions. Third, it tells the student why his behavior is unacceptable. Fourth, it derives its authority from "we" or the group, not from the demands of the teacher. Fifth, the talk ends on a note of humor, letting the student know that the teacher has not become overly involved in the events that happened in class.

Special Suggestions for Music Teachers

Are music classes more susceptible to student behavior problems than other areas? In some respects they have less. Many students like music better than they do their other school subjects, and in secondary schools many performing organizations are elective, often only by the permission of the teacher. Therefore student interest is higher and students with serious behavior problems are not present. Music classes are often active, which means that the students are kept busy at constructive activities, which in turn means that they have less opportunity for deviant behavior.

In other ways music classes are more prone to behavior problems. Music lacks the concreteness of some academic subjects in terms of work to be covered and tested. An eighth grader may be held back in school for failing English but not for failing music. In the secondary schools music classes are sometimes very large, especially the performing groups. Having more students means a greater chance for students' misbehavior.

Here are some suggestions that apply to the teaching of music groups:

Maintain eye contact with the class. Minor behavior problems are sometimes encouraged by teachers whose attention is focused more on their music than on the class. If a teacher hovers over the music and does not look at the class, the chances are that some students will lag in participation and behavior. In other cases music teachers cannot tear themselves away from the piano. Either the piano is a "crutch" to help them through their teaching or a "fortification" standing between them and the class. Whatever the reason, if the music of the piano is such an attraction for a teacher, he or she should deliberately teach part of each class without using the piano or looking at music.

Learn the students' names. Teachers of elementary and junior high school general music classes usually see a great many students each week. For this reason they have many names to associate with the faces they see. However, part of the preparation for teaching such classes should be the learning of the students' names. Sometimes class pictures are available from the previous year, and they may help in learning names. If such pictures are not available, the teacher simply has to work harder at learning names. For the first class or two in the fall, music teachers in elementary or middle school can request that the students wear name tags.

Names are important because students feel more free to misbehave if they think that the teacher is not sure who they are. Also, if teachers want to praise the good work of a student—and it is hoped that they will—then saying the student's name is essential. It is not very effective to say, "You with the green shirt, you did a good job of singing with us that time."

Problem Areas for Music

There are areas in which policies have to be made for almost every music class. Here are some suggestions that may serve as guides in dealing with these areas.

Talking. It is difficult for most people to sit for a half hour or more without talking to someone. Anyone who has observed a meeting of teachers will quickly realize that they are no different from anyone else in this regard. Complete silence is, therefore, not a reasonable expectation of American school students. What the students need to learn is that there is a time for talking and a time for keeping silent. The times for talking that the class can consider in setting up rules might be (1) during changes of music or activity, (2) before class starts, and (3) any time that the teacher is not trying to teach, such as when conferring with an individual student. Uncontrolled talking should be prohibited at other times.

The two spots that appear to cause the most trouble with talking are when teachers work with one group of students and leave the others sitting with nothing to do, and when they stop a group to make a suggestion on the performance of the music. *Teachers should not give suggestions or directions to the class if some students are talking.* The students who miss the directions will make the same errors again, and the teacher will need to repeat the directions especially for the talkers. In classes of much size the students should raise their hands and be recognized before speaking. That procedure makes for a more orderly class and offers the students a more equal chance to be heard.

Inability to Participate. Students are sometimes present but unable to sing because of colds or laryngitis. Instrumental teachers have to deal with broken or forgotten instruments, cut lips, and sprained fingers. These situations should be handled in basically the same way. The students should report their afflictions to the teacher *before* class begins. Then they should sit in their regular places and follow the class activities, learning as much as possible without actually participating.

Sometimes students in secondary schools who cannot participate will ask permission to do homework during music class. If doing homework under such circumstances is allowed, it is surprising how many students develop throat problems or broken instruments on days in which there are important examinations in other subjects! Unless students are allowed to practice music in their other classes (which of course they are not), then students should not study other subjects in music class.

Attendance.　　　Usually there are schoolwide policies and procedures for handling excessive tardiness and unexcused absences. When this is so, music teachers need to do little about these problems.

Problems with attendance may arise in conjunction with out-of-school performances. Music teachers, who for the most part have been taught throughout their lives a sense of obligation and responsibility, are distressed when a few students fail to appear for a performance. Legally students can be required to be present, and grades lowered or other penalties administered, *if* two conditions are met. One is that the students enrolled in the music course know that out-of-school performances are involved. This situation is not true for performances in which an entire fourth grade sings at a PTA meeting, for example; it only applies when the students have elected the class. The other condition is that the students be notified a reasonable amount of time in advance of the performance. Ideally teachers should hand out a list of the performances for the group or class the first week or two of the semester. If these conditions are met, then teachers cannot allow missed performances to pass without notice. Failing to show up for a performance mocks the efforts of the rest of the students who did appear. Again the class should help formulate the penalties, which will probably vary according to the nature and importance of the performance.

A situation that appears to be increasing at the secondary school level is a time conflict between school activities for some students on days of performances. As school calendars become more crowded, students run a greater chance of conflicts with athletic events, school plays, or field trips. Music teachers need to work with the school administration to keep such conflicts of dates to a minimum. If conflicts do arise, the student should, with everyone's knowledge, alternate his or her presence equally between music and the other activities. Because a student is on the swimming team does not mean that he performs with the music group *only* when there is no swim meet.

Other Problem Areas.　　　Chewing gum and making music do not go together. Students should be asked to dispose of their gum before class begins. To get this practice started, teachers can designate a different student each day to pass around the wastebasket.

All students in music classes, but members of performing groups especially, should maintain good posture. It increases alertness and improves behavior. Slouchers can be reminded that they are starting to look like a question mark or a pretzel. Good-natured remarks by teachers usually bring about better posture. In most classes slouching can be corrected by having the class stand, and this suggestion includes instrumental groups as well as choral.

*T*he following suggestions about what specifically teachers might do in handling discipline situations should be viewed in light of all that has been said earlier in this chapter about good teaching procedures and the motivation of students. Without effective teacher methods the procedures for handling behavior situations will be of limited value. The suggestions are offered because prospective teachers like the security of knowing some things they can say and do in various situations.

Students have an uncanny way of knowing when teachers are confident in what they are doing, and they are especially discerning when teachers are hesitant. Teachers should make sure that the rules have been clearly established, that the class understands them, and that students are dealt with in some manner when they violate the rules.

Handling Minor Disturbances

It is often wise not to make an issue of a small offense. Everyone makes small infractions of rules on occasion. When motorists are caught overparking the time on the meter, they get a ticket. They are wrong and they know it, but they don't want to be treated like criminals. Students feel the same way about their small offenses.

There are many ways to pass out mild reprimands for rule infractions. The following illustration describes how one case *might* be handled.

> Helen Oliver was telling the Girls' Glee Club about the procedures they would follow at the concert for getting on and off the stage. Denise turned and whispered to her neighbor. Helen stopped talking for a moment, looked at Denise and said in a firm voice, "Denise." She waited a moment more for her to stop whispering. Denise stopped, and Helen went back to explaining the stage procedures for the concert.

Most small violations can be handled in a similar manner. With less sensitive students it is necessary to be quite blunt, but most students will respond to a short reminder.

What does a teacher do if a student continues to talk even after a reminder? This situation probably will not happen, but it can. Here is how it might be handled.

> Leon Russell was working with the tenor section. One of the basses turned around in his seat and started to talk and laugh with one of his friends. Leon said, "Jack, sometimes I think you should've joined a speaking chorus instead of a singing one." Before Leon could finish working with the tenors, Jack resumed his talking and laughing. Leon then said in a firm voice, "Jack, you were just told to stop the chatter. Now do it!" He kept looking at him until Jack turned around and gave him his full attention.

What would happen if Jack still persisted in violating the rules? The teacher would have no choice but to deal with him outside the class. The ways of doing so will be discussed shortly.

Another type of situation involves no particular individual but rather a sizable portion of the entire group.

> To Sandra Babcock, it seemed as if the whole general music class was talking and not yet ready to work. She held up her hand and said in a clear voice, "A moment of silence, please." She waited about fifteen seconds for the group to quiet down, meanwhile catching the eyes of several students and looking directly at them. After a few seconds of silence she said, "Ah, what a wonderful sound—silence." Then she immediately started to work on the day's activities.

How much better this solution is than standing in front of the group and shouting for attention, making everyone tense and irritable. For the technique to be effective, teachers must wait for real silence, and by their manner they must insist on it. Their duty is to keep a cool head, get the attention of the students, and give firm, clear requests. They should put the group to work as soon as possible and make their own remarks pertinent to teaching the class.

Handling Persistent Rule Violators

If a student persists in violating standards of conduct in spite of good, positive teaching and the employment of reminders and mild reprimands in the classroom situation, he or she should be dealt with outside of class. Usually a friendly private conference is the most effective means of working with such a student. It does not bring any additional class attention to the troublemaker, and attention in some form is frequently what is wanted. Furthermore, it avoids embarrassing the student in front of the other students.

Teachers should keep in mind several points when speaking with a student in such a conference.

1. Be friendly, honest, and unhurried. Remember to make a distinction between disliking the student as a person and disapproving of what he or she has done. Sarcasm, ridicule, and anger are ineffective.

2. Approach the student positively. Something like this is usually effective: "Look, Mandy, you could be a lot of help to the chorus. We need singers who know their parts and can sing on pitch. You could be a big plus in chorus, if you wanted to be. Why don't you spend your energies building up the group, rather than seeking attention for yourself by talking so much?" Such an approach is better than

emphasizing the negative by saying, "Don't do this, and don't do that."

3. Give the student a chance to talk. A conference is a two-way affair; both parties should have the opportunity to express themselves. Ask the student if there is anything that can be done to help him or her behave better in the future. Sometimes a change of seat in the group will largely solve the problem.

Sometimes students will try to talk their way out of a situation, even when they are clearly at fault. Some of these statements are so predictable that they have become almost "time honored." One defense basically asks, "Why are you picking on me?" The answer teachers can give is the obvious truth: "You were doing something you shouldn't, and that is why you got caught." Another standard defense essentially says, "I wasn't the only one; others were doing it, too." The previous teacher response is appropriate here also, with the added comment that if others continue doing it, they will be in trouble, too. Some persistent perpetrators of small offenses offer a justification that runs, "All I did was ask Sherri a question (pick up Aaron's music, take a comb out of Mike's pocket—a great variety of actions fit the statement), and I got in trouble." The teacher response can simply be that the question should have been asked of the teacher. In addition, the teacher should point out that the student is being called in because of the accumulation of many small infractions of the rules that the class developed.

Handling Serious Problems

If a private conference with the student does not work, then more forceful action is required. It is best to work with the principal or counselor on serious behavior problems. Often a student who is causing a problem in music is also a problem in other classes. The principal or counselor can study the situation and suggest a course of action. In some cases this action may involve calling in a parent or a temporary suspension of the student from class. Also, the student might be assigned to do something constructive for the music department after school hours, or the poor behavior might be reflected in the student's grade. However, the lowering of a grade has little effect on students who don't care about what grades they receive.

Should a problem student in an elective secondary school course be permanently removed from the course? Yes, under certain conditions. One condition is that the teacher and the school have tried to work with the student and can demonstrate that fact with written records, if necessary. The second condition is that the benefits to the individual are outweighed by the negative effect of the student on the group or class. Teachers have a clear obligation to the majority of the students who do behave properly; they deserve the best instruction in music that can be offered in the available time and facilities. One or two students should not be permitted to spoil it for everyone else.

Although the extremely serious school disruptions—threats of physical violence, knife pullings, fights—are rare in music classes, a word should be said about them. Under no circumstances should a teacher attempt to wrestle a weapon from a student or hold two combatants apart. Besides inviting injury, physical intervention complicates the determination later of what really happened. Instead, send a fleet-footed, responsible student for the principal or school security officer if the school has one. Do not panic outwardly or lose self-control. Meanwhile, in the most determined, forceful tone of voice possible, tell the student or students to stop fighting or put down the weapon. Surprisingly, this command will sometimes work. But in any case, unless the teacher issues a clear directive, during a later investigation it may not be possible to establish the point that the teacher did all that was reasonably possible to maintain control. Again such violent behavior problems are rare, but for a number of reasons they have been increasing in the last twenty years. A little forethought helps in handling a potentially dangerous situation that might arise.

For teachers who demonstrate a positive approach combined with consistency and reasonableness in handling student behavior problems, the amount of effort required for such matters seems to go gradually away. What was a major concern becomes an occasional minor challenge.

Questions

1. Why is it necessary for students in music classes to behave properly?

2. What factors present in most classrooms contribute to good student behavior? What factors contribute to undesirable behavior?

3. Suppose that you are a secondary school choral or instrumental teacher. You receive a telephone message that a member of the group cannot be present for the big spring concert because the student has to work that night at a local fast-food establishment. What reasons can you give the parent as to why the student should be present? Can you require that the student be present for the performance?

4. For each of these incidents, decide what teachers can do to prevent it from occurring and what teachers should do if they do happen.

(a) Bob, a sophomore, is somewhat of a "show off." A student running errands for the principal's office enters the room with a notice for the teacher. Bob shouts to the girl bringing the note, "Patty! Baby!"

(b) Linda is a quiet freshman in the clarinet section. As the teacher is explaining a point, he notices that Linda is talking quietly to her neighbor.

(c) Howard has caused trouble in the eighth grade general music class before. Feeling that he is seeking attention, the teacher assigns him a report to make to the class, with the hope that this would provide him with attention and the class with useful information. While giving the report, Howard talks and talks, uses the occasion to be a "clown," and is clearly not interested in giving a real report.

(d) The seventh grade general music class is attempting to adapt an Autoharp accompaniment to a song. Herb is usually reasonably well behaved. However, as he holds the instrument waiting to play the chords the class decides on, he can't resist strumming lightly on it.

(e) The ninth grade girls' glee club is practicing its music for a performance at the annual Mothers' Recognition Dinner. As the teacher walks by frivolous, talkative Diane, he notices that she is looking at a *Glamour* magazine in her folder.

(f) A nearby store is featuring inexpensive plastic water pistols this week. Nearly every boy entering Mrs. Hixson's seventh grade general music class has a loaded water pistol in his pocket.

Project

1. While observing teachers in school situations, notice the following:

   (a) the proportion of approval/disapproval actions of the teacher

   (b) whether or not class begins on time

   (c) what behavior the teacher reinforces and how it is reinforced

   (d) the existence of behavior guidelines for the class

   (e) how matters such as talking and gum chewing are handled

   (f) whether the teacher maintains eye contact with the students

Suggested Readings

Fargo, G., C. Behrns and P. Nolan. *Behavior Modification in the Classroom.* Belmont, Calif.: Wadsworth, 1970.

Johnson, L. V., and M. A. Bany. *Classroom Management.* New York: Macmillan, 1970.

Jessep, Michael H., and Margaret A. Kiley. *Discipline: Positive Attitudes for Learning.* Englewood Cliffs, N.J.: Prentice-Hall, 1971.

References

[1]Henry Clay Lindgren, *Educational Psychology in the Classroom*, 3rd ed. (New York: John Wiley, 1967), pp. 370–371.

[2]R. V. Hall et al., "Instructing Beginning Teachers in Reinforcement Procedures Which Improve Classroom Control," *Journal of Applied Behavior Analysis*, I, (1968), pp. 315–328.

[3]"Ac-cen-tchu-ate the Positive." Johnny Mercer and Harold Arlen, © 1944 Harwin Music Company; renewed 1972, Harwin Music Company.

[4]Charles H. Madsen, Jr., and Clifford K. Madsen, *Teaching/Discipline*, 3rd ed. (Boston: Allyn & Bacon, 1981), p. 185.

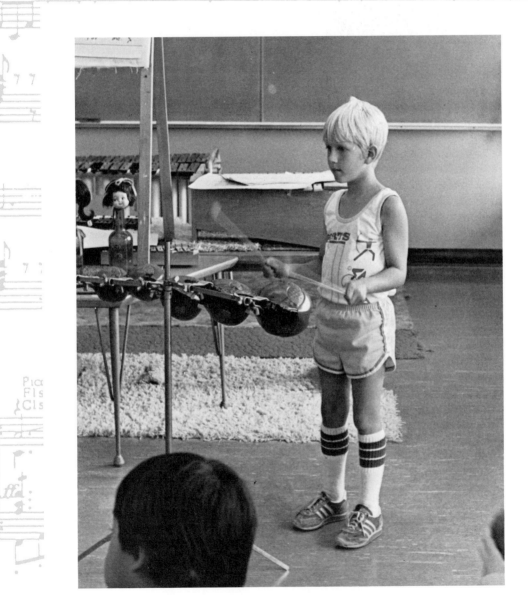

5 | Evaluating Results

I shot an arrow into the air,
It fell to earth, I knew not where.

THESE LINES FROM LONGFELLOW describe in a poetic way what many teachers do. They lead an activity designed to teach the students something, but they never find out the results of their effort. In a sense they carry on a one-way conversation and do not know what impact, if any, their words have on the listeners. If teaching is more than just dispensing information—and it is—then evaluating the results of teaching is essential. Unlike poets, teachers should know where their "arrows" land, and this topic is introduced in Chapter Eleven.

CHAPTER ELEVEN

AT FIRST GLANCE it may seem odd to talk about planning and assessment in the same chapter. Planning is concerned with organizing for instruction, while assessing involves finding out how much the students have learned. The reason they go together is that they are actually two sides of the same coin, so to speak. Planning concentrates on what will be learned and how it will be learned, and assessment centers on how well the students learned what was planned.

Using Objectives

The key to both planning and assessing is the formulation of objectives—statements of what the students should gain from the instruction. Without clearly defined objectives, both planning and assessing will be ineffective and largely a waste of time. It is, of course, possible to have effective planning without any assessment of whether or not learning took place, but the opposite is not possible: teachers cannot assess learning if no objectives have been spelled out to assess.

Objectives are most useful when they are stated (1) specifically and (2) in terms of what the students should be able to do to indicate they have learned. Here are three examples of objectives that meet the two criteria just mentioned.

George Edwards is teaching his seventh grade general music class about major and minor chords. He wants the students to be able to recognize by ear the difference between major and minor triads.

Aaron Feldman wants his band members, among other objectives, to tell the difference between harmony and counterpoint when they hear them in a band composition.

Lori Petrosky is teaching her high school fine arts class about the main features of romanticism—its fondness for nature and the "long ago and far away," its trusting of emotions instead of intellect, and the like—and wants the students to recognize those characteristics in works of art, music, and literature.

These objectives can be stated in actions or behaviors that the students do to show that learning has taken place. All that is needed is the filling in of three points: (1) what the students will do, (2) under what conditions, and (3) sometimes with what degree of success. Here is how the three teachers just mentioned might assess the objective they had selected.

George Edwards: "The students will indicate by answering questions after a triad has been played or by raising their hands during the playing of the music that they recognize the difference between major and minor triads."

Aaron Feldman: "Nine out of ten band members will be able to answer correctly in rehearsal whether the music they are playing at the moment is basically a melody accompanied by chords or counterpoint."

Lori Petrosky: "Given a short romantic poem not previously studied in class, most of the students will be able to locate and list in writing three characteristics of romanticism in the poem."

The following figure presents visually the three essential components of a behavioral objective.

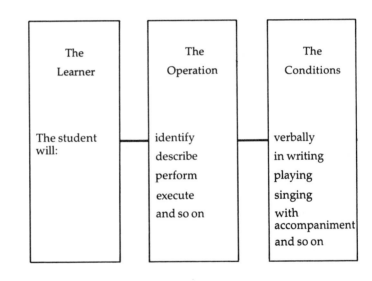

The Learner	The Operation	The Conditions
The student will:	identify describe perform execute and so on	verbally in writing playing singing with accompaniment and so on

You may have noticed that one of the teachers established a standard or criterion level for student learning: nine out of ten were to answer correctly. The setting of a level is done arbitrarily by the teacher as a goal for his or her teaching and in some cases for the students to complete a portion of a course. Specifying a standard is not an essential part of assessing learning, but it can be a valuable guide to teachers and students. Teachers can use the criterion level in making decisions about what should be done in future classes or rehearsals. Students can use criterion levels in completing tasks that are part of a larger program of study. Many students find the learning of a program bit by bit much more effective than dealing with large segments of learning.

A clear statement of objectives in terms of what the students should be able to do is not just an intellectual exercise. It is necessary for good teaching, and in many ways it represents an important change of emphasis from the way teachers have usually thought about planning and assessing. With behavioral objectives the attention is shifted from what teachers do to what students are able to do. This change is more the way it should be because, in the end, schools exist so that students learn, not to provide employment for teachers (as desirable as that may be).

Furthermore, looking for student actions to indicate the amount of learning prevents teachers from simply assuming that their students have learned. Too often teachers have had objectives that were so general that no one could tell if the students had achieved them or not. Having students understand this or that point may be a desirable objective, but teachers must be specific about what the students will be able to do as a result of the instruction and not trust their luck that learning has taken place.

Planning

*S*ince planning precedes assessing in terms of when it takes place, it is logical to begin with it. Some points concerning planning merit explanation: why it is needed, how much of it do music teachers do, how it can be done, and what aids exist in making plans.

Need for Planning

The reasons for planning in teaching any subject may be so obvious that they are sometimes overlooked. The main reason planning is done is to enable teachers to know what they are trying to accomplish and how they will accomplish it. Without planning, teachers are not clear about what they are hoping to teach or the way they will use to help the students learn.

There are other benefits of planning. One benefit is the feelings of confidence and security it encourages, which usually helps a teacher be more effective. Another benefit of planning is that time and effort are not wasted because of uncertainty and confusion. Time is wasted when teachers try improvising in front of a class. Making up instruction on the spot seldom helps students learn.

Amount of Planning by Music Teachers

Many music teachers, especially those who direct performing groups, do not do much planning; in fact, a few teachers seem to do none at all, except for the setting of some dates for performances and other nonteaching matters. Planning is not a popular topic in the music education profession. If planning has the benefits just described, then why do music teachers not do more of it? Probably there are several reasons. One is that some music teachers see the function of school music as the providing of entertainment, not the education of students. As long as the students seem to be having a good time, these teachers are not worried about learning. Although they may not be aware that they have made such a fundamental decision, by their actions, as Chapter Three points out, they have indicated their beliefs.

Some teachers wonder if anyone cares whether or not the students in their classes learn much about music. Sometimes, or so it seems, the principal is favorably impressed if there are few complaints about music class from the students and almost never is anyone sent to the office for disciplinary reasons. Other music teachers and some parents want a performing group to win high ratings at contests or present entertaining performances, and they don't care about other aspects of music education. In other words, the rewards (or reinforcement, to use a psychological term) to teachers for teaching students about music are not strong in many situations.

Many music teachers carry a heavy teaching load. They hurry from one class to another for six hours a day, and after school they have special rehearsals or help students. There simply is not much time or energy left for planning by the end of the day.

It is clear that there are aspects of music teaching that cannot be fully planned for. When teaching a song in two parts to a general music class, no one can predict exactly how well the class will sing the song or the places where mistakes will occur. Therefore, some on-the-spot decisions must be made by the teacher, regardless of the amount of prior planning.

Some music teachers are suspicious of planning because they think it might encourage teaching that lacks flexibility and spontaneity. This might be true if teachers were unwilling to make any changes in their plans or allowed their plans to shackle their enthusiasm and adaptability. Clearly, if it seems wise to alter a plan and it appears that the students will learn more if a change is made, then no teacher should hesitate to change what has been planned. Although some plans may be altered before they are used, the original planning was not a waste of time. The unused planning was a foundation on which the teacher built a better lesson; it provided something for the teacher to work from, which is better than stumbling about without objectives and ideas of how to achieve them.

Aids in Planning

It is not a sign of weakness or incompetence to take advantage of books and curriculum guides in planning, especially if you are not an experienced teacher. Music teachers in the secondary schools see five and sometimes six classes a day, and elementary music specialists often teach music at six different grade levels and see each classroom twice a week. That amount of teaching requires a lot of planning. A new teacher has no reservoir of ideas from previous years, so an even greater effort in planning is required. Any help that a teacher can utilize in planning and teaching should not be avoided.

Several sources are available that provide suggestions and ideas on which teachers can build. Some school districts have developed curriculum guides or courses of study for parts of their music curriculum. Some of these guides are quite useful, but others are very general and of limited value to teachers. Many states publish curriculum guides, and some of them can be a source of ideas for teachers. Elementary and middle school music specialists can take advantage of the ideas offered in the music series books. These books contain not only materials and lessons, but also suggestions and teaching aids. One need not use everything in a book or guide; teachers can choose what will be useful to them and omit portions that are not of value.

Planning for Different Types of Classes

Music classes tend to divide into two types. One type consists of the classes found in the elementary and junior high or middle schools. The other type of music class is the rehearsal of performing groups found mostly in the secondary schools. The general music classes study music through a variety of activities such as singing, listening, creating, discussing, and reading.

An important difference between general music classes and the rehearsals of performing groups lies in the much greater amount of on-the-spot judgments and decisions that teachers make when rehearsing. There is also a difference in that rehearsals of performing groups do not entail the wide variety of musical learning that is found in general music classes.

Long-Range Planning

Where does a teacher start in planning for an entire school year? Since this is no easy task, the beginning teacher should feel free to take ideas from any source—books, curriculum guides, and other teachers. And there should be no hesitation about coming up with one's own ideas. But what kind of ideas? Ideas about what you want the student to learn, to be able to do.

At the beginning these ideas may be rather general and vague. They need to be honed and sharpened so that they can be stated clearly and in terms of student actions. For example, suppose you have an idea that you would like to see the students understand and read music notation better. That is a perfectly good but vague notion.

The next step is to sharpen the idea so that you can express more clearly what you want them to know about or do with notation. It might be that among other things you want them to become conscious of the size of intervals in a melody. You hope they notice that adjacent intervals sound closer than wide intervals, and you also hope that the students can identify the basic intervals such as thirds and fifths when they see and hear them. What began as a general idea has now become more specific.

Although it may not be easy to "fill in the blanks" for classes meeting a couple of months in the future, planning should be attempted for an entire semester or school year. Long-term planning allows for thinking through the sequence in which topics will be presented. Without such plans, there is a good chance that gaps or duplication will occur. For example, one teacher was teaching about the jazz influences in music, and wanted to have the students learn about blue notes. When he got to the point where he wanted to explain how the third, fifth, and seventh notes of the scale are lowered, he realized that the students did not know the pattern of the major scale.

Planning for a course or a school year concentrates on the main topics and their order of appearance. Making detailed lesson plans for classes that will be taught three months in the future probably is a waste of time, because changes will be needed by the time the plans are to be taught. For these reasons prospective and beginning teachers should think of long-term planning as the first step. They should expect to make changes in them; in fact, they can expect to make quite a few changes.

Sometimes inexperienced teachers plan for much more than can be covered adequately. The extra material presents no problem, as long as it does not frustrate the teacher or cause him or her to skim over topics in an effort to cover the content. It is better to have more ideas than can be used than it is to have too few and run out of things to teach.

Unit Planning

In a sense, planning for a group of classes or rehearsals is half way between planning for a course and planning for just one class. Unit plans have elements of long-term planning in that they cover three or more classes, but are much more specific about what will be taught and how it will be taught. It is at this point that the objectives become more specific. Sometimes the plans for a small number of classes or rehearsals can be written at the same time.

The idea of unit planning makes it possible for a topic to act as a unifying thread for a number of classes. A topic is not treated in just one short presentation, but rather is developed and studied in enough depth to help the students remember it better.

The unit idea can be overdone, of course. Conceivably, an entire year could be spent on music of Russia, with all theoretical learnings, songs, recordings, and class activities revolving around that single topic. Instead of aiding learning, such an excess could become excruciatingly boring.

One guideline that music teachers should follow in developing or selecting units is that they be centered on something to do with music. Rather than selecting a group of songs about rivers or lines from plays, both of which are nonmusical topics, units in general music classes should be about sound, types of music, uses of music, playing or singing, and so on. The difference between building around a musical or a nonmusical topic may seem like hairsplitting, but it can lead to rather different types of lessons. In the case of the nonmusical topic, music is included when appropriate for the topic. In the case of a musically centered unit, other information is included as it pertains to the music being studied.

Because class situations vary greatly, and because each unit has its own particular requirements, it is impossible to provide a model plan that can be used for all units. Essentially the unit should focus on some phase of music and integrate as much as possible the activities of singing, listening, creating, discussing, and reading. It is neither possible nor desirable for every unit to encompass in each class period the wide variety of activities that could be included. Some topics suggest singing, while others invite discussion and study. Teachers should not strain to achieve subject matter integration where it does not logically exist. If a unit does not in itself suggest appropriate songs, then the class can work on songs that are not directly related to the unit and that will not detract from the unit. When possible, films, books, bulletin board displays, field trips, and appearances by outside authorities should be integrated into the unit of study—not forcibly, but as a logical extension of the learning experience.

The rehearsals of performing groups can also be planned in units. If, as is hoped, the course of study consists of more than preparing for one public performance after another, then units can be formed around types of music, forms, or technical problems. For example, a unit for studying choral music could be formed about particular aspects of works from Russia or the Renaissance, a unit of band music developed around overtures, and a unit for orchestras created around types of bowing. While such learning is going on, the group is also rehearsing some of the music for performance.

Lesson Planning

When all is said and done, lesson planning is merely the process of organizing the things a class will do to learn music. Although several approaches can be used to develop lesson plans for teaching music, certain guidelines should be considered:

1. Consider what most of the students know and what would be worthwhile for them to learn in music. Finding out the students' present knowledge or skills may involve giving a test. However, because of practical limitations of time and energy, music teachers cannot do this very often. Furthermore, after a teacher has taught a group of students for awhile, he or she should have a rather clear idea about what the students know and can do musically. In performing groups each performance of music provides the teacher with information about what the group can do. Observing student responses to questions and other learning activities provides some information in music classes. Although teachers need not give formal pretests often, they should consciously look for and consider where the students are in terms of the subject and what has been covered in previous classes.

2. Select two or three specific topics or skills to teach in music classes or one specific topic or skill in each rehearsal. Students, especially those in elementary and middle school, become restless and their attention wanes if any one activity is continued for too long a period of time. One activity is satisfactory for rehearsals because quite a bit of time is spent playing or singing.

3. State the points to be studied specifically. An objective such as "to learn about music composed in the Renaissance style" is too vague and too broad. An objective such as "to identify aurally and in notation the points of imitation in Renaissance madrigals and motets" is much clearer and more manageable.

4. Formulate the objectives for the class or group in terms of what the students should be able to do as a result of the instruction. Unless the students can provide evidence of how much they have learned, it is hard for a teacher to determine what should be taught in subsequent classes. Behavioral objectives can apply to skills; for example, "The group will learn to sing Palestrina's 'Sanctus' with a light tone and accurate pitch." Other objectives can apply to cognitive learning with a criterion level added if the teacher so desires; for example, "Ninety percent of the students will be able to locate in the notation three examples of imitative entrances in 'Sanctus' by Palestrina."

5. Select appropriate materials. The teacher who wishes to teach about Renaissance madrigals should try to secure the most authentic version of each madrigal that is available and to play recordings of madrigals being sung in an authentic style.

6. Decide on how the content is to be taught. Suppose that a class is learning to identify *A B A* form. There are several ways in which this could be done. If the class knows a song that is in *A B A* form, they could sing it through and identify the different sections. A recording of a work with clearly delineated sections in *A B A* could be played. The students could create a simple piece in three-part form using classroom instruments. They might think of ways to represent visually the different sections of a piece of music, such as with different symbols or colors for the various sections of the work. Each of these ways—and many others—is appropriate under the right circumstances.

7. Assess the results of each portion of a class or rehearsal. Assessing learning is discussed in the second half of this chapter.

These seven guidelines are based on the basic questions raised in Chapter One about teaching: What? To whom? How? With what results? Lesson plans should contain the "in action" answers to those four basic questions. Of course, there is a fifth question that underlies all teaching: Why? The reasons for knowing music are basic to all planning and teaching, but they do not need to be restated for each lesson.

The exact manner in which a lesson plan is put down on paper is not of major importance, but planning for the main points to be taught is. What follows is a sample plan built around the basic questions of what, how, and with what results. In the sample plan these questions are indicated along the left-hand side of the page by the words "Objectives," "Materials," Procedures," and "Assessment of Results." Notice that the categories are used for both of the main topics to be presented in the lesson. Estimates of the amount of time to be consumed by a topic are also included. Such estimates provide a teacher with some guidance on how much time to spend, but should not be followed slavishly. The "If time permits" heading allows for some latitude in using time and saves a teacher from the uncomfortable position of completing the planned lesson with ten or more minutes of class time remaining. As you become more experienced in teaching, it may not be necessary to write plans in as much detail as the one presented here. Often one-word cues are enough. The amount of detail in a plan is a matter on which teachers have their own individual preferences.

Sample Lesson Plan for General Music

Objectives	1. Learn about the music and words of typical ballads.
	2. Become informed about the gestures used in conducting, the conductor's score, and interpretations and how they differ.
Materials	1. *The Music Book*, 7 and recordings.
	2. *Silver Burdett Music*, 7 and recordings.

Procedures

1. Ballad (15 minutes):
   (a) Review "Henry Martin" (*The Music Book*, p. 76), by singing the song again. Give the class the seventh and eighth verses.
   (b) Ask if most songs they sing express feelings or tell a story. Discuss the text. Does it tell a story? Is it happy? Does it repeat lines or words? Does it contain any words they don't understand?
   (c) Ask about the characteristics of music. Does it need much accompaniment? Does it have several verses to the same melody? Does it contain any portions that are similar or the same? Is it highly expressive music? What's unusual about the rhythm?
   (d) Listen to the recording of "Henry Martin."
   (e) Sing the song again with improved expression and style.

2. Conductor (25 minutes):
   (a) Read and discuss the pages on conducting in *Silver Burdett Music* (pp. 122–124).
   (b) Discuss the musical decisions of conductors. Point out how the size and style of gestures give an idea of the style of the music.
   (c) Study the page of the score of "O Fortuna" from Orff's *Carmina Burana* and explain any words the students don't know.
   (d) Play the recording of the two versions of "O Fortuna." Which is faster? Louder? How does the tone quality differ between them?
   (e) Ask if one version is better than the other or just different. Discuss personal preferences and their validity.

3. If time permits (5 minutes):
   Review "Frog Went A-Courtin'" (*The Music Book*, p. 150). Compare with "Henry Martin." Discover what chords are used in the accompaniment.

Assessment of Results As a result of the lesson, the students will be able to:

1. Describe the characteristics of story-telling, strophic form, rather detached quality in the ballad, and find similar measures. (Check for participation in singing.)
2. Describe how conducting gestures reflect style of music, describe the basic pattern of an orchestral score, and state differences between two versions of "O Fortuna."

Lesson plans can be arranged in several different formats. One has just been presented. Another example shown below presents a different type of format in which the information is to be written in columns according to the portion of the teaching process.

Lesson plans should not be like scripts for a play that teachers read almost line by line to a class. Such plans are very time consuming to prepare, and few people can read a lecture to a class and make it seem interesting and vital. Some materials available to teachers do provide ready-made questions and lines to read to the class; these are the actual content of a lesson, not plans for a lesson. There is a difference between a plan and something to read.

Lesson Plan

Aspects of music to be taught through materials or activity.	Materials and/or activities.	Method or procedures to be used to teach topic or skill.	Actions of students to be observed for evaluation of amount of learning.

Planning for Rehearsals

To prepare for rehearsals, teachers must decide which pieces will be studied, which places in the music should receive special attention, and what should be accomplished or learned in conjunction with the music. In addition, teachers need to study the score and parts to the music they don't already know. The music is studied by the teacher prior to class or rehearsal to analyze it, to learn the score, to work on any special conducting techniques, and to decide on the best interpretation of the work. Also, the study should anticipate spots that are likely to be difficult for the group. When the students reach a troublesome passage, teachers should be quick to come up with the alternative fingering for G on the trumpet, a bowing technique that will help the strings to coordinate the bow with the left hand, or a suggestion for getting the woodwinds to play a particular rhythmic figure correctly. *No teacher or conductor should be caught unprepared for such problems in the music; plans should have been made for overcoming them.*

No single outline of activity is suitable for all rehearsals of performing groups, of course. The methods and content will vary according to what has been learned previously, the closeness of a performance, and the type of music being studied. Many teachers begin rehearsals with a combination warm-up and technique-developing routine. This portion of the rehearsal should be varied from day to day and be relevant to the other activities in the course. In singing, for example, attention can be centered on producing the sound correctly or singing in tune. In instrumental music, playing techniques can be stressed, or a scale or exercise can be played to practice correct fingerings or bowings. This type of work should be brief—not longer than five or seven minutes.

To close a class, the students can review something they do well or put together something on which they have been working. The idea is not to leave the group hanging in the middle of learning a piece of music when the period ends. Between the opening and closing of the rehearsal, the group can begin studying new music, review familiar works, perfect its current repertoire, and learn aspects of music theory and literature relevant to the music being rehearsed.

It is probably possible to get by without spending time in planning for teaching. However, music educators should set their goals higher than just getting by. If students in music classes and performing groups are to learn the most they can in the time available, teachers need to plan carefully for what they will do.

Assessing "*W*hat did the students learn?" has become an important question, for a number of reasons. First, teachers have become increasingly aware that they need to have evidence on how well their students are learning. Without such evidence, they have no solid basis for making educational decisions. Second, federal, state, and local school agencies have grown more concerned about the results of education. To put it bluntly, the taxpayers want to know what they are getting for their money. Giving a lot of attention to the immediate, visible results of learning may be shortsighted, but it is understandable.

A third reason for securing evidence of learning is that it helps teachers in planning subsequent instruction. A teacher whose band has not learned to play dotted-eighths and sixteenths correctly should be aware of that fact and try different methods to teach the playing of this pattern. At least the original approach should be tried again, perhaps more thoroughly than before. Unless past results are confronted and assessed, planning for the future is an exercise in guesswork.

It is surprising how careful some teachers are in preparing for a class and how careless they are about finding out what is really learned in that class. It is easy to assume that learning is taking place. Also, sometimes teachers think that if the students do not learn, it is the students' fault. And then, some music teachers are unsure of how or what to evaluate, and some teachers may fear that evaluating student learning will show that the teachers have not taught as much as they thought they had.

Ways of Assessing

Doing assessment well is not easy, because it is not possible to measure many aspects of learning directly. For example, the concept of *musicianship* is not something that can be weighed, seen, or held in the hand. It exists only as a concept or mental construct in people's minds. To most people, actions such as performing the music accurately, phrasing at suitable places, and changing dynamic levels carefully and sensibly are indications of it. However, no two people mean exactly the same thing when they use the word *musicianship*. This situation presents a bit of a problem, because people look for slightly different things in musicianship. What, then, can be measured about musicianship or any mental construct? The answer is *indicators*. Indicators of musicianship probably include keeping a steady tempo, performing in tune, phrasing at the right places, using an appropriate tone quality, and so on. It is very unlikely that a student who plays with poor intonation, breaks up phrases, and seldom varies the dynamic level will be considered musical. Although seeking evidence about indicators of something does not solve all the assessment problems (for example, some people may not agree that keeping a steady beat or knowing where a breath should be taken are valid indicators), such evidence is far more valid in assessing learning than trying to deal with general ideas.

Assessing the effectiveness of instruction does not mean giving one test after another. It is not necessary to involve all the members of the class in every evaluation situation. A sample of four or five students selected at random to answer questions or in other ways indicate what they are learning is usually enough to provide a good idea of how much learning is taking place.

Tests and Testing

Since grading is involved in most courses, and since school administrators, boards of education, and parents want reports on student achievement, teachers usually need to construct and give tests. Their informal observations of student learning are valuable for their own use, but inadequate for purposes of grading. So a more formal assessment of students is needed, in addition to the evaluation of instruction.

What is being discussed here is the evaluation of achievement—what the students have learned—and not aptitude. Admittedly there is a rather close relationship between the two types of tests—achievement and aptitude—but the correlation is not so high that the two can be used interchangeably.

As was pointed out in Chapter Nine, the nature of instruction, and therefore evaluation, differs somewhat according to the type of learning—cognitive, affective, or psychomotor. The discussion of testing is, therefore, divided into these three types.

Cognitive Tests.   One type of cognitive test is the essay examination. It gives the students latitude in organizing their responses and expressing their ideas fully. But different test graders vary in their assessment of the answers, and even the same grader will vary from one time to another. Also, verbally adept students have an advantage over the less articulate students on this type of examination. For many instructors, the essay examination is simply not feasible because the grading can be too time-consuming when large numbers of students are involved.

The true-false examination is generally unsatisfactory. The 50 percent chance of guessing the correct response requires that many items be written to cancel the effects of chance and achieve significant results. Furthermore, it is difficult to write true-false questions that probe an area in depth.

The completion question requires the students to fill in the correct word. For example, "The stick held by the conductor is called a _____." Completion questions are satisfactory when a precise term is required. The question should be worded so that there is no ambiguity about the correct answer. For example, the question "A feature of Baroque music is _____" could be answered by the words *continuo, harpsichord, metrical rhythm,* or a number of other terms. Such a question should be avoided.

The multiple-choice question has several advantages. It can be scored easily either by hand or by machine, so a large number of tests can be graded quickly. Its chance factor is usually one in four or five—much lower than the true-false item. With imagination and planning, multiple-choice questions can be written to test general understanding as well as specific facts. A correct response does not depend on a student's ability to verbalize an answer.

A multiple-choice question consists of two parts. One is the statement called the "stem," the statement that applies to all the choices. For example: "In sonata form the first large section is called . . ." The stem must be relatively short. The choices to complete the stem are called "foils" or "distractors." If teachers have trouble inventing enough logical foils for four or five choices, they can write foils such as "None of the above," "All of the above," "True of both (a) and (b)," and so on. In the preparation of such a test, there is a tendency to put a disproportionate number of the correct choices in the last distractor, which causes an undesirable overbalance on it. Apparently there is a subconscious desire to withhold the right answer until the students have read the other choices. In addition, the correct choice often contains the most words because it must be accurate; the wording of the incorrect foils seldom matters. Here is a typical multiple-choice item:

The song "Scarborough Fair" is from:
(a) the Appalachian mountains
(b) France
(c) England
(d) the western United States
(e) Mexico

The difficulty of an item can be varied by adjusting the specificity of the question. For example:

"Scarborough Fair" is:
(a) a ballett
(b) an aria
(c) a broadside
(d) a ballad
(e) an art song

is a much more demanding question than

"Scarborough Fair" is:

(a) an opera
(b) a ballet
(c) a folk song
(d) a church hymn
(e) none of the above

A statement or question employing a negative in the stem is useful when you can't think up enough logical foils. An in-depth examination of an area can be accomplished through a series of multiple-choice questions. Sometimes several questions can be built to refer back to a single descriptive paragraph or musical example.

The most important criterion of a test is whether it is valid—whether it tests the students on the real content of the course. If the general music class spends most of its time singing, and the band spends most of its time getting ready for public appearances, it is hardly fair to test the students on the keys of Beethoven's symphonies, since this information is not a logical outgrowth of their experiences in the course.

No matter which tests are favored, the teacher should include questions that involve varying degrees of complexity and comprehensiveness. There is a big difference between these two questions: "What does the word *accelerando* mean?" and "Which of these two musical examples is most representative of the Renaissance polyphonic style?" The first question is confined to a specific musical fact, one that can be learned by rote without much understanding. The second requires pulling together knowledge, experiences, and comparative judgment for evaluating music. The first type of question is certainly acceptable; factual knowledge has its place in any subject. But the rudimentary level of comprehension should not be the only one tested, as was pointed out in Chapter Nine.

The most notable published achievement tests are the *Music Achievement Test* by Richard Colwell[1] and the *Achievement Tests in Music* by William Knuth.[2] Both use a recording and both are designed for evaluating students in upper elementary grades and junior high school. The Music Achievement Test includes subtests on pitch, intervals, major/minor, meter discrimination, auditory-visual discrimination, feeling for tonal center, tonal memory, melody, pitch, instrument recognition, and identification of style, texture, and chords. Its reliability is high, and its validity has been established by correlations with other tests, by performance ratings of students made one year after taking the test, and a variety of teacher ratings of students. The norms were developed from a sample of 9600 students, a far greater number than was used in standardizing any other music test.

Knuth's Achievement Tests in Music is neither as comprehensive nor as well standardized as Colwell's. It consists mainly of detecting errors in notation from hearing the phrase played. Its reliability is satisfactory, and its validity has been established by analyzing the content of basal music series, inviting the judgment of six authorities in music education, and correlating it with success in school music classes. The norms provided in the test manual are not as complete as most teachers would desire.

Psychomotor Tests. Music teachers are often concerned with the development of skills. Administering ear-training examinations, adjudicating at contests and festivals, and deciding who will be first-chair clarinet are three examples of situations that require the teacher to evaluate technical skills. Often this area is not handled in as capable a manner as the testing of cognitive achievement.

The problem in assessing skills well is apparent in the contest situation. Adjudicators must rely solely on their impressions of one performance. Even when an adjudication form is available, it calls for general observations about various aspects of the performance—tone quality, technical proficiency, and so on.

Most of the rating forms are general categories of technical skills required in performance, and this does encourage more consistent reporting. They do include some space for the adjudicator's comments and criticisms. However, merely listing grades for each category is not very informative. For example, what does a grade of B on technique mean? That the group was not together? Some notes were missed? Some rhythmic figures were not executed properly? Some articulations were incorrect or sloppy? The tempo slowed down in the difficult places? Teachers and students can assume that B is better than C but not as good as A, and that's all. In some respects, adjudicators might have given a more useful report if they had been provided a blank sheet of paper on which to write comments.

Sometimes adjudicators vary widely in their assessment of a performance. For example, in one contest the same band received a first division rating from one judge, a third division from another, and a fifth (the lowest possible rating) from the third judge. Some states allow adjudicators to confer about their ratings so that such embarrassing disagreements can be avoided. Differing opinions are not confined to contest adjudicators, either. Varying evaluations of performing ability occur regularly among juries of applied music teachers who hear individual performances of college music majors.

The probable cause for varying ratings by teachers and adjudicators is not that they are incompetent but that they are each listening and looking for different things—the problem of mental constructs mentioned earlier in the chapter. For assessments to be useful, they must be made on specific points that are agreed on by the panel or jury and should be specifically stated, preferably in writing.

Within the class or rehearsal room, assessment should also consider specific aspects—the more specific, the better. How can this specificity be accomplished? One method is to tape-record a performance and replay the example enough times to hear everything thoroughly. This long and involved procedure is used in research studies, but it is too time-consuming for most teachers to undertake. The answer to the dilemma between the need for accurate assessment and limited time is to select a sample of the music and aspects of performance.

Suppose that in the "Hallelujah Chorus" from Handel's *Messiah*, the teacher decides to test the basses by concentrating on three phrases from the bass part. (The students may sing more than the three phrases. They need not know the exact places selected for adjudication.) One of the phrases is:

From this phrase the teacher might choose three places for precise assessment: (1) the tone quality and pitch of the high D, (2) the accuracy and evenness of the two eighth notes, and (3) the diction and tone quality of the last note of the phrase. Other aspects could have been chosen, of course, but these three can be used to secure some solid evidence for assessment. Since these three places occur several beats apart, which allows the teacher time to think, it is possible for their quality to be assessed during a live performance.

A published test employing some of the ideas advocated here is available for specific instruments: the *Watkins-Farnum Performance Scale* by John Watkins and Stephen Farnum.[3] The test consists of sixteen graded levels of achievement. Reliability is rather good. Validation was made by correlating an overall ranking with the test scores. The correlations are high, from .86 on some brass instruments to .68 on drums. The test is carefully developed and norms are provided. The most common complaint of teachers who have used this test is the rather complicated scoring process. Actually, teachers can pursue the idea of specific, precise assessment without using this particular test by carefully developing their own performance examination.

A word of caution needs to be given about employing tape recordings for evaluation, especially when large groups are involved. Even the finest equipment under the best conditions cannot reproduce exactly what the human ear hears. In some cases the recording is a distortion of the actual sounds. School recording equipment and recording conditions are usually not the best, and they do not faithfully reproduce some aspects of the music, especially timbre and overall balance. Ideally, one could evaluate those aspects during live performance and then use the tape recording to check for wrong notes, phrasing, and the like.

The tape recorder can be a valuable aid in hearing students individually without consuming a large amount of rehearsal time. The recorder can be set up in another room, with its volume level, treble and bass setting, and microphone placement properly adjusted before the auditions begin. Each student individually goes into the room, pushes the "record" button, announces his or her name, plays or sings the assigned music, then stops the recording and returns to class. The teacher can listen to the audition tape at a more convenient time.

How should a test of skill development be scored? The rating system used in some state contests assigns a specific number of points to the grade given in each category. The points are then totaled to determine the overall rating. The practical result in some states is that as long as the student or group shows up and performs, it is impossible for that entrant to receive the lowest overall rating. This fact may reduce anxiety for the participants but it undermines the integrity of the ratings. A more serious flaw in assigning points is that they tend to blur valid distinctions among performers. For example, if a group does well on almost everything, but has terrible intonation, it can still be placed in the highest rating. In actual practice, adjudicators adjust points in other areas so that this does not happen. But adjusting points to achieve the correct overall rating is evidence of the weakness of such a point system. Another weakness is that each piece of music is different: in one work the tone quality and expression may be most important, while in another it is the execution of the notes. If points are assigned to areas of performance, they need to be reapportioned for each musical work in order to be valid.

The best answer is to assign points to the specific places selected. Returning to the phrase from the "Hallelujah Chorus" cited earlier in this chapter, the teacher-adjudicator should determine how many points can be earned by the best possible execution of the three places selected. Then points should be assigned—so many for the timbre on the high D, so many for the accuracy of its intonation, so many for not sustaining the r sound on the final note, and so on. As in all testing, some subjective judgment is involved in assigning points. However, by observing skills as objectively and systematically as possible, teachers can assess performance as accurately and fairly as they do cognitive learning.

Affective Assessment.   Assessing attitudes presents obstacles not found in assessing factual learning or skills. First, is it possible to test attitudes? Either students know what a diminished seventh chord is, or they don't. But if asked, "Do you enjoy the sound of a diminished seventh chord?" the students can give the answer they think the teacher wants to hear. Furthermore, words are not always indications of true belief and practice. Some people profess honesty, but cheat on their golf score and income tax.

Second, there also remains the question of whether beliefs and values *should* be graded, a point mentioned in Chapter Four.

To be valid, the assessment of attitudes should be separate from grading students. Freeing the assessment of attitudes from grades encourages the students to respond honestly by removing the influence of rewards or penalties from their answers. To assure the students that they may express their attitudes freely, teachers can suggest that written responses to questions of attitude be made anonymously.

Assessing students' attitudes accurately requires skill both in gathering information and in interpreting it. Although music teachers are not expert researchers, they still can gain insight into how students' attitudes are being affected by observing the choices students make regarding musical activities. Do they go to concerts voluntarily? Do they seem to listen to music or just daydream? Did more students attend concerts this year than last? What records do they check out of the library? Has there been a significant change during the year? What songs do students ask to sing? Do they read about musical events in newspapers and magazines?

Questioning students directly can also provide information, but the questions should be subtle. Asking "Do you like Benjamin Britten's music?" is too obvious an approach. Teachers will find out more by asking, "Would you like to hear Britten's *A Ceremony of Carols* again?" or "Would you like to hear other music by Benjamin Britten?" or " 'This Little Babe' from Britten's *A Ceremony of Carols* is (a) a sissy piece, (b) weird and dull, (c) okay but not as good as many other pieces I know, (d) different but interesting to hear." Another way to ask questions about choices is: "Suppose you've won the lucky number drawing at the music store. You can have *free* any five records of your choice. Which would you choose?" Many variations of this question are possible: "Which composer would you most like to meet? Why?" "Is 'This Little Babe' from Britten's *A Ceremony of Carols* a piece that people will listen to a hundred years from now? Why or why not?"

A somewhat different type of questioning asks students to register their feelings on a scale from *strongly disagree, disagree, neutral, agree,* to *strongly agree*. The statement might be this: "Benjamin Britten's *A Ceremony of Carols* is fascinating music." In this type of item, the wording of the statements should vary. Students circle their choices from the five possible responses.

The projective question is another testing technique: " 'This Little

Babe' from Britten's *A Ceremony of Carols* sounds like _____
_____.'' The problem with this type of question is the interpretation required of the answer, especially in the case of students who are not articulate. Playing pairs of musical examples and then asking the students which of the two they prefer can also be used to assess musical attitudes. Several unpublished tests are based on this technique.[4] Unless a teacher can devote considerable time to developing such a test, the results will not be valid.

None of the techniques described here can provide conclusive data about students' attitudes, but each can indicate whether the students are becoming more receptive to and interested in music.

Grading Students

*M*usic teachers often consider grading students as a necessary nuisance and feel justifiably that any grading system is inadequate to reflect what a student is accomplishing in music class. Therefore, teachers sometimes tend to consider grading a rather insignificant, routine duty. The students look at grades with interest and concern, even though, paradoxically, grades as such are not a primary motivation for most teenagers. Because many students are sensitive about grades, and because what is learned in music class is less often subjected to concrete examination in written form, it is important that the manner of giving grades be seen by the students as fair and understanding. If grading is handled brusquely or carelessly, it can hinder the establishment of good relationships between students and teachers.

Teachers should establish clear-cut criteria for grading that are consistent with the overall evaluation procedures of the school. So that later misunderstanding is prevented, these standards can be written down and given to each student. The criteria may or may not carry definite point or percentage values. Assigning a certain number of points for effort, for deportment, for technique, and the like gives students a sense of concreteness, but the objectivity is more apparent than real.

The purpose of grading is to provide parents, students, and teachers with an accurate picture of the student's work. A single grade cannot do this. If the report card allows for only a single grade, which is often the case, music teachers can give students and parents a clearer understanding of the evaluation by providing supplementary information. A narrative paragraph is often helpful. Another possibility is a form on which teachers check statements about singing, completion of assignments, progress during the marking period, concert attendance, aspects of playing, or whatever is significant for the class. The supplementary sheets should be mailed to the home if teachers want to be sure they are received; students are unreliable couriers, even of favorable reports.

Music teachers face two dilemmas in grading: one between pupil growth and a fixed standard, and the other between musical accomplishment and class deportment. Marks can be determined in relation to some standard, with an A or 100 representing perfection in this system, or they can be decided in relation to the progress and effort that the student has shown. Both methods are valid when applied to the right situations. In college a grade should represent fulfilling some standard. In the elementary schools, however, the concept of rigid standards is not appropriate. It is somewhat unfair to grade a child with many musical advantages by the same standard as another child with an impoverished musical background. Still, by the time students reach secondary school, teachers cannot ignore the existence of some standard of achievement.

A number of practical actions are available to music teachers for making the student grading process more useful to everyone concerned. However, these specific procedures are beyond the scope of an introductory textbook. Whether they are giving grades or not, music teachers should devote much attention to planning and assessing the learning in their classes and rehearsals. These actions are the guides to and gauges of a teacher's work and an integral part of the teaching process.

Questions

1. How can teachers present well-planned lessons and at the same time allow for some flexibility and spontaneity in their teaching?

2. What are the main differences between music classes and rehearsals with regard to planning? Should plans even be made for conducting a rehearsal? Why or why not?

3. What are the benefits of unit plans over planning for individual lessons?

4. Where can music teachers look for ideas to help in planning for classes or rehearsals? Why should beginning teachers be especially interested in ideas and suggestions about what they might teach?

5. Which of the following statements are objectives adequately stated in behavioral terms?

(a) The students will not throw paper in class.

(b) The students will learn the song "Chester" by Billings.

(c) Each singer will be able to sing his or her part in "Chester" in tune, with a clear tone, and at tempo, while the piano fills in the remaining parts.

(d) The students will learn about the Baroque style.

(e) The students will be able to describe verbally the pattern of the exposition of a typical fugue.

6. Why are educational objectives and assessment so closely related?

7. Name two music achievement tests, and describe how they assess learning in music.

8. What are the advantages and disadvantages of essay examination questions? Of true-false? Of multiple choice?

9. Describe some techniques for assessing students' attitudes and feelings.

Projects

1. Plan a unit of four general music classes for any grade 1–8. Assume class periods last for about thirty minutes for elementary school and forty-five minutes for junior high school. Plan several different topics and/or activities for each class. Allow for some student involvement in each class. Use either format presented in this chapter.

2. Plan a unit of four rehearsals for any performing group from grades 7–12. Assume rehearsal periods last about fifty minutes. Plan one or two points to teach in each rehearsal in addition to playing or singing pieces of music. Use either format presented in this chapter.

3. Administer the Watkins-Farnum Performance Scale to an instrumentalist friend.

4. Write objectives in behavioral terms for this chapter.

5. Examine and evaluate tests given you in this and other courses in terms of validity and reliability.

Suggested Readings

Colwell, Richard, *The Evaluation of Music Teaching and Learning.* Englewood Cliffs, N.J.: Prentice-Hall, 1970.

Klotman, Robert H. *The School Music Administrator and Supervisor: Catalysts for Change in Music Education.* Englewood Cliffs, N.J.: Prentice-Hall, 1973. Chapters 9 and 10.

Labuta, Joseph A. *Guide to Accountability in Music Instruction.* West Nyack, N.Y.: Parker, 1974.

Lehman, Paul R. *Tests and Measurements in Music.* Englewood Cliffs, N.J.: Prentice-Hall, 1968.

Mager, Robert F. *Preparing Instructional Objectives.* Belmont, Calif.: Fearon, 1962.

Popham, W. James, and Eva L. Baker. *Establishing Instructional Goals.* Englewood Cliffs, N.J.: Prentice-Hall, 1970.

References

[1] Available from Richard Colwell, 406 West Michigan Street, Urbana, Ill. 61801.

[2] Creative Research Associates, Monmouth, Oreg., revised 1967.

[3] Hal Leonard Music, Inc., Winona, Minn., 1954; string edition, 1969.

[4] Newell H. Long, "A Revision of the University of Oregon Music Discrimination Test" (Ed. D. dissertation, Indiana University, 1965). Long's revision is based on the work of Kate Hevner (Mueller), "Appreciation of Music," *Studies in Appreciation of Art* (University of Oregon Publication), IV, no. 6 (1934), pp. 83–151; and George Kyme, "The Value of Aesthetic Judgments in the Assessment of Musical Capacity" (Ph.D. dissertation, University of California, 1954).

6 | The Music Education Profession

PROSPECTIVE MUSIC TEACHERS are preparing for a profession. Whether they like it or not, their work will be affected by what others in the profession have accomplished in the past and are doing now. In many ways, as Chapter Twelve points out, the music education profession is one in which its members can take pride. No one, however, is claiming that it has no blemishes or problems. Therefore, prospective teachers can take comfort in the accomplishments of the music education profession, but they should be prepared to work for its improvement.

CHAPTER TWELVE

MUSIC TEACHERS are never alone in their work, even though they may be the only music teachers in a particular school or district. They are identified as "music teachers," whether they like it or not. Their work is affected to some degree by what others who teach music have done in the past and are doing now. This happens in several ways.

To begin with, teachers usually succeed other music teachers, and so they inherit a legacy from their predecessors. If, for example, the previous choral teacher devoted his or her main efforts on a big musical each year, it may be hard to wean the students and community away from the annual spring entertainment.

Another influence is that administrators and teachers are aware of what goes on in neighboring school districts, and they tend to make comparisons among schools in relation to enrollments, curriculum, number and length of class meetings, and the size and quality of the performing organizations. There is an unfortunate tendency on the part of some school board members and administrators to be guided more by what similar schools are doing than by what is best for their particular situation. More than one music teacher has been asked: "Why should we start a string program (add more classes of general music, buy some quality instruments for music in the elementary classrooms—the same sentiment can be applied to many matters) when Duxbury and Westfield don't have one?"

Also, all school music teachers are involved in the same general type of work. Like it or not, the same conditions and public attitudes affect everyone who teaches music in the schools. If a school music program succeeds and music is made stronger, music education in general benefits. And, unfortunately, every teacher or program that fails hurts music education a little bit.

What Is a Profession?

*M*usic education is often spoken of as a profession, but is it? What characteristics should a type of workers possess in order to earn the distinction of being a "profession"? Four factors seem essential for a profession. One is that their jobs require extensive education and preparation, usually a baccalaureate degree from college and often several years of additional study. A medical doctor graduates from college and completes three or four years of medical school plus several more years of internship and residency. Music teachers do not have quite as much training, but they usually hold a college degree plus at least one year of graduate study. So they qualify in terms of amount of education.

A second characteristic of a profession is the responsibility for making decisions. An architect plans—makes decisions about—the design and construction of a building; the electricians, plumbers, bricklayers, and other workers carry out specific tasks according to the blueprints of the architect. Music teachers make decisions about how and what students learn in music classes, but they are usually also responsible for carrying them out. Nevertheless, they do make decisions about how something is done.

A third characteristic of a profession is the commitment to their jobs possessed by the membership. Most professionals do not think of their work as only a 9-to-5 undertaking. They work more than the minimum number of hours, and they work when no one tells them to work. Nor is it unusual for them to take some work home with them from the office. Most music teachers (but not all!) possess a real sense of commitment to their chosen work. In fact, their deep sense of commitment sometimes causes problems for them if the public and school administrators do not view the teachers' work as particularly important and do not support it well.[1] That situation can cause frustration and conflict.

Finally, a profession has an organization that is mainly concerned with the advancement of the profession, not with the welfare of its members. This is the main difference between a union and a professional association. A union's main obligation is to improve the pay and working conditions of its members; a professional organization seeks to keep its members current on developments in the field and to provide for their continued growth in carrying out their work. This is not to say that unions are wrong or bad (because they have an important role in society) but only that the nature of a professional association is different.

The professional organization of school music teachers in the United States is the Music Educators National Conference (MENC). Although it engages in a wide variety of activities, its two main efforts are professional in-service conferences and publications. In recent years MENC has also spoken for music education to various legislative and governmental agencies at the federal and state levels. To the degree that MENC is successful in promoting music education, all music teachers and students benefit. And the success of MENC depends on how well music teachers are united in supporting it.

Smaller, specialized groups within music education such as choral directors and elementary music specialists in one method or another cannot speak for music education as a whole. Teachers who feel attracted to a specialized organization should still retain their commitment and membership in MENC. If they do not, the profession becomes more fragmented and easier prey to the wolves of poor financial and educational support. As Abraham Lincoln quoted from the gospel of Mark, "A house divided against itself, that house cannot stand."

The Profession in the Past

*T*here has been music in America since the first Indians migrated to this hemisphere thousands of years ago. European music came with the first settlers to Jamestown and Massachusetts, but it is not clear when professional instruction in music started. The first music instruction books were the product of John Tufts, a minister, who in the early eighteenth century wanted to teach the churchgoing colonists to sing psalms and hymns. He devised a tetrachord system of notation in which the octave is broken into two identical halves. Tufts chose the tetrachords E F G A and B C D E, which he identifed by the first letters of the syllables *mi, fa, sol,* and *la*.[2] His system was later adapted into "shape notes" in which each of the four shapes of note head indicates a syllable. Shape notes are still seen occasionally in the notation of some hymnals, especially in the southern states.

Tufts's efforts were followed by the "singing school movement" in which music teachers traveled from one town to another to give lessons for a few weeks. The singing school was primarily to teach church music. One of the leaders in this movement was Lowell Mason, who in 1837 was able to persuade the Boston Board of Education to initiate singing in the school curriculum. New York had instituted music in the common school program a few years earlier in 1829. Mason was a strong advocate of the ideas of the Swiss educator Johann Heinrich Pestalozzi, as were other music educators of that era.

Prior to the twentieth century, education consisted mainly of a common elementary school for children; high school education was mostly preparation for college. Only a small percentage of teenagers attended school, and their education was limited and routine by today's standards. Teachers were poorly prepared and paid and were generally treated as second-class citizens.[3] Along with many other subjects, music received only rudimentary treatment at best.

The first organization of music teachers, called the National Music Congress, assembled in 1869. This organization grew into the Music Teachers National Association, which created a committee on public school music in 1884. Shortly before the twentieth century the leadership in school music passed to the Music Section of the National Education Association (NEA). The present MENC began in 1907 in Keokuk, Iowa, as a meeting of music supervisors. Two years later the group met again and adopted the name Music Supervisors National Conference, which was not changed to Music Educators National Conference until 1934. The first issue of the *Music Supervisors Bulletin* was published in 1914, and the name was changed to *Music Supervisors Journal* in 1919 and later to the *Music Educators Journal*.

The first elementary basal series music books were published by Edwin Ginn in 1870. The emphasis in these books was on music reading, and it remained so for at least the next half century. The first instrumental groups appeared early in the twentieth century in Winfield and Wichita, Kansas, and in Richmond, Indiana. They were orchestras and were initially combined school-community efforts. Bands became significant in the 1920s, and the first group method books for winds were also published in that decade.

Music education as we know it today did not develop until after 1920 with the growth of the high school, a point mentioned in Chapter Five. Even by 1940 music education did not reach into many schools; that would not happen until the 1950s and 1960s. A 1963 report stated that elementary music specialists had the entire responsibility for music instruction in about 20 percent of the upper-grade classrooms and between 12 and 15 percent of the lower-grade rooms.[4] Virtually all secondary schools had a band and most of them had a chorus; orchestra was offered in only one secondary school in four.[5] By the end of the 1970s it was clear that the rate of growth had slowed down considerably. However, in spite of some distressing local situations, more school music programs continue to report increases than decreases in staff and students enrolled.

Has the growth of music education been a steady, smooth climb from its small beginnings? In a pig's eye it has! For some reason music educators have had a tendency to think that their programs were only a step away from elimination when, in fact, they were thriving. In the early 1930s one of the leaders of music education, Jacob Kwalwasser, advised his students that music education had been a great experiment; but now the depression was here and music probably would not last in the schools, and they should plan pursuing work in their teaching minor area or another field.[6] In 1958 the National Defense Education Act was passed by the U.S. Congress. It contained support for the physical sciences, foreign languages, and a few other related educational areas such as counseling, but nothing for the arts and humanities. Also this was the time of the shock caused by Sputnik. The great fear was that the sciences would greatly reduce the arts in the schools, and many music educators were filled with pessimism. Yet when the data finally came in for the years 1958–1963, they turned out to be some of the best ever for the growth of music education.[7] So while at the time of this writing in the early 1980s, things do not appear as bright as they did a decade or two earlier, it is reassuring to know that doubts about the future of school music have a long tradition among music educators—all while the profession was continuing to grow.

Concerns and Opportunities

$\mathcal{B}$y 1980 music education programs were being threatened in many places with cutbacks and reductions, and their preservation had become a major concern of many music teachers. However, other concerns from previous decades are still around. Music educators are questioning the adequacy of what is being offered. Is it affecting a large enough share of the students? Is it meaningful to the students? Are too many hours spent in entertaining the public at the expense of what the students are learning? In addition, other long-term problems remain: the rather high rate of turnover among music teachers, the tendency for many music teachers to have a "looking out for No. 1" attitude (only half of them belong to MENC), the limited musicianship of some persons currently teaching music, and the excessive amount of attention 'given to the portions of the music curriculum that the public sees, to say nothing of all the problems that affect education in general.

What should you, as a future teacher of music in the schools, do about the situation? Here are some suggestions to consider.

1. Be committed to your ideals and goals, but yet be flexible in achieving them. Granted, this sounds like asking someone to be rigid and flexible at the same time, which is a bit inconsistent. The answer to the dilemma lies in being firm in what you want to accomplish as a teacher but flexible in how you achieve those goals. No one can expect to have his or her way all the time, or even most of the time; accommodations and maybe an occasional retreat will have to be made. For example, you may want to have your students perform a certain piece of music, but there is little to be gained if they do not like it at all or are unable to perform it. Is is better to put it away for another year when circumstances should be more favorable. However, do not lose sight of the "big picture" of what you are trying to do. It is easy to lose perspective when you become immersed in the day-to-day activities involved with teaching, and this temptation should be resisted.

2. Keep in mind a view of music education that is greater than just your individual teaching assignment. There really is more to being a music educator than meeting your classes, even though that does require a great deal of ability and energy to do successfully. For instance, unless you and your colleagues educate the school administration and community about the purpose and progress of the music program, there may not be any classes for you to meet in a year or two. Remember that the more unified music educators are in educating the public and school administrators, the more effective they will be. Try to work with music teachers you may hardly know and even those you may not like personally. Like it or not, you are all together in the same profession. Also, there will be times when the music teacher's day should not end with the close of school. Sometimes students need extra help, and there are evening performances.

3. Continue learning and growing professionally. This point was made in Chapter Two but it is so important that it bears repeating. Although you may have had excellent training in your undergraduate years (and the "benefits" of reading this book!), that preparation is only a good start toward becoming a good music teacher. There is much more to learn, far more than could be learned in only four years and a semester of student teaching. As a part of growing professionally, learn about and evaluate carefully new ideas and practices in teaching music. Examining new practices does not mean that you must adopt them. Some of these practices should be rejected or modified in their application to your teaching situation. The real criterion is not the newness of a method or proposal but rather the contribution it can make toward educating students in music. Try to strike a happy medium between one who jumps on each new bandwagon and adopts the latest buzzwords and one who has closed his or her mind to any new thoughts.

4. Try not to let a few weak or cynical colleagues discourage you from becoming a good teacher. Keep in mind the fact that every profession, even medicine and law, have members of whom the profession isn't particularly proud. Because it is a large profession and its admission requirements not as high as some professions, teaching may have a somewhat greater number of them. The thing for you to do is make sure that you do not end up being cynical or ineffective (which is one reason for continuing to grow professionally) and make yourself into the best teacher possible. You can do something about your own teaching; there is very little you can do about teachers with low aspirations or abilities. So work with them when you must, as was suggested in point 2 of this discussion, but do not let yourself be dragged down or disenchanted by them.

5. Enjoy teaching music for what it offers young people and society, without becoming overly concerned about the modest financial rewards that teaching provides. In the long run it is far more satisfying and important that you work at something you enjoy and believe in than to make more money doing something you don't enjoy and don't think is worth much to humanity. For the reasons presented in Chapter One, teaching can be interesting and enjoyable. For how many types of work can the same thing be said to be true? Not very many. Yes, every job, including music teaching, has its good and bad points. Rather modest financial rewards is perhaps teaching's worst feature. However, there are other personal benefits, such as less days of work each year than most occupations and after tenure is achieved a higher degree of job security, in addition to the satisfaction and enjoyment. However, if making money is your main goal in life, then a reexamination of your choice of occupation seems called for, because teaching will probably not provide a high enough income to satisfy you.

The Future

*T*he profession of music education not only has a long and distinguished past but also is alive and vital today, and it is seeking to improve and to do better in the future. To the first sentence in this book—". . . you have chosen a profession that is interesting, challenging, and important"—should be added the word *dynamic* or *vigorous*. This vitality is a good sign, and it bodes well for the future of music education. Not only does it attract the type of person who seeks a continuing challenge, but it ensures that music education will progress and keep pace with education and society as a whole. Music education cannot afford to rest on its laurels, and if the current scene indicates anything about the future, the profession is in no danger of standing still.

An active and dynamic profession that is seeking to do an even better job produces differences of opinion. And so it is in music education. A kaleidoscope of opinions can be found on almost every aspect of music teaching. To beginning teachers, the lack of agreement may seem confusing. They may wonder why a committee of recognized music teachers cannot be formed, perhaps under the auspices of MENC, and write comprehensive and detailed publications on the best way to teach this or that. The answer is that music education, because it is trying new practices and considering divergent views, can agree only on general statements. Experimentation and differing ideas are not necessarily bad. In fact, they generally indicate intellectual curiosity and professional vitality.

Music education will continue to evolve in the years ahead. Twenty years from now it will not be exactly what it is today. There may be diversions and even regressions, but if the first eighty years of the twentieth century are indicative, there will be continued growth. Generally the changes will be evolutionary, not revolutionary. Real progress in human affairs, education included, seems to come in small increments.

The prospects for the future contain some encouraging signs—and also one that may not be good news, depending on how you look at it. Because of the leveling off in the size of the school population, employment prospects for music teachers in the 1980s are only moderately favorable, although so far supply and demand have remained in balance. No longer is there a teacher shortage, so schools can be more selective in employing teachers. This fact contributes to uneasiness and uncertainty for prospective teachers, but in the long run it should mean a better quality of education for the students.

Two major trends in American society are favorable for the future of music education. One of these is the increased emphasis on education (sometimes not matched in financial support) in general, and the other is an increasing interest in the fine arts, especially music. Partly because of the vast sums of money it requires, but more because of society's need for it, education receives much support from local and state sources. Not only are more people going to school, but they are staying in school longer, and many others are returning to school in adult education programs. The percentage of persons between the ages of 14 and 17 enrolled in school has increased from 11.4 in 1900, to 32.3 in 1920, to 73.3 in 1940, to 86.1 in 1960 and to 94.1 in 1978.[8] Although there has been some increase since 1968 in the defeat of local school tax building proposals, a slight majority of the elections have supported the proposed funding.[9] The percentage of the gross national product spent on education has increased from 2.6 in 1941, to 3.4 in 1951, to 5.6 in 1961, to 7.5 in 1969, but slipped back to 7 percent in 1979.[10]

As for the fine arts, greater leisure and economic affluence have enabled artistic interests to develop throughout the population. Radio, television, and the electronic reproduction of music have contributed to the trend. Certainly the great American experiment in mass education can also claim some credit for the increasing interest in the fine arts. For the first time in the long history of the human race, society has the means, the time, and the financial resources to make great music and other arts available to practically everyone. Evidence of this trend is seen in the number of community orchestras, the number of musical instruments purchased, the sales of recordings and sound-producing equipment, the money spent for musical events, and the establishment of fine arts centers and arts councils in many cities and almost every state.

The future of music education will partly be what music educators make of it. The challenges and opportunities are available. To be more complete and accurate, the sentence that opened this book should now be further expanded to read ". . .you have chosen a profession that is interesting, challenging, important, and dynamic, and one with a promising future."

References

[1] Charles R. Hoffer, "Work Related Attitudes of Indiana Music Teachers" (Paper presented at the Music Educators National Conference meeting, San Antonio, 1982).

[2] Irving Lowens, *Music and Musicians in Early America* (New York: W. W. Norton, 1964), Chapter 3.

[3] Myron Brenton, *What's Happened to Teacher?* (New York: Avon Books, 1970), Chapter 4.

[4] *Music and Art in the Public Schools,* Research Monograph 1963–M3 (Washington, D.C.: National Education Association, 1963), p. 12.

[5] *Course Offerings, Enrollments, and Curriculum Practices in Public Secondary Schools, 1972–73* (Washington, D.C.: U.S. Government Printing Office, 1976).

[6] Letter from William R. Sur. April 1982.

[7] *Music and Art in the Public Schools.*

[8] National Center for Educational Statistics, *Digest of Educational Statistics* (Washington, D.C.: U.S. Government Printing Office, 1980), p. 44.

[9] Ibid., p. 72.

[10] Ibid., p. 23

Index

Date Due

NOV 2 6 1996			